Göttinger Wirtschaftsinformatik
Herausgeber: J. Biethahn† · L. M. Kolbe · M. Schumann

Band 101

Schahin Tofangchi

Towards a Theory for Designing Machine Learning Systems for Complex Decision Making Problems

CUVILLIER VERLAG

Herausgeber

Prof. Dr. J. Biethahn† Prof. Dr. L. M. Kolbe Prof. Dr. M. Schumann

Georg-August-Universität
Wirtschaftsinformatik
Platz der Göttinger Sieben 5
37073 Göttingen

Bibliografische Information der Deutschen Nationalbibliothek
Die Deutsche Nationalbibliothek verzeichnet diese Publikation in der Deutschen Nationalbibliografie; detaillierte bibliografische Daten sind im Internet über http://dnb.d-nb.de abrufbar.
1. Aufl. - Göttingen : Cuvillier, 2020
  Zugl.: Göttingen, Univ., Diss., 2019

© CUVILLIER VERLAG, Göttingen 2020
  Nonnenstieg 8, 37075 Göttingen
  Telefon: 0551-54724-0
  Telefax: 0551-54724-21

Alle Rechte vorbehalten. Ohne ausdrückliche Genehmigung des Verlages ist es nicht gestattet, das Buch oder Teile daraus auf fotomechanischem Weg (Fotokopie, Mikrokopie) zu vervielfältigen.
1. Auflage, 2020
Gedruckt auf umweltfreundlichem, säurefreiem Papier aus nachhaltiger Forstwirtschaft.

  ISBN 978-3-7369-7200-1
  eISBN 978-3-7369-6200-2

Towards a Theory for Designing Machine Learning Systems for Complex Decision Making Problems

Dissertation

zur Erlangung des wirtschaftswissenschaftlichen Doktorgrades
der Wirtschaftswissenschaftlichen Fakultät der Georg-August-Universität Göttingen

vorgelegt von

Schahin Tofangchi, M.Sc.

aus Hamburg

Göttingen, 2019

Betreuungsausschuss

Erstbetreuer: Prof. Dr. Lutz M. Kolbe
Zweitbetreuer: Prof. Dr. André Hanelt
Drittbetreuer: Prof. Dr. Jan Muntermann

Tag der mündlichen Prüfung: 06. Februar 2020

Preface

This dissertation tells the tale of researching and designing practicable machine learning systems, while being targeted at an audience that is not required to have in-depth knowledge of machine learning. More importantly, upon closer inspection, this dissertation speaks about the value of cooperation and friendship for pursuing any kind of achievement. For this reason, I would like to take this chance to show my appreciation and gratitude for all the people that were, in one way or another, involved in creating this piece of work. I feel grateful to have been given the opportunity to work on this dissertation and conduct research in those areas which I am most passionate about. I'd like to thank Prof. Lutz M. Kolbe and Prof. André Hanelt for this opportunity, for the years of cooperation not only in research, and for all the challenges along the way they helped me overcome. The trust and the creative freedom I received is immeasurable and can't be taken for granted. I am also thankful for Prof. Jan Muntermann's insightful comments at each stage of my research process, through which I was able to get on the right track. Special thanks go to Prof. Hanelt as my mentor, who not only guided my academic and professional life but also fostered my personal growth. I'm looking forward to our further cooperation in the future!

I thank all the colleagues with whom I had the pleasure to work, laugh, and share an office during my time at the University of Göttingen. You are the ones who gave substance to my work and brought life to the workplace. I hope you will look back on these memories with the same joy as I do and wish you all the best on your future paths. All my close friends that I have made somewhere along the line, especially in Hamburg, Berlin, and Göttingen: You help me get by from day to day and I know that I can count on you the same way you can count on me. Stay the way you are and maintain your wonderful personalities, your kindness, and openness.

Thank you to my love, Lara, who stays by my side and whose affection is the antidote to all evils and everyday stress. I'm unable to express the extent of my gratitude for having you in my life and I wouldn't want to imagine it without you. At the same time, I am incredibly grateful for my family, who have supported me from the very beginning. Thanks to my parents, Manijeh and Masoud, for constantly and persistently caring for me and for the enormous amount of patience you have always managed to find in order to show me the right direction. All my achievements are indebted to your guidance. I thank my sister, Nadia, for always being there for me and for being the funny and kindhearted person she is. You have been my trusted confidante since our early childhoods and the one I could rely on when I was going through hard times. To my cousin, Sharareh. You are like a sister to me and have become an essential part of my family who I wouldn't want to do without. I am grateful for your warmth, joy, and positive impact on my life. I love all five of you and wish you nothing but the best. I'd also like to express my appreciation to all other relatives in Tehran, Urmia, and all over the world. I think about you all the time. Finally, I would like to thank the reader for taking a look into this work. I hope you enjoy my modest contribution to the world of research.

Dedicated to Aziz-joon.

Abstract

The ubiquitousness of data and the emergence of data-driven machine learning approaches provide new means of creating insights. However, coping with the great volume, velocity, and variety of data requires improved data analysis methods. This dissertation contributes a nascent design theory, named the Division-of-Labor framework, for developing complex machine learning systems that can not only address the challenges of big data but also leverage their characteristics to perform more sophisticated analyses. I evaluate the proposed design principles in three practical settings, in which I apply the principles to design machine learning systems that (i) support treatment decision making for cancer patients, (ii) provide consumers with recommendations on two-sided platforms, and (iii) address a trade-off between efficiency and comfort in the context of autonomous vehicles. The evaluations partially validate the proposed theory, but also show that some principles require further attention in order to be practicable.

Die Allgegenwart von Daten und das Aufkommen datengetriebener Methoden des maschinellen Lernens bieten neue Möglichkeiten, Erkenntnisse zu gewinnen. Die Bewältigung großer Datenmengen sowie deren Geschwindigkeit und Vielfalt erfordert jedoch verbesserte Datenanalysemethoden. Diese Dissertation befasst sich mit der Entwicklung einer, in Entstehung befindlichen, Designtheorie mit dem Namen "Division-of-Labour-Framework" zur Entwicklung komplexer maschineller Lernsysteme, die nicht nur die Herausforderungen von Big-Data bewältigen, sondern speziell ihre Eigenschaften nutzen, um komplexere Analysen durchzuführen. Ich evaluiere die vorgeschlagenen Entwurfsprinzipien in drei praktischen Situationen, in denen ich die Prinzipien auf den Entwurf von maschinellen Lernsystemen anwende, die (i) die Entscheidungsfindung bei Krebspatienten unterstützen, (ii) Verbrauchern Empfehlungen auf zweiseitigen Plattformen geben und (iii) eine Abwägung zwischen Effizienz und Komfort im Kontext autonomer Fahrzeuge umsetzen. Die Evaluationen bestätigen teilweise die vorgeschlagene Theorie, zeigen jedoch auch, dass einige Prinzipien weiterer Aufmerksamkeit bedürfen, um praktikabel zu sein.

Table of Contents

List of Figures vii

List of Tables x

Acronyms xii

A.		**Foundation** 1
I.		**Introduction** 2
	I.1	Motivation 2
	I.2	Research Agenda 3
	I.3	Structure of the Dissertation 6
	I.4	Research Context and Design 7
	I.5	Contributions 10
II.		**Theoretical Background** 13
	II.1	Intelligence and Intelligent Agents 13
	II.2	Machine Learning and Big Data Analytics 16
	II.3	Computational Data Analytics in Information Systems Research 20
B.		**Developing and Validating a Design Theory for Complex Machine Learning Systems** 25
I.		**Distributed Cognitive Expert Systems: Deriving Design Principles from Existing Theory** 26
1		**Study 1: Towards Distributed Cognitive Expert Systems** 27
	1.1	Introduction 28
	1.2	Related Work 28
	1.3	A Design Theory for Distributed Expert Systems 29
	1.4	Conclusion 39
II.		**Distributed Cognitive Expert Systems in Action: Developing Specific Instantiations of Machine Learning Systems** 40
1		**Study 2: Distributed Cognitive Expert Systems in Cancer Data Analytics: A Decision Support System for Oral and Maxillofacial Surgery** 41
	1.1	Introduction 42
	1.2	Background 43
	1.3	Context and Data 46
	1.4	Design of a Real-time Decision Support System 48
	1.5	Results 55
	1.6	Discussion of Findings 59

	1.7	Implications	61
	1.8	Limitations	63
	1.9	Conclusion	64
2		**Study 3: Advancing Recommendations on Two-Sided Platforms: A Machine Learning Approach to Context-Aware Profiling**	**65**
	2.1	Introduction	66
	2.2	Background	68
	2.3	Designing a Time-Series-Based Machine Learning Approach for Collaborative, Content-Based, and Context-Aware Recommendations	71
	2.4	Evaluation	74
	2.5	Limitations	81
	2.6	Implications	82
3		**Study 4: A Machine Learning Approach to the Efficiency-Comfort Trade-Off in Everyday-Life Automation – The Case of Autonomous Vehicles and Sharing Business Models**	**85**
	3.1	Introduction	86
	3.2	Background	87
	3.3	Research Setting	91
	3.4	A Division-of-Labor Application for Resolving the Efficiency-Comfort Trade-Off in Autonomous Driving	93
	3.5	Evaluation	97
	3.6	Discussion	100
	3.7	Appendix A: Data and Preprocessing	104
	3.8	Appendix B: Tuning LSTM Hyperparameters	106
	3.9	Appendix C: Evaluation of the Prediction Modules	111
	3.10	Appendix D: Variables used for Personalization in Prior Studies	120
C.		**Contributions**	**123**
I.		**Findings**	**124**
	I.1	Reflections on the Development of a Decision Support System for Cancer Treatments	124
	I.2	Reflections on the Development of a Consumer-Centric Recommendation system for Two-Sided Platforms	125
	I.3	Reflections on the Development of an Efficiency-Comfort Trade-Off System for Autonomous Vehicles	127
	I.4	Synthesizing the Artifact Designs: Lessons Learned and Revisitation of the Division-of-Labor Framework	128
II.		**Limitations and Implications**	**135**
	II.1	Limitations	135
	II.2	Implications for Practice	137

II.3	Implications for Research	140
III.	**Conclusion and Outlook**	**148**

References 151

Appendix xiii

List of Figures

Figure A:1. Overview of the research agenda. 4

Figure A:2. Structure of the dissertation. 7

Figure A:3. Research design. 8

Figure A:4. Agents perceive their environment through sensors, decide upon actions based on their percepts, and carry out these actions using their actuators (based on Russell and Norvig (2010)). 15

Figure A:5. The four V's of big data (based on Gandomi and Haider (2015) and Yoo (2015)). 17

Figure A:6. The information value chain (based on Abbasi et al. (2016)). 21

Figure B:1. The Division-of-Labor framework. Gray and black arrows indicate the transmission of (sub-) tasks and their solutions, respectively. Hierarchical re-distribution of tasks is enabled through agents that serve as both experts and central executives. 35

Figure B:2. The Division-of-Labor framework. Gray and black arrows indicate the transmission of (sub-) tasks and their solutions, respectively (Tofangchi, Hanelt and Kolbe 2017). 50

Figure B:3. The potential of clustering in prediction tasks. Part (a) depicts a simple regression line and part (b) depicts regression lines that were computed based on three clusters in the original data. All regression lines were computed using the method of least squares (Legendre 1806). 52

Figure B:4. The Division-of-Labor framework. Gray and black arrows indicate the transmission of (sub-) tasks and their solutions, respectively (Tofangchi, Hanelt and Kolbe 2017). 72

Figure B:5. Long short-term memory neural network (Chauhan and Vig 2015). 73

Figure B:6. The proposed DoL recommendation system. 74

Figure B:7. Reconstruction errors of IsoMap models for different projected dimensions and neighborhood sizes. The highest errors are depicted in dark-red and the lowest in dark-blue. 78

Figure B:8. The Division-of-Labor framework. Gray and black arrows indicate the transmission of (sub-) tasks and their solutions, respectively (Tofangchi, Hanelt and Kolbe 2017). 92

Figure B:9. Architecture of the Division-of-Labor application for autonomous driving based on a trade-off between efficiency and comfort. 97

Figure B:10. Architecture of the recurrent layer in an LSTM (non-peephole adaptation based on Chauhan and Vig (2015)). Arrows indicate the propagation of a vector to a recipient. Black triangles indicate that two vectors are added before being forwarded to the recipient. 106

Figure B:11. Mean absolute errors of efficiency predictions (y-axis) for hidden layer sizes in the range [5, 150] (x-axis) averaged over five trials......................................107

Figure B:12. Mean absolute errors of efficiency predictions (y-axis) for hidden layer sizes in the range [1, 5] (x-axis) averaged over five trials. 107

Figure B:13. Mean absolute errors of efficiency predictions (y-axis) for different activation functions (x-axis) averaged over five trials. 108

Figure B:14. Mean absolute errors of efficiency predictions (y-axis) for different forget gate biases in the range [0.2, 2] (x-axis) averaged over five trials........................108

Figure B:15. Mean absolute errors of efficiency predictions (y-axis) for different forget gate biases in the range [0.2, 2] (x-axis) averaged over five trials........................109

Figure B:16. Mean absolute errors of efficiency predictions (y-axis) for different learning rates in the range [0.001, 0.15] (x-axis) averaged over five trials. 109

Figure B:17. Mean absolute errors of efficiency predictions (y-axis) for hidden layer sizes in the range [5, 150] (x-axis) averaged over five trials......................................110

Figure B:18. Mean absolute errors of efficiency predictions (y-axis) for different activation functions (x-axis) averaged over five trials. 110

Figure B:19. Mean absolute errors of efficiency predictions (y-axis) for different forget gate biases in the range [0.2, 2] (x-axis) averaged over five trials........................111

Figure B:20. Mean absolute errors of efficiency predictions (y-axis) for different learning rates in the range [0.001, 0.15] (x-axis) averaged over five trials. 111

Figure B:21. Efficiency prediction errors (y-axis) over time (x-axis) for the first two drives of user #0. 112

Figure B:22. Efficiency prediction errors (y-axis) over time (x-axis) for the first drive of user #100. 112

Figure B:23. Average efficiency prediction errors (y-axis) per drive (x-axis) for user #100..113

Figure B:24. Average efficiency prediction errors (y-axis) per user (x-axis) for all users. 113

Figure B:25. Efficiency prediction errors (y-axis) over time (x-axis) of baseline models for a random drive, compared to the LSTM's error (green curve). 115

Figure B:26. Preference estimation errors (y-axis) over time (x-axis) for the first two drives of user #0. 115

Figure B:27. Preference estimation errors (y-axis) over time (x-axis) for the first and the third drive of user #15. 116

List of Figures

Figure B:28. Average preference estimation errors (y-axis) per drive (x-axis) for user #15. 116

Figure B:29. Preference estimation errors (y-axis) over time (x-axis) for the first drive of user #100. ...117

Figure B:30. Average preference estimation errors (y-axis) per user (x-axis) for all users. .117

Figure B:31. Average preference estimation errors (y-axis) per drive duration in seconds (x-axis) for the last drive of all users. ...118

Figure B:32. Preference estimation errors (y-axis) over time (x-axis) of baseline models for a random drive, compared to the LSTM's error (green curve). ...119

Figure C:1. Revisited research design: the relationship and interactions between the four studies presented in this dissertation. ...130

Figure C:2. Entity-relationship models describing potential ways of task division and recombination in the DoL framework. ...133

Figure C:3. Overview of the practical implications of this dissertation. ...140

Figure C:4. Overview of the theoretical implications of this dissertation. ...147

List of Tables

Table A-1. Overview of studies included in the thesis. 6
Table A-2. Overview of research design and core research questions. 10
Table A-3. Summary of anticipated contributions. 12
Table B-1. Fact sheet of Study no. 1. 27
Table B-2. Definition of the study's core constructs. 33
Table B-3. Fact sheet of Study no. 2. 41
Table B-4. Properties of experts and central executives in the Division-of-Labor framework (based on Tofangchi, Hanelt and Kolbe (2017)) 51
Table B-5. F1 scores of different classifiers for the prediction of therapy intentions and each treatment type. The overall score is the average of the scores for all prediction tasks, weighted by the number of samples in the respective test sets. The best score is highlighted for each prediction task. 55
Table B-6. True positive (TP) and true negative (TN) rates of the classifiers for the prediction of therapy intentions and each treatment type. The overall rate is the average of the rates for all prediction tasks, weighted by the number of samples in the respective test sets. 57
Table B-7. Most important attributes and their scores for each prediction task. The scores of the overall most important attributes are their average over all prediction tasks, weighted by the number of samples in the respective test sets 58
Table B-8. Fact sheet of Study no. 3. 65
Table B-9. Variables of the Expedia hotel booking data set. 75
Table B-10. Hyperparameters considered for logistic regression, decision tree, random forest, and NN. 77
Table B-11. Results of dimensionality reduction (rounded to three significant figures) 77
Table B-12. Hyperparameters considered for SVD, NMF, and LSTM. 80
Table B-13. Prediction scores (rounded to three significant figures). 81
Table B-14. Fact sheet of Study no. 4. 85
Table B-15. Properties of experts and central executives in the Division-of-Labor framework (Tofangchi, Hanelt and Böhrnsen 2017). 92
Table B-16. Variables used in the evaluation. 104
Table B-17. LSTM hyperparameters for efficiency predictions and preference estimations. 106

List of Tables

Table B-18. Error rates of energy efficiency predictions for different models. 114

Table B-19. Error rates of preference estimates for different models. 119

Table B-20. Variables used in related work. 121

Table C-1. Contribution of Study 2..124

Table C-2. Title, research question, and main contribution of Study 3. 125

Table C-3. Title, research question, and main contribution of Study 4. 127

Table C-4. Overview of Studies 2, 3, and 4 and their individual contributions. 128

Table C-5. Title, research question, and main contribution of Study 1. 129

Table C-6. Properties of experts and central executives in the Division-of-Labor framework. 130

Table C-7. Overview of Studies 2, 3, and 4 and their individual contributions. 134

Acronyms

AI	Artificial Intelligence
AV	Autonomous Vehicles
DoL	Division-of-Labor
IS	Information Systems
IT	Information Technology
ML	Machine learning
RI	Research Inquiry

A. Foundation

This cumulative dissertation is concerned with developing and examining a theory for designing machine learning (ML) systems that support complex decision making processes. Part B constitutes the main part, in which multiple interrelated studies are carried out to fulfill the overall purpose of this dissertation. The dissertation further includes a Foundation part preceding the individual studies, and three subsequent parts in which the findings and their implications are described and discussed and the work is finally concluded.

The Foundation is divided into the Introduction (Chapter A.I) and the Theoretical Background (Chapter A.II). In the Introduction, I motivate my research and present the research gaps that are addressed by this dissertation as well as its structure and anticipated contributions and the research contexts in which the individual studies are carried out. In the Theoretical Background, I review existing literature and provide relevant definitions and the theoretical foundations for the presented research.

I. Introduction

The introduction to this dissertation comprises the motivation for my research, the description of the research gaps, the structure of the dissertation, and outlines of the contexts and designs of the studies carried out in Part B. In Section A.I.5, I conclude this chapter by describing the anticipated contributions for research and practice.

I.1 Motivation

Purposeful decision making in organizational contexts is an essential competence that determines the path of an organization and its positioning within an industry. The amount of consideration put into making decisions can make the difference between success and failure of organizations. Top-performing organizations "make decisions based on rigorous analysis at more than double the rate of lower performers" (LaValle et al. 2011, p. 22) and are significantly less likely to rely on intuition (LaValle et al. 2011).

For organizations, the transformational value of information technology (IT) has been long discovered (Gregor et al. 2006). IT-enabled organizational transformation may yield "productivity increases by reducing costs and, more importantly, by allowing organizations to increase output quality, along with offering new products and improved customer service" (Gregor et al. 2006, p. 250). More recently, algorithmic decision making (Newell and Marabelli 2015), as a consequence of IT-related progresses, has had successful applications. As a specific instance of algorithmic analyses, the transformational impact of business intelligence and data-driven analyses on organizational decision making processes has been recognized (Sharma et al. 2014). Researchers highlight their great potential for obtaining "insights ... from the highly detailed, contextualized, and rich contents of relevance to any business or organization" (Chen et al. 2012, p. 1168), especially due to the progressing digitalization across all areas of life and the datafication (Galliers et al. 2017) that steadily increase the availability of data as well as the means of collecting them (Berente and Seidel 2014). However, while decision making is one of the main areas affected by business intelligence, it is also clear that data-driven decision making does not automatically guarantee increased value for an organization (Sharma et al. 2014). For an IT- or business-intelligence-enabled transformation, it is also necessary to apply changes to the processes and the structure of an organization to accommodate new technology and capture its potential benefits (Sharma et al. 2014).

With the emergence of big data, researchers and practitioners witness a hitherto unseen opportunity of gaining valuable insights from rich data. Given the increasing availability of individual-level data – for example, through computing in everyday life (Yoo 2010) –, analysts can unveil complex and fine-grained relationships between entities of interest. Big data is associated with two properties that are deemed to carry the greatest potential benefits for information systems (IS) research and practice, namely volume and variety (Abbasi et al. 2016).

The opportunities arising from the new kinds of data call for adequate methods of ML-based analysis tailored to big data (Chen et al. 2012). With the emergence of big data tools and the growing number of sophisticated ML models that are able to learn highly complex relationships from data, both research and practice may benefit from increasingly intelligent methods of generating insights from data (Shmueli and Koppius 2011). We have already witnessed researchers developing automated data analysis methods and tools to support decision making processes on both operational and strategic levels in diverse industries (Kruse et al. 2016; Lucas Jr et al. 2013; Newell and Marabelli 2015; Woerner and Wixom 2015). In practice, however, due to managerial barriers based on a lack of understanding of how to effectively use analytics, the adoption of data-driven decision making methods progresses slowly, despite many organizations having large amounts of rich and high-quality data at their disposal (LaValle et al. 2011). This lack of understanding is partially owed to the fact that complex ML models often constitute black boxes, in the sense that the process through which they generate their outputs are incomprehensible to outsiders (Abbasi et al. 2016). Regarding the design of ML models, their explanatory power and predictive power are often viewed as mutual antagonists (Shmueli 2010; Shmueli and Koppius 2011): By increasing a model's complexity to achieve higher predictive accuracies, the model forfeits part of its explanatory power.

Given the knowledge base and the research methods of the field, Goes (2014) views IS researchers as being excellently positioned to contribute to big data research. He argues that big data constitutes an interesting field of research for a community traditionally engaged in interdisciplinary research. Similarly, Agarwal et al. (2014) state that the IS community possesses knowledge of data management as well as value creation through data. They suggest that the IS community, therefore, holds a comparative advantage for conducting research on big data. Thus, this dissertation draws on this body of knowledge and on contributions from the ML and artificial intelligence (AI) communities to address the challenges associated with big data analytics and data-driven decision making for complex problems. More specifically a nascent design theory (Gregor and Hevner 2013) is developed based on existing ML and AI theory that guides the design of ML systems towards being able to cope with large volumes of data that flow through the system with a high velocity, as well as exploit these properties along with a potentially high data variety to uncover complex relationships between entities of interest. At the same time, the principles proposed in the design theory enable a better understanding of the results produced by ML systems without reducing their overall complexity, which enables in-depth analyses of given problems. At the end of this dissertation, I review the contributions of the individual studies, describe their combined overall contribution, and discuss limitations and implications for research and practice.

I.2 Research Agenda

The development of the nascent design theory and its exemplary application to three different research problems are divided into two parts. The first part deals with the development of the theory itself, whereas the second part applies the theory in different contexts in which ML can be used to drive decision making. Figure A:1 sketches the research studies carried out in this dissertation, which I briefly describe in the following paragraphs, along with their roles in the overall research design and their relationships among each other. Chapter A.II details the theoretical background to the relevant topics covered in the remainder of this dissertation.

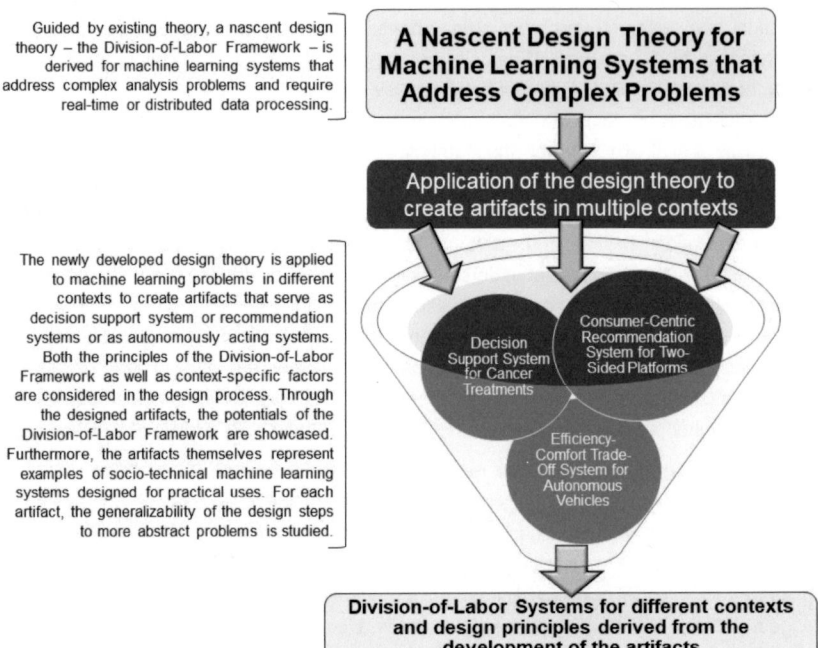

Figure A:1. Overview of the research agenda.

The focus of this research lies on analysis tasks that aim to model non-shallow relationships among data. Existing research has extensively dealt with creating ML models and fine-tuning them to different tasks (e.g., decision trees (Breiman et al. 1984), support vector machines (Cortes and Vapnik 1995), and neural networks (Cybenko 1989)). However, employing ML in practice typically goes beyond applying a single ML model to a given task. Instead, an ML system often constitutes a composition of multiple ML models and data processing modules. While we increasingly witness research contributions in the form of level one design science artifacts (Gregor and Hevner 2013) in the IS literature that provide ML systems for particular practical problems, the body of literature on ML lacks formal guidelines regarding the design of such systems.

In the previous section, I described the benefits of ML systems for analytical decision making and the typical challenges they entail. Given the ubiquitousness of IS (Vodanovich et al. 2010), the, thereby, increasing availability of data (Berente and Seidel 2014), and the cruciality of delivering information in a timely manner (Kiron et al. 2012), ML systems carry great potential for supporting decision making processes. However, in order to so, they have to cope with and take advantage of a high volume, velocity, and variety of data. The given problem leads me to the main research inquiry (RI) of this dissertation, which seeks to answer the following question:

RI 1. *How can ML systems be designed to address complex decision making problems while taking advantage of big data and adequately handling its technical and managerial adoption barriers?*

In answering this research question, a nascent, level two design theory (Gregor and Hevner 2013) is developed, which I name the Division-of-Labor (DoL) framework. This framework provides design principles for supervised ML problems that deal with data sets of intermediate to large sizes. This design theory is particularly suited for data analysis problems revolving around big data sets with high volumes and varieties (Abbasi et al. 2016). Furthermore, it addresses issues regarding data distributions of complex shapes, high-velocity data, and the interpretability of ML systems. It is applicable in different use cases such as any kinds of forecasts that require consideration of a large number of factors (e.g., user behavior predictions), analyses of large company data that flows into a system in a rapid manner, analyses that require a high level of anonymity and protection of consumer data (e.g., medical analyses), self-organizing systems that not only analyze data but also perform actions autonomously (e.g., autonomous vehicles), and complex, descriptive analyses in research. In order to showcase the design theory's potential, three expository instantiations (Gregor and Jones 2007) are provided. First, a decision support system is designed for making treatment decisions for head and neck cancer patients. This area of application is characterized by the extraordinary cruciality of decisions, which can spell the difference between life and death (Aron et al. 2011). Second, a recommendation system is designed for consumers on two-sided digital platforms that typically involve an intermediate or high number of interactions. Knowing the consumers' preferences to match them with providers is of the highest importance for digitally enabled two-sided platforms (Parker et al. 2016). However, being able to predict consumers' choices is a highly complex problem with platforms on which diverse consumers and products or services are brought together. Third and finally, the efficiency-comfort trade-off in autonomous vehicles (i.e., the trade-off between optimizing for efficiency and the passenger's individual driving preferences) is formulated and a real-time ML system is designed that addresses this trade-off.

The development of the expository instantiations based on the nascent design theory are, thus, subdivided into the following three research inquiries:

RI 2. *Defining the requirements for designing an ML-based decision support system for head and neck cancer treatments; designing the system according to the DoL framework to enhance the decision making process.*

RI 3. *Determining the specific characteristics of consumer data generated on two-sided platforms; designing an ML system according to the DoL framework that maintains highly individual user profiles to models their preferences in detail.*

RI 4. *Conceptualizing an ML system based on the DoL framework that models driving preferences of users, learns efficient driving patterns, and resolves the trade-off* between the preferred and an efficient driving behavior; designing the system as a real-time system that can be used in dynamic situations that occur with autonomous vehicles; evaluating the system in a simulation environment based on real carsharing data.

In order to evaluate the proposed artifacts, they are implemented as computer programs using the programming languages *Java*, *Python 2.7*, and *Python 3.6* in combination with data processing and ML libraries such as *NumPy*, *SciPy*, *Scikit-learn*, and *TensorFlow*. The implementations comprise the constructs of the design theory and abstract definitions of their functions as well as concrete formulations of the processes involved in the expository instantiations. The implementations correspond to the formulae provided in this dissertation, which allow for a precise replication of the findings.

I.3 Structure of the Dissertation

This cumulative dissertation is comprised of three parts. In Part A, I describe the motivation for my research (A.I.1), present the research agenda (AI.2), outline the structure of the dissertation (AI.3), define the research context and design (AI.4), and state the contributions of the dissertation (AI.5). Chapter A.II is concerned with the theoretical background of this dissertation comprising (artificial) intelligence in general, ML and big data analytics, and computational data analytics in IS research.

Part B constitutes the main part of this dissertation. In that part, four studies are carried out that address the design of ML systems for complex decision making problems (see Table A-1). Chapter B.I comprises one research article, in which a nascent design theory for ML systems is derived. In the three articles comprised by Chapter B.II, the design theory is applied to design applications for specific problems in different contexts.

Table A-1. Overview of studies included in the thesis.

No	Outlet	Status	Ranking (VHB)	Section	RI	Main contribution
1	Proceedings of the Twelfth International Conference on Design Science Research in Information Systems and Technology	Published	C	B.I	1	Nascent design theory (DoL framework) for machine learning systems dealing with complex analysis problems. The theory addresses real-time (incremental) machine learning and the benefits of computing machine learning models in a distributed manner.
2	Proceedings of the Thirty-Eighth International Conference on Information Systems	Published	A	B.II	1, 2	Medical decision support system that uses machine learning to provide physicians with treatment recommendations for head and neck cancer patients. The system adheres to the principles of the DoL framework and lays the foundation for deriving design principles for machine-learning-based decision support systems for chronic diseases in general.
3	Proceedings of the Fortieth International Conference on Information Systems	Accepted	A	B.II	1, 3	Recommendation system for consumers on two-sided platforms with the purpose of recommending the most desirable content/products for each user. It adheres to the DoL framework and employs a novel technique based on time-series embedding, using a combination of feedforward and recurrent neural networks to create content-based, context-sensitive, and user-specific recommendations.

A.I Introduction

4	Journal of Management Information Systems	Submitted (second round)	A	B.II	1, 4	Machine learning artifact for autonomous vehicles that need to resolve a trade-off between resource efficiency and behavioral preferences. It adheres to the principles of the DoL framework to allow for a novel way of gradually learning a trade-off based on two machine learning models in an autonomous and real-time manner. The artifact was tested in a simulation environment with a minimal data set obtained from a carsharing provider.

In Part C, I summarize and synthesize the findings of Part B, discuss limitations and implications for theory and practice, and finally conclude the dissertation and briefly state future research opportunities. The structure of the dissertation is illustrated in Figure A:2.

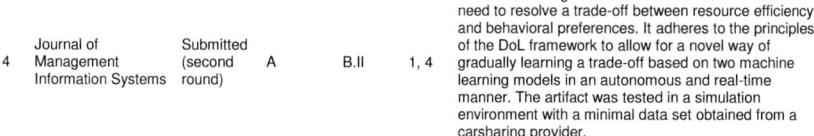

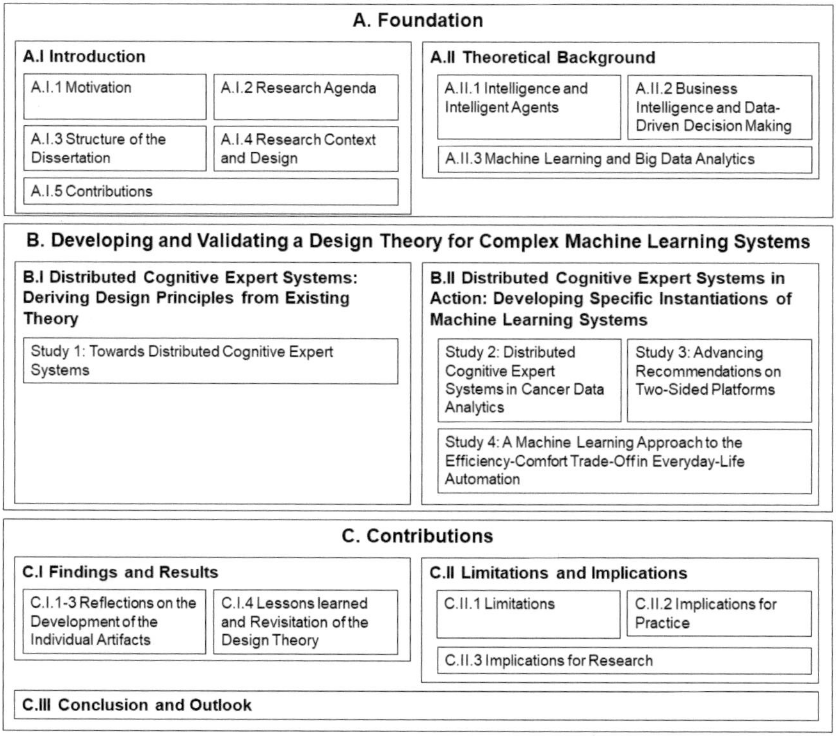

Figure A:2. Structure of the dissertation.

I.4 Research Context and Design

As stated in the Research Agenda Section, the studies are carried out in different settings. Study 1 is a purely theoretical approach to designing ML systems. Drawing on existing theory on AI, mathematical optimization, and basic economics, a nascent design theory is derived. In order to provide the theory's practicability (Gregor and Hevner 2013), expository instantiations (Gregor and Jones 2007) are provided in three subsequent studies.

Study 2 considers data on cancer patients collected by the Department for Oral and Maxillofacial Surgery of the University Medical Center Göttingen. These data and data collected in medical environments in general are characterized by a large number of missing values (Wells et al. 2013). Treatment decisions embody great impacts for both patients and physicians and the large number of factors that determine the outcome of a treatment makes it exceptionally difficult for physicians to make the right decision. Furthermore, they are hesitant to adopt IS partially due to the additional administrative efforts that would arise thereafter (Romanow et al. 2012). An artifact is designed that considers these circumstances to make a step towards practicable ML for medical decision support systems. Study 3 addresses shortcomings of contemporary recommendation systems, which are well known because they have been studied in regard to a large variety of recommendation techniques (Çano and Morisio 2017). A novel user-specific, context-aware, content-based, and collaborative recommendation system is developed that may effectively process static and time-varying variables of users and take into account their history and similarities to other users in order to make more precise predictions regarding their future actions on two-sided, digital platforms. The proposed system is evaluated using data gathered on Expedia's hotel booking platform. Finally, Study 4 designs an artifact for a real-time environment, namely autonomous vehicles. More specifically, an ML system is developed composed of three ML modules: a module for modeling users' preferred driving behaviors, a module for modeling the relationship between driving behavior and efficiency, and a module that builds upon these two modules to resolve a postulated trade-off between efficient and comfortable driving. The proposed design may be adapted for other situations in which individuals' goals, especially regarding processes that play a role in people's everyday lives (Yoo 2010), may run against system-level goals.

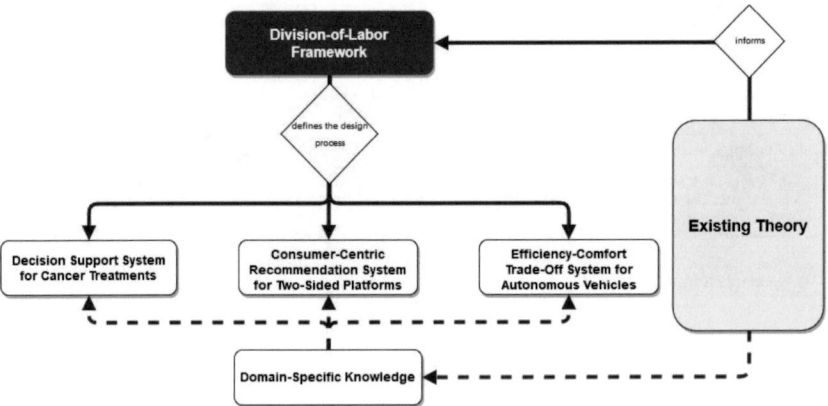

Figure A:3. Research design.

Studies 2, 3, and 4 not only provide new ways of addressing ML problems in different application areas. Combined with Study 1, they also become part of a nascent design theory that is put to work in different contexts to showcase its effectiveness in addressing different challenges when employing ML and big data analytics. The overall design of the research is depicted in Figure A:3.

In the field of IS, we may distinguish five general streams of research, which I describe in the following according to Banker and Kauffman (2004). The research stream *value of information* is concerned with understanding the value that information may contribute. It determines the worth of certain information for individual decision makers and firms in a market context. The stream of *human-computer systems design* studies cognitive processes based on behavioral decision theory to model individual and group dynamics when interacting with IS. *IS organization and strategy* is a research stream that considers the value of IS investments on levels of analysis that go beyond the individual level, for example, the system level, business process level, strategic level, and organizational level. The research stream *economics of IS and IT* deals with the value of IT, the adoption of network technologies, and IT-based coordination for organizations, markets, and industries. Finally, the *decision support and design science* research stream – a science of the artificial (Gregor 2009; Simon 1996) – deals with designing and implementing IS. This dissertation, taking action with respect to complex decision making problems by designing ML systems, contributes to the latter research stream. In contrast to behavioral science – a traditional paradigm in IS research –, which is rooted in natural science and aims to explain and predict social phenomena (Hevner et al. 2004; Shmueli and Koppius 2011), design science research is concerned "not with how things are but with how they might be" (Simon 1996, p. xii). Research conducted based on the design science paradigm, thus, produces prescriptive knowledge, which describes the steps to achieve a certain goal (Gregor and Jones 2007). In IS research, design science contributions build IS, which gather, process, and provide information and, thus, often take on the shape of decision support systems (Arnott and Pervan 2012), which are also a point of focus of this dissertation in dealing with decision support and autonomous decision making systems. Here, the design of these systems follows a top-down approach by first developing a design theory, which represents a meta artifact with the purpose to address a class of problems (Iivari 2015), and then applying this design theory to specific instances of the problem class.

From a philosophical perspective, inquiries in IS research – and social science research in general – each follow one of two main epistemologies, namely positivism and interpretivism (Gregor 2006). "Positivism is largely concerned with the testing, confirmation and falsification, and predictive ability of generalizable theories" (Wynn and Williams 2012, p. 788) and assumes the existence of an objective reality, whereas interpretivism considers reality to be a subjective view of each individual on a given phenomenon in a specific context (Wynn and Williams 2012). According to Gregor (2006), design theories require some kind of realist ontology. In social science research, we witness the increasingly important role of a realist epistemological view, namely critical realism (Bhaskar 1998), which states that there exists an independent reality, albeit not fully understandable or observable by humans, and requires research to examine the shape of components and interactions in this reality based on given observations (Wynn and Williams 2012). This dissertation is concerned with developing methods to automatically derive insights from data. For this purpose, I follow the ontology of critical realism, assuming that given observations are indicators that an observer may use to model relationships that they believe to exist in a hidden reality. Furthermore, with human knowledge of reality being fallible (Wynn and Williams 2012) and assuming that this statement holds true for any observer that obeys the laws of this reality (i.e., both biological and artificial agents (Pfeifer and Bongard 2006)), the proposed design theory advocates for adaptive systems that not only create representations of their perceived realities but also adapt these representations when new observations are made.

Table A-2 summarizes the research design of this work.

Table A-2. Overview of research design and core research questions.

No.	RI	Epistemology	Paradigm	Methodology (Seminal work)	Data collection	Data analysis
1	1			Top-down development of a design theory (Gregor and Hevner 2013)	-/-	-/-
2	1, 2	Critical Realism	Design Science	Design according to the DoL framework (Tofangchi, Hanelt and Kolbe 2017)	Collection of structured and unstructured patient data by the medical staff of the University Medical Center Göttingen	Machine learning (clustering, different kinds of classification models)
3	1, 3			Design according to the DoL framework (Tofangchi, Hanelt and Kolbe 2017)	Quantitative consumer data automatically collected through the Expedia platform	Machine learning (dimensionality reduction, different kinds of classification models)
4	1, 4			Design according to the DoL framework (Tofangchi, Hanelt and Kolbe 2017)	Real-time usage data automatically collected in carsharing vehicles	Machine learning (different kinds of regression models, density estimation)

I.5 Contributions

The major contribution of this dissertation is a nascent design theory (Gregor and Hevner 2013) that builds upon existing theory (i.e., "kernel theories" (Hevner et al. 2004, p. 76)) in artificial intelligence, mathematical optimization, and economics to provide design principles for complex ML systems. It can be classified as a *theory for design and action* (Type V according to Gregor (2006)) and comprises prescriptive knowledge for a given class of problems. As a theory involving constructs, methods, models, and design principles to address a certain class of problems, it constitutes a level 2 (nascent) design theory (Gregor and Hevner 2013). The design theory deals with how to address complex decision making problems (diverse data sets and complex relationships to uncover) through ML based on a composition of models while maintaining the interpretability of the designed systems, the durability of employed models (i.e., efficient incorporation of new data), and their adaptability to environmental changes that may alter previously identified relationships. Although ML research has contributed individual methods for addressing some of the above-mentioned challenges (e.g., ML based on composing multiple models through bagging (Breiman 2001) or boosting (Schapire 1990)), there exists, to the best of my knowledge, no extensive theory for the design of ML systems that addresses the technical challenges that occur in business contexts that involve big data. From the perspective of AI research, this dissertation contributes to the research stream of collective intelligence (al-Rifaie et al. 2012; Beni and Wang 1993; Lévy 1997; Reynolds 1987; Rosenberg and Pescetelli 2017): It shows how a complex autonomous system can be constructed by using simple ML models as buildings blocks that compose a recursive collective system. The system may exhibit diverse behavior that is determined by the behavior of its building blocks, which are agents that act autonomously towards a common goal. With respect to big data analytics in IS research, design principles are contributed that not only allow addressing the challenges of big data but also leverage the high volume and variety of big data to build systems that process tasks of a high complexity. For these reasons, I classify this contribution as an "invention" (Gregor and Hevner 2013, p. 345). That is, the design theory deals with an application domain with a low maturity (ML and big data research in general is still at an early stage, with many uncertainties regarding the suitability of different ML models for different kinds of problems) and a low solution maturity (the given problem has not been adequately addressed yet).

Aside from the main contribution, this work includes several minor contributions: The provided expository instantiations (Gregor 2007) for three different application contexts, which require building models to get an understanding of the studied problems, contribute to theory for explaining (Type II) and theory for predicting (Type III). More specifically, this work develops (1) data science methods for head and neck cancer treatments that identify patient attributes that are most crucial to making treatment decisions and predict optimal treatments, (2) a recommendation system for the Expedia platform that makes hotel recommendations based on users' historical behavior, their similarity to other users, and uses a novel approach to model user contexts, and (3) a real-time system for autonomous vehicles that uses data-driven techniques to resolve a user-specific trade-off between efficient and comfortable driving. These situated artifacts – brought into material existence by applying the nascent design theory – can be, in themselves, understood as contributions to design science research (Gregor and Hevner 2013). Each of these artifacts solves a particular problem and may be the first step in the emergence of new theory that addresses a broader spectrum of related phenomena (Gregor and Hevner 2013). Moreover, the research framework surrounding these artifacts offers more abstract method descriptions and design principles that can be operationalized in further contexts. These contextual studies (1) describe how, in typical medical environments in which physicians decide upon treatments and log their decisions, patient attributes crucial to treatment decisions can be discovered in a data-driven manner and which design principles for treatment decision support systems can be generalized to chronic diseases, (2) show that a recommendation system for two-sided platforms, in general, learns more effectively by taking into account collaborative, content-based, contextual, and user-specific variables at the same time and how to integrate static and time-varying data, and (3) provide design principles for a trade-off module for autonomous agents whose interactions with humans is characterized by conflicting system-level goals (e.g., efficiency) and individual-level goals (e.g., comfort of users). On a more abstract level, these artifacts are expository instantiations (Gregor and Jones 2007) of the design theory and therein contribute to our understanding of it. Being in a nascent state, this theory requires practice-oriented research to test its propositions and drive its maturity.

Finally, the proposed design theory also constitutes a contribution to business practice, dealing with increasingly significant issues related to employing big data systems. While big data enables more sophisticated analyses of business problems, their accommodation requires new methods and models (Chen et al. 2012) because standard ML methods are often not suited for big data analytics. The design theory addresses the challenges arising from a high volume, variety, and velocity of data (Abbasi et al. 2016) through design principles that guide the development of durable, self-sufficient ML systems, in the sense that they continuously and autonomously adapt to changing environments without interference by developers. Furthermore, design principles are proposed for task division to address complex analysis problems through ML while maintaining a high level of interpretability of employed systems, thereby mitigating managerial barriers for data-driven decision making that may arise from a lack of understanding of the approaches (LaValle et al. 2011).

The complete set of contributions is summarized in Table A-3.

Table A-3. Summary of anticipated contributions.

Audience		Anticipated Contribution
Business Practice	Developing and Employing Big Data Systems	(1) Design principles for developing durable, self-sufficient ML systems that can process sets of diverse data and continuously and autonomously enhance their models of phenomena of interest. (2) Design principles for a task division system to allow for the processing of complex analysis problems while maintaining the comprehensibility of the acquired solutions for business analysts.
Research	Information Systems	(1) A nascent design theory that guides the development of ML-based systems such as decision support systems, recommendation systems, and autonomous systems. (2) Specific design science artifacts that show (a) how to increase the acceptance of ML-based recommendations, (b) how to improve the personalization of services based on observations of user actions, and (c) possible means to address the increasingly relevant trade-off between the efficiency of services provided to users and their satisfaction. (3) Contributing to big data research in the field of IS by showing how to build upon existing ML models to compose systems whose values go beyond the isolated employment of said ML models.
	Artificial Intelligence	(1) Recursive design of cognitive systems that allows for a composition based on similarly structured modules. The recursiveness enables the design of autonomous agents at an individual level as well as the hierarchical design of a population of agents, thereby contributing to research on collective intelligence.
	Machine Learning	(1) Theoretically justified use of collective intelligence to address complex decision making problems, showing that the division of such problems into a set of sub-problems may increase the efficiency of the analyses. (2) Showing how to create sophisticated methods of analysis that mitigate the black-box effect of commonly used deep neural networks.

II. Theoretical Background

In this chapter, I lay the theoretical foundation to the research conducted in the following part of the dissertation. Centered around ML and big data analytics for creating intelligent machines that automatically solve problems and offer decision support, the theoretical background comprises, at an abstract level, the definition of intelligence and intelligent agents (Section II.1) and, at a more concrete level, the current state of research in ML and big data analytics (Section II.2) and data analytics in the field of IS (Section II.3).

II.1 Intelligence and Intelligent Agents

Defining intelligence has been a concern of research for quite a long time. Based on a sound definition, researchers and practitioners would be able to measure intelligence and compare the intelligence of living beings more effectively. In the realm of AI research, which studies, replicates, and aims to improve upon biological intelligence (Russel and Norvig 2010), an explicit definition of intelligence is crucial to designing scientific studies. However, to date, there is no generally agreed-upon definition of intelligence. Furthermore, the philosophical question of whether AI could (at least theoretically) be deemed equivalent to biological intelligence may have an influence on the way researchers address AI problems. In the following, I review different viewpoints on these matters and provide a definition of intelligence and intelligent agents that is suited for this work and describe the notion of AI that this dissertation follows.

First, I briefly present dictionary definitions of intelligence. They range from short or vague definitions to more elaborate definitions. Short or vague definitions of intelligence include "the faculty of understanding" (Intelligence 1989), "the ability to learn or understand or to deal with new or trying situations" (Intelligence 2003), "the ability to acquire, understand, and use knowledge" (Intelligence 2011), "the ability to learn, understand, and make judgments or have opinions that are based on reason" (Intelligence 2013), "the ability to learn, understand, and think about things" (Intelligence 2014), and "the capacity to learn, reason, and understand" (Intelligence 2019a). All of these definitions have in common that they rely on other explicit concepts such as understanding, having opinions, thinking about things, and reasoning. In order to make use of these definitions as a basis for research, one requires definitions of these newly introduced concepts.

That being said, defining these concepts is an issue in itself: While people have an intuitive grasp on the meaning of understanding, thinking, and reasoning, providing a formal definition is at least as challenging as finding a definition for intelligence. I look at two further, more elaborate definitions provided in dictionaries to obtain a broader perspective on the different views on intelligence: "capacity of mind, especially to understand principles, truths, facts or meanings, acquire knowledge, and apply it to practice; the ability to comprehend and learn" (Intelligence 2019b) and "the general mental ability involved in calculating, reasoning, perceiving relationships and analogies, learning quickly, storing and retrieving information, using language fluently, classifying, generalizing, and adjusting to new situations" (Intelligence

2006). While the former is also based on vague concepts such as understanding, the latter describes properties that subjectively define a high level of intelligence (instead of providing an objective, abstract notion of intelligence) and relies on highly specific factors that it considers to determine intelligence. Furthermore, by referring to calculating and using languages fluently, it appears to treat intelligence to be exclusive to humans rather than a trait that is commonly shared by living beings in general.

From a psychological view, intelligence is defined by some as the "ability to understand complex ideas, to adapt effectively to the environment, to learn from experience, to engage in various forms of reasoning, to overcome obstacles by taking thought" (Neisser et al. 1996, p. 77), being "aware, however dimly, of the relevance of his behavior to an objective" (Drever 1952, p. 175), "the capacity for knowledge, and knowledge possessed" (Henmon 1921, p. 195), "a mental trait, is the capacity to make impulses focal at their early, unfinished stage of formation ... therefore the capacity for abstraction, which is an inhibitory process." (Thurstone 1924, p. 159) and being based on judgement, initiative, and the ability to adapt to changes (Binet and Simon 1905). Several attempts have been made to quantify intelligence (e.g., the Wechsler adult intelligence scale (Kaufman 2016) and the Stanford-Binet intelligence scales (Janzen et al. 2004)), with the most popular quantification being the, now infamous, intelligence quotient (Neisser et al. 1996). Such intelligence tests have in common that they exclusively address the intelligence of humans, neglecting other entities that may exhibit intelligent behavior. For this reason, their underlying notion of intelligence is not suited for the work in this dissertation.

Many definitions of intelligence and intelligence tests are either human-centric and, thus, unsuited for this work or revolve around the concept of understanding, assuming that intelligent behavior is determined by the degree to which an entity can understand its environment. This concept has also sparked discussion in the AI community about whether an artificially intelligent entity can develop a mind and a consciousness similar to living beings. This discussion is typically referred to as the strong AI versus weak AI discussion. Putnam (1967) argues that the human mind can essentially be considered an information processing system and consciousness arises through neural computations. His work, thus, argues in favor of strong AI – the general possibility of AI reaching the same level of consciousness as humans. On the other hand, Searle (1980) – a proponent of weak AI – states that a digital computer program cannot develop a consciousness of its own regardless of how intelligent its outputs are considered. To exemplify his position, he proposes the Chinese room experiment (Searle 1980). This thought experiment assumes the existence of a computer program that can take Chinese writings as inputs and presents other Chinese writings as responses to these inputs, being able to hold convincing written conversations with Chinese native speakers. A computer running this program, along with a human being, is locked in the Chinese room whose interior is unobservable to outsiders. Through a slot in the door, outsiders may provide Chinese inputs, which the human inside the Chinese room inputs into the computer according to the steps given in a manual. They then return the outputs to the outsiders, creating the impression that the entity in this room is a native Chinese speaker and possibly even passing the Turing test (Turing 1950) – a test designed to determine whether a machine performs a certain task in a human-like manner. Through this thought experiment, Searle (1980) likens the machine to the human. Just like the human obtains Chinese writings by following a set of rules, the machine, internally, also uses a set of rules to compute the writings and appear capable of holding and understanding a conversation.

The question "Can machines think?" (Turing 1950, p. 433) is deemed difficult to answer. Whether or not they are able to understand is an issue of similar difficulty. The Chinese room experiment intends to show that exhibiting human-like behavior does not necessarily imply human-like understanding. However, the same can be said about humans and other living beings. How can one be sure that a human has actually understood their actions? Although unintended by Searle (1980), his Chinese room shows that, in general, when judging an entity's intelligence, we can rely only on observations of this entity. For this reason and for the reason that one may endlessly debate the concept of intelligence without arriving at a solution (Drever 1952), in this dissertation, I adopt a pragmatist's view on intelligence that is based on the notion of agents: all entities that sense their environment through sensors and act upon this environment through actuators (Pfeifer and Bongard 2006). Aside from animals, the term "agents" also comprises artificial agents that possess these traits. In this regard, an agent's intelligence is its ability to manipulate its environment to achieve a certain goal, which is effectively determined by how well it perceives its environment and puts plans into action (see Figure A:4). This definition refrains from using abstract concepts such as understanding and consciousness and reduces intelligence to observable behavior. Although this dissertation is not exclusively concerned with developing systems that have a physical embodiment, they all satisfy the given definition of agents because they sense their environment through data and perform actions either on their own or through human decision makers by providing them with recommendations.

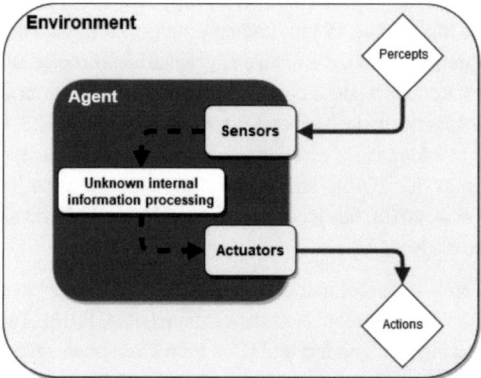

Figure A:4. Agents perceive their environment through sensors, decide upon actions based on their percepts, and carry out these actions using their actuators (based on Russell and Norvig (2010)).

Having specified the definitions of intelligence and (intelligent) agents that I use, I present a further aspect of (artificial) intelligence that is essential to this work before concluding this section. This aspect is most commonly referred to as collective or collaborative intelligence, which has gained notable interest starting with the observation of ant colonies (Wheeler 1911). Studying the behavior of organisms, Wheeler (1911) takes the ant colony as an example to show that collectives of organisms are, in fact, distinct organisms themselves. Therefore, the collectives exhibit behavior that is different from the behavior of the individuals within the same collective (Wheeler 1911). For example, upon finding a source of nutrition, ants leave pheromone trails that allow other ants to locate the source. This fact has inspired the ant colony optimization algorithm, which is based on the following principles (Dorigo 1992): The higher the pheromone density the more likely are the ants to follow the respective path. Since pheromones evaporate over time, pheromone trails that lead to food sources that are closer to the ant colony are typically denser. Thereby, ant colonies can determine the distance of food sources, despite each individual following the simple rule of leaving pheromones when finding food without being aware of the bigger picture. Similarly, Reynolds (1987) has, among others, shown that a flock of birds can be simulated by having each bird follow three local rules: avoid collision with other birds, match velocity with neighboring birds, and maintain a close proximity to neighboring birds. These examples show that a modular composition of autonomous agents that follow individual goals may collaboratively form a more complex system that pursues higher-level objectives (al-Rifaie et al. 2012). This dissertation exploits the great potential of collective intelligence by studying and developing modular ML systems.

II.2 Machine Learning and Big Data Analytics

Digital technologies are computational IS that process information and enable communication through connectivity technologies (Bharadwaj et al. 2013). Due to their continuous growth in terms of memory, computational power, and communication speed, as well as their miniaturization and the rapid decline of their price-to-performance ratio (Bharadwaj et al. 2013; Yoo 2010), they have widely spread into everyday business and people's private lives (Vodanovich et al. 2010), leading to the gradual emergence of ubiquitous computing (Yoo 2010). With the homogenization of data, enabled by digital technologies, allowing for accessing a variety of information through a single device (Yoo et al. 2010), firms may acquire information in a way that not only speeds up decision making (Bharadwaj et al. 2013) but also allows them to consider a variety of information, which improves the quality of decisions. The process of datafication (Galliers et al. 2015), having emerged from a wide availability of digital technologies (Tilson et al. 2010), has increased the significance of data analytics for research and business practice alike.

The use of sophisticated statistical models can enable unveiling complex relationships and insights that are hidden in vast amounts of data (Abbasi et al. 2016). The discipline of ML is concerned with developing such models that learn from given observations and, thus, acquire knowledge that is not explicitly injected by a programmer. ML research has taken great steps since the middle of the 20th century when it started to gradually distance itself from symbolic AIs such as the general problem solver (Newell et al. 1959) and move towards statistical and less symbolic models such as k-Means (Lloyd 1982), support vector machines (Cortes and Vapnik 1995), and different kinds of regression models. The history of the now-famous neural networks has started with the perceptron (Rosenblatt 1958) with the aim to mimic biological intelligence. Having been out of sight for some time, they have regained attention with the emergence of the multi-layered perceptron (Cybenko 1989) and, subsequently, deep neural networks (Deng and Yu 2014). Through these developments, ML has achieved great success in some areas including document analysis (Devlin et al. 2018), speech recognition (Dahl et al. 2012), and object detection in images (Krizhevsky et al. 2012). In contrast to business intelligence, the primary focus of ML lies on developing predictive and prescriptive, data-driven models that automatically classify entities, predict outcomes of certain processes, and provide action recommendations (Han et al. 2012). While it also deals with descriptive data analytics such as clustering, density estimation, and visualization, its models typically neglect explaining phenomena for the sake of increasing predictive performance (Shmueli 2010). On the other hand, business intelligence, pursuing the objective of informing managers and decision makers, is concerned with explaining the *why* of phenomena of interests or historical events and, thereby, supports the decision makers' understanding of certain situations.

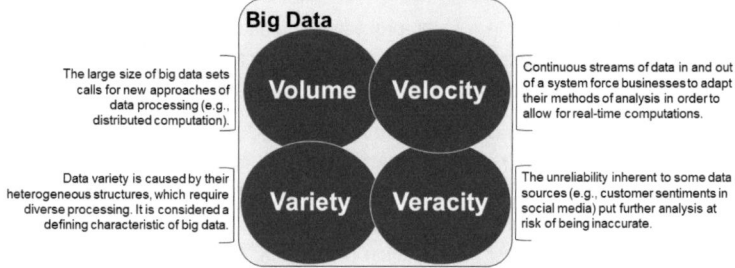

Figure A:5. The four V's of big data (based on Gandomi and Haider (2015) and Yoo (2015)).

Being based on the models developed through ML research and enabled by the ubiquitousness of IS (Vodanovich et al. 2010), big data analytics promises to support research and drive decision making through a plethora of methods of analysis including text and audio analysis and social media analytics (Gandomi and Haider 2015). Before discussing the advantages and challenges of big data analytics, I provide a definition of big data. In this work, I define big data in terms of four V's that are widely recognized in the literature (see Figure A:6), namely volume, variety, velocity, and veracity (Abbasi et al. 2016; Goes 2014; Müller et al. 2016; Yoo 2015). *Volume* refers to the large sizes of big data sets; many practitioners consider big data as data whose size exceeds a terabyte (Gandomi and Haider 2015). While such classification may be justified in practice, its arbitrariness and generality make it unsuited for research. Instead, I consider the volume of a data set as *big* if it cannot be processed, as a whole, inside the main memory of a machine. This way, the volume of a data set is classified relative to the machine on which it is processed and the algorithm according to which it is processed. This classification rule emphasizes the significance of a data set being too large for a machine and a data analysis setting classified as *big* according to this rule is certain to require special treatment and the design of entirely new algorithms to allow for an out-of-memory analysis. Approaches have emerged to address this very issue – among others, distributed computation (e.g., Dean and Ghemawat (2008)). The *variety* of big data sets comes about by firms' technological capabilities to collect, store, and analyze various kinds of structured, semi-structured, and unstructured data" (Gandomi and Haider 2015). Unstructured and semi-structured data, making up 95% of all existing data (Cukier 2010), constitute the most significant source of variety. Not only are there different kinds of unstructured data (e.g., texts, images, audio, and video) but also does each instance of each kind assume a different shape (e.g., different document/video length, number of pixels, and pitch of one's voice). The *velocity* of data is "the rate at which data are generated and the speed at which it should be analyzed and acted upon" (Gandomi and Haider 2015, p. 138). Due to the ubiquitousness of computational connected devices (e.g., smartphones), the rate at which data are generated has exploded, desperately calling for new methods of analysis that employ real-time (or online) computation (Gandomi and Haider 2015). That is, in order to acquire insights from the complete and large flows of data, firms require ML models that process the data on the fly. This requirement implies the need for updatable ML models (Constantiou and Kallinikos 2015) that, upon receiving new data, adapt their understanding of their environment rather than having to entirely recompute it in a batch-processing manner. Finally, *veracity* refers to the uncertainty of big data, which are typically collected in order to obtain a diverse rather than a completely reliable view of a particular topic (Gandomi and Haider 2015).

I note that some researchers have introduced further V's (Gandomi and Haider 2015) to the definition, whereas others do not explicitly state veracity as an essential part of big data (Gandomi and Haider 2015; McAfee and Brynjolfsson 2012). In this work, I neglect further V's because they do not contribute to understanding the foundation of my research and are generally questionable as part of the definition of big data. Regarding veracity, I argue that collecting big data is characterized by agnosticism, that is, data are often collected without a predefined purpose (Constantiou and Kallinikos 2015). This approach contrasts with traditional approaches to data collection, which were guided by certain (business) problems that were to be addressed. Consequently, only small numbers of variables were collected in a controlled manner that were deemed significant for the respective problems. Big data, on the other hand, is collected without a predefined purpose, flipping "the traditional strategy-making from top-down to bottom-up" (Yoo 2015, p. 63). Large numbers of variables are, thus, gathered without extensive care for quality control. Such data collection process may give rise to the postulated veracity of big data.

For the same reason – that is, agnostic data collection –, big data sets comprise large varieties of data often from different sources and in different formats (e.g., numbers, texts, and images). Some scholars believe that, while the high volume and velocity of data is a (rather technical) challenge to be addressed by big data systems (Goes 2014), it is the variety associated with big data that accounts for its value (Goes 2014; Yoo 2015). In contrast, this work is based on the concept that a high volume of data is also valuable in itself, allowing analysts to employ increasingly complex ML models, which may only be trainable based on a large number of examples. At the same time, I acknowledge the potentials that high-variety data can bring. Data sets with a high variety (e.g., a combination of related audio, image, textual, and structured data) offer richer ways of analysis through which diverse information can be generated. Apart from these opportunities, big data also brings some challenges. That is, to accommodate the large volume and velocity of data (i.e., the large and rapid flow of data in and out of the systems), organizations have to apply changes to their IT infrastructure (Abbasi et al. 2016). Moreover, the variety of data requires the combination of multiple methods of data processing and analysis to deliver integrated insights. Finally, data veracity leads to a lack of confidence in insights and conclusions obtained through data-driven analyses and can be addressed by improving the data collection process or consulting multiple sources of data to mitigate the veracity. While my research deals with the volume, velocity, and variety of data, their veracity is out of the scope of this dissertation.

While data analytics and ML have traditionally been predominantly studied by different subgroups of the computer science discipline such as the database and ML communities, the management and IS community has increasingly been targeted as an audience for such research. Due to the knowledge base (e.g., on data management and analytics and their contribution to value creation) and research methods (in particular, related to behavior and design science research) available to IS scholars, they have also begun to conduct research on these topics and particularly on big data analytics, for which they hold a comparative advantage (Agarwal et al. 2014; Goes 2014). Big data analytics bears the potential to transform business and research alike (Constantiou and Kallinikos 2015; Goes 2014; Markus 2015).

In practice, big data analytics can be used not only to optimize a firm's internal processes, effectively provide personalized products and services, and create autonomous systems that make decisions on their own rather than supporting other decision makers (Parasuraman et al. 2000) but also to generate entirely new business models (Günther et al. 2017). The firm can leverage big data to "develop whole new value propositions, target different customers, or interact with customers in different ways" (Günther et al. 2017, p. 197). Netflix serves as one of the most prominent examples of such an innovation. Moving away from a disc rental business model to streaming, Netflix has started using big data analytics for its successful recommendation system (Koren et al. 2009) and even produces data-driven content (Lycett 2013). Aside from these practical application areas, big data analytics also bears the potential to enhance research methods. While it can be used to generate more sophisticated insights from structured (i.e., numerical and categorical) data, its benefits are even greater with unstructured data. Most of all available data is unstructured (Cukier 2010) and qualitative research, in particular, relies on such data, whose analyses have traditionally required extensive human labor. Grounded theory (Glaser and Strauss 1967), a popular qualitative research method, is concerned with an inductive, bottom-up theory generation and is, thus, aligned with the philosophy of big data that "research can start with data or data-driven discoveries" (Müller et al. 2016, p. 291). For these reasons, quantitative and qualitative research, especially grounded theory, are particularly suited to be assisted by big data analytics, which may analyze large amounts of data to provide researchers with hints throughout the research process (Agarwal and Dhar 2014; Berente and Seidel 2014). We have witnessed the emergence of data-analytics-based tools that assist research through the analyses of unstructured data. Examples include topic modeling through latent Dirichlet allocation for assisting grounded theory (Müller et al. 2016; Rai 2016) and semantic-indexing-based tools for literature review (Koukal et al. 2014).

While the literature is dominated by articles that call for increased big data research (e.g., Abbasi et al. (2016); Goes (2014)), point out the potentials of big data (e.g., Günther et al. 2017; Constantiou and Kallinikos (2015)), and propose system designs that address a particular problem (e.g., Atahan and Sarkar (2011); Lin et al. (2017)), it lacks a clear guidance on how to develop practically employable big data systems and carry out their implementation while addressing the typical challenges that arise.

II.3 Computational Data Analytics in Information Systems Research

With increasingly ubiquitous data and consumers being regarded as "walking data generator[s]" (McAfee and Brynjolfsson 2012, p. 5) that leave their traces all over the world wide web through their use of, for example, mobile devices, online shopping, social networks (McAfee and Brynjolfsson 2012), firms are provided with large amounts of individual-level data that can be mined to obtain insights that allow for optimizing different business processes and individualizing consumer experiences (Martens et al. 2016). Similarly, research may profit from appropriate methods of analyzing the newly available data. Quantitative researchers, which often rely on simple statistical models such as linear regression (Legendre 1806) or structural equation modeling (Kaplan 2008), may take advantage of increasingly accurate ML methods to uncover complex relationships in data (Shmueli and Koppius 2011). While this new IT-enabled opportunity to gain insights and drive efficiency and business value calls for research on its ethical and societal implications and requires the careful consideration of privacy issues (Galliers et al. 2017), this dissertation is concerned with the design of computational methods of analysis that effectively extract knowledge from given data.

Firms have long understood the value of systematically collecting data regarding both the market in which they operate and their internal processes, using data to improve their understanding of their customers and competitors (Constantiou and Kallinikos 2015). IS and management research considers their situation and has produced various kinds of (big) data analytics systems for different business problems. Examples include financial fraud detection through a meta learning approach (Abbasi et al. 2012), healthcare analytics such as logistic-regression- and density-estimation-based prediction of the readmission of patients diagnosed with heart failure (Bardhan et al. 2015; Muus et al. 2010) and the estimation of risks of adverse events related to chronic diseases through Bayesian multitask learning (Lin et al. 2017), profiling techniques (i.e., techniques for identifying user attributes based on their behavior) based on the real-time application of the Bayesian rule (Atahan and Sarkar 2011), and a framework for designing self-reflective, dynamic, intelligent DSSs (Meyer et al. 2014). Thereby, ML and big data analytics automate practical processes that include intelligent tasks traditionally performed by humans, while also holding implications for IS research regarding the design of socio-technical systems (Gasson 2003) in which not only the social but also the technical part also exhibits intelligent behavior.

I refer to the processes involved in data-driven decision making as the *information-value chain* (Abbasi et al. 2016). With data-driven decision making pursuing the ultimate goal of increasing the value of a business, Abbasi et al. (2016) define the information-value chain (see Figure A:5) as follows.

> The information value chain is the cyclical set of activities necessary to convert data into information and, subsequently, to transform information into knowledge (Fayyad, Piatetsky-Shapiro, & Smyth, 1996a, 1996b; Han, Kamber, & Pei, 2006), which individuals use to make decisions and take action. The decisions and actions then result in outcomes such as business value and additional data (Sharma et al., 2014). (Abbasi et al. 2016, p. iii)

The information value chain is divided into different stages, each of which involves different actors, technologies, and processes (Abbasi et al. 2016). While the first few steps of collecting data and transforming them into information and knowledge are carried out by technical employees and data analysts, decision making is performed by managerial employees and executives in cooperation with data scientists who assist in interpreting machine-generated knowledge.

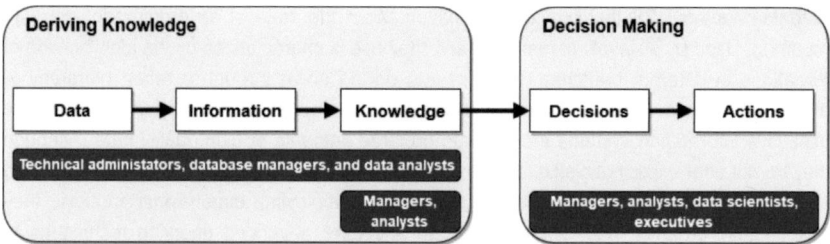

Figure A:6. The information value chain (based on Abbasi et al. (2016)).

Datafication and the rise of big data have led to the transformation of the information-value chain regarding the actors and technologies involved in its different stages (Abbasi et al. 2016). Business intelligence based on big data increasingly relies on database management systems that can handle unstructured data (e.g., NoSQL systems), distributed data processing systems (e.g., Hadoop (Dean and Ghemawat 2008)), and data scientists across all stages, guiding the analysis processes (Abbasi et al. 2016). Being concerned with data-driven decision making, decisions support systems (DSSs) are the main tools used in business intelligence (Arnott and Pervan 2008). DSSs are systems that support and improve managerial decision making (Arnott and Pervan 2005). Rather than having to make a choice between alternative actions, a decision maker undergoes a creative process to discover such alternatives (Frisk et al. 2013). The high complexity of decision making (Sharma et al. 2014) makes the design science paradigm (Hevner et al. 2004) essential for DSS research (Arnott and Pervan 2012), which conceptualizes and implements practically relevant systems and studies their influence on decision makers and a firm's success (Arnott and Pervan 2008; Chen et al. 2012) and requires the consideration of rigor and relevance through a structured development and a systematic analysis of managerial requirements (Arnott and Pervan 2012). Arnott and Pervan (2005) identify seven kinds of DSSs frequently designed by researchers, which they describe as follows. *Personal DSSs* are developed for a single decision problem dealt with by an individual or a small group of independent individuals. Personal DSSs support individual managers as opposed to the previously dominant, but ultimately unsuccessful management information systems that intended to serve whole organizations. Contrasting personal DSSs, *group DSSs* target problems that require the involvement of multiple managers who share the decision responsibility. They make use of software, hardware, language components, procedures, and communication and information processing tools to influence the group decision process. Similarly, n*egotiation DSSs* are also concerned with group dynamics, but, being conceptually based on game theory, are specifically designed to facilitate negotiations. One may distinguish two types of negotiation DSS, namely problem-oriented negotiation DSS, which offer support for a specific problem type, and process-oriented negotiation DSS, which support the general process of negotiation. *Intelligent DSSs* comprise rule-based expert systems, which use explicitly programmed domain knowledge to assist decision makers, and the currently trending ML-based systems. Research in the latter domain has partly been concerned with achieving a human-machine symbiosis (Döppner et al. 2016) and partly with the full replacement of humans by computers. *Executive information systems and business intelligence* are described as data-oriented DSS that provide information about the state of an organization through reporting. Used by all levels of management, their use is characterized by the identification of deviations in different branches of a firm and drilling down through a report hierarchy to discover the cause. *Data warehouses* address an issue emerging with the need for large-scale executive information systems that operate on large amounts of high-quality data. Although they do not offer explicit decision recommendations, they assist decision making by providing raw data from an integrated set of databases. Employing dimensional models, they meaningfully organize high-dimensional data and offer advanced querying techniques to obtain more sophisticated reports of organization-wide matters. Finally, *knowledge-management-based DSS*s

The different kinds of DSSs are not mutually exclusive. A DSS may simultaneously belong to multiple categories. While Arnott and Pervan (2005) group business intelligence with executive information systems, they also clarify that "business intelligence ... is a poorly defined term and ... some even use ['business intelligence'] for the entire range of decision support approaches" (Arnott and Pervan 2005, p. 71). Finally, they provide a definition that I consider purposeful for this work: Business intelligence is "the contemporary term for both model-oriented and data-oriented DSS that focus on management reporting" (Arnott and Pervan 2005, p. 71). This definition moves the focus away from the way data are processed to the kind of information that is presented (i.e., managerial reports). However, in this dissertation, I focus methods centered on data processing. More specifically, I deal with intelligent (decision support) systems. This dissertation designs intelligent systems that can be used, among others, for business intelligence purposes. Regarding the application domain, business intelligence has proven to be effective in numerous areas. In IS research, we observe the development of data-driven methods that can be used for business intelligence in different areas such as healthcare, customer experience, and entertainment (Kruse et al. 2016; Lucas Jr et al. 2013). Prominent examples of algorithmic decision making include "IBM's Watson (Markus, 2015); self-driving cars (Newell and Marabelli, 2015); fraud detection algorithms (Sharma et al., 2014); loan processing algorithms (Chae, 2014), and recommender systems (Lycett, 2013)" (Günther et al. 2017, p. 196). Specific applications include descriptive analytics for optimizing processes, predictive analytics for risk identification, and visual analytics for surgical assistance in healthcare (Gianchandani 2011), individualized targeting of customers by analyzing their demographics, locations, and related contextual data (Hormozi and Giles 2004; van den Poel and Lariviere 2003), as well as recommendation systems and social media analytics through sentiment analysis based on natural language processing for e-commerce and market intelligence (Chen et al. 2012). Business intelligence applications may range from simple reporting tools that, for example, visualize the performance of different branches of a firm to more complex ML-based analyses that automatically generate action recommendations to managers. Thus, ML and, more recently, with the exponentially growing amount of data (Müller et al. 2016), big data analytics provide the techniques that allow for an effective business intelligence (Chen et al. 2012).

While ML in the context of AI has at times been concerned with finding ways to replace human intelligence or humans altogether (Arnott and Pervan 2005), IS research views data analytics as a way to support human decision makers through DSSs. ML and big data artifacts (Gregor and Hevner 2013) contributed in the IS community mostly constitute level 1 artifacts. Rather than developing their own ML models, they are characterized by making use of and adapting algorithms and models from external communities dedicated particularly to ML and big data. Being an interdisciplinary field, IS research borrows and benefits from concepts contributed by other fields. Thus, the fact that IS research does not primarily yield new kinds of ML models is not necessarily a disadvantage of the field. On the contrary, IS research, being concerned with IT-based value generation, can build upon existing models and combine them to develop practically relevant big data systems and design their interaction with human actors. I argue that, enabling a symbiosis of human and machine by using intelligent algorithms that can integrate human inputs, one may take advantage of autonomous machines, which can process large data sets in richer ways than humans (Constantiou and Kallinikos 2015), without discarding their unique experiences and grasps of complex situations. Collective AI, described in the previous section, constitutes an approach to data analytics that is well suited to achieve such human-machine symbioses. Collective AI not only can enhance the predictive performance of analytics systems (Rosenberg and Pescetelli 2017) but also enables the integration of humans as part of the collective. This integration requires carefully designed interfaces between humans and machines, but ultimately allows for human involvement throughout the analysis process. The collaborative and modular nature of collective AI has recently led researchers to acknowledge its potential for business decision making by getting "beyond the limitations of machine learning AI and [bringing] humans with all of their knowledge – both explicit and tacit – into the loop" (Metcalf et al. 2019, p. 85).

B. Developing and Validating a Design Theory for Complex Machine Learning Systems

This part deals with the development of a nascent design theory that can be used to design ML systems for analysis problems involving complex data potentially in a real-time or distributed environment. Following the design principles, one may build multi-agent systems that perform high quality analyses and offer explanatory insights into their analysis processes. The application of the design theory is showcased by three exemplary artifacts that address prediction problems in different contexts. To achieve these goals, the studies comprised by Chapters B.I and B.II carry out the four RIs (derived in Section A.I.2).

Chapter B.I, comprising Study 1, derives the design theory – named the Division-of-Labor framework – from existing theory. In Chapter B.II, I present Studies 2, 3, and 4, which, guided by the design theory developed in Study 1, address different practical data analytics problems through ML. While each study addresses an individual research problem, they all contribute to RI 1 by providing a better understanding of the nascent design theory.

Note that the original manuscripts of the studies were edited to correct spelling, phrasing, and minor formal errors.

I. Distributed Cognitive Expert Systems: Deriving Design Principles from Existing Theory

To address the lack of principles for designing practicable ML systems for complex decision making problems, the design science approach (Hevner et al. 2004) is followed to develop a design theory. Aiming to cover a broad range of data analysis problems, this design theory is developed in a top-down manner. That is, rather than solving a problem in a particular context (Gregor and Hevner 2013; Iivari 2015), "an IT meta-artefact (Iivari, 2003) is constructed as a general solution concept (van Aken, 2004) ... to be instantiated (March & Smith, 1995) into a ... concrete IT artefact (application) to be adopted and used in a specific context" (Iivari 2015, p. 107).

1 Study 1: Towards Distributed Cognitive Expert Systems

Table B-1. Fact sheet of Study no. 1.

Title	Towards Distributed Cognitive Expert Systems
Authors	Schahin Tofangchi*, Andre Hanelt, Lutz M. Kolbe Chair of Information Management, University of Göttingen, Platz der Göttinger Sieben 5, 37073 Göttingen, Germany * Corresponding author. Tel.: +49 (0)551 / 39 - 22254. E-mail address: schahin.tofangchi@uni-goettingen.de
Outlet	Proceedings of the Twelfth International Conference on Design Science Research in Information Systems and Technology, Karlsruhe (Germany), 2017
Abstract	The process of Datafication gives rise to ubiquitousness of data. Data-driven approaches may create meaningful insights from the vast volumes of data available to businesses. However, coping with the great volume and variety of data requires improved data analysis methods. Many such methods are dependent on a user's subjective domain knowledge. This dependency leads to a barrier for the use of sophisticated statistical methods because a user would have to invest a significant amount of labor into the customization of such methods in order to incorporate domain knowledge into them. We argue that machines may efficiently support researchers and analysts even with non-quantitative data once they are equipped with the ability to develop their own subjective domain knowledge in a way that the amount of manual customization is reduced. Our contribution is a design theory – called the Division-of-Labor framework – for generating and using experts that can develop domain knowledge.
Keywords	Machine learning, domain knowledge, distributed computing, real-time analytics, deep learning

1.1 Introduction

Due to the growing ubiquitousness of data as a result of technological advances in areas like mobile computing, social networking, and smart vehicles, businesses have the opportunity to gain previously unobtainable information about their customers and market position (Baesens et al 2016). However, in order to gain business value from these data, businesses require better data analytics architectures that can extract relevant information from data (Baesens et al 2016). With the growing attention paid to big data analytics in information systems (IS) research, Abbasi et al. (2016) outline a research agenda and identify great opportunities for design science research for big data and real-time analytics artifacts. Goes (2014) describes how the knowledge of the IS community and its research methods can positively impact big data research. He argues that big data constitutes an interesting field of research for a community traditionally engaged in interdisciplinary research. Similarly, Agarwal et al. (2014) state that the IS community possesses knowledge of data management as well as value creation through data. They suggest that the IS community, therefore, holds a comparative advantage for conducting research on big data.

Abbasi et al. (2016) call for new design theories aimed at gaining not only information but insights through data analyses. Although methods for automated data analyses exist, the process of gaining insights from data is often accompanied with great amounts of human labor (Bengio and LeCun 2007). Despite these amounts of human labor, the results obtained are, especially with unstructured data, not always satisfactory due to shallow learning algorithms (Bengio and LeCun 2007). In an attempt to get more informative results from the analyses of unstructured data, researchers and practitioners often incorporate more prior knowledge into algorithms, essentially relocating human labor from the postprocessing step to the preprocessing step. While this approach may indeed improve the results of the analysis step, a decrease in human effort will not be observed because the incorporation of prior knowledge is usually not a trivial task, but has to be performed individually for each given problem.

We suggest that an efficient solution to complex data analysis problems lies in a modular design of the analysis process – that is, a design comprising independent and possibly reusable data analysis modules. Our contribution is, thus, a design theory for distributed expert systems. Our design theory, named "the Division-of-Labor (DoL) framework", addresses the issue of solving complex information extraction tasks from any combination of numerical, categorical and unstructured data. The DoL framework handles complex tasks by treating them as compositions of less complex sub-tasks, which are distributed among several processing units. Aside from reducing the complexity of tasks, task distribution also enables horizontal scalability of learning and data analysis algorithms, making the framework suitable for analyses of big data (Grolinger et al. 2014).

1.2 Related Work

The presented design theory is a framework that employs multiple consecutive layers of feature learning and information extraction to solve data analysis problems. As such, it can be considered a "deep learning" framework. As an emerging field of research, deep learning does not have a clear, established definition (Deng and Yu 2014). However, deep learning methods are said to learn "feature hierarchies with features from higher levels of the hierarchy formed by the composition of lower level features" (Bengio 2009, p. 5). Deng and Yu. (2014, p. 201) name two commonly identified aspects of deep learning: "(1) models consisting of multiple layers or stages of nonlinear information processing; and (2) methods for supervised or unsupervised learning of feature representation at successively higher, more abstract layers". We proceed by giving a short overview of contributions made to this field.

Many deep learning methods have been developed in the recent past such as Deep Feedforward Neural Networks and Deep Recurrent Neural Networks (Goodfellow et al. 2016), Convolutional Neural Networks (LeCun et al. 1995), Deep Boltzmann Machines (Salakhutdinov and Hinton 2009), and Deep Belief Networks (Hinton et al. 2006). In addition to these methods, other machine learning (ML) methods have been developed, which do not themselves constitute deep learning methods, but serve as important building blocks of deep learning architectures. Examples for such methods are Autoencoders and representation learning methods (Bengio et al. 2013), which extract important features from data that can be used in subsequent processing steps to perform more meaningful analyses. Bengio (2009) describes principles for the implementation of deep learning algorithms.

In addition to deep learning, the DoL framework draws on concepts of "ensemble learning". We describe these concepts in Section 1.2.1 and relate them to our framework.

1.2.1 Relationship to Ensemble Learning

Ensemble learning describes a class of ML methods that combine a set of weak, supervised learning models to obtain a single, ideally more accurate, model (Schapire 1990). One generally distinguishes ensemble methods in "bootstrap aggregating" (bagging) (Breiman 2001) and "boosting" (Schapire 1990) methods. Bagging methods combine weak models by averaging or taking a majority vote of their individual predictions (Breiman 2001). Random Forests are a prominent example of bagging learning systems, making use of Decision Trees as a base set of weak classifiers (Breiman 2001). Boosting methods, in turn, not only specify a way of combining the output of models but also affect the training procedure of these models. They train different models with emphases on different subsets of the data such that individual models perform particularly well on different subsets (Zhou 2012). The output combination may be performed through (weighted) averaging/voting (Zhou 2012).

Our DoL framework builds on concepts used by ensemble learning and distributes data among multiple learning models. However, it applies less strict conditions on the individual models and the way data are distributed. That is, it not only allows a developer to employ bagging and boosting methods but also allows for the application of different kinds of ensemble methods. The principles of data/task distribution in the DoL framework are described in Section 1.3.4.

1.3 A Design Theory for Distributed Expert Systems

In response to the call for IS research in the context of data analytics by Abbasi et al. (2016), we propose a design theory – the Division-of-Labor framework – following the steps developed by Gregor and Jones (2007). We adopt these steps to develop our design theory because they encourage and enable formalization of knowledge of the artifact's shape and configuration, rather than incorporation of implicit knowledge in the artifact.

The goal of our design is a product, namely a distributed cognitive expert system. We label this product as "cognitive" because of its increased employment of self-governance and interaction with its environment (see Section 1.3.2). We describe the purpose and scope of our framework in Section 1.3.1, our justificatory knowledge – underlying knowledge giving an explanation for our design – in Section 1.3.2, constructs of our theory in Section 1.3.3, principles of form and function – the framework's architecture – in Section 1.3.4, principles of implementation in Section 1.3.5, artifact mutability – anticipated changes of the artifact in future research – in Section 1.3.6, and testable propositions – predictions about the outcome of artifact implementations – in Section 1.3.7. We omit the optional step of presenting an expository instantiation for space reasons[1].

1.3.1 Purpose and Scope

The purpose of the proposed design theory is to provide guidelines for the development of systems that deal with complex data analysis tasks – that is, analysis tasks that aim to model non-shallow relationships between some attributes. In contrast to traditional ML algorithms that are often equipped with rather high amounts of prior knowledge and deep neural network architectures that require relatively little prior knowledge but in turn much computational power (LeCun et al. 1995), our design deals with computational scalability by distributing the workload on multiple processing units and requires a moderate amount of prior knowledge. This prior knowledge typically assumes the form of specifications on how to distribute incoming data analysis tasks. For example, in the context of customer churn prediction, a developer may incorporate prior knowledge into a system developed according to the DoL framework by specifying that customers are to be segmented based on their age, income, and location.

Our design theory is applicable to supervised and unsupervised ML problems based on structured and unstructured data. However, the design theory is particularly interesting in the context of unstructured data such as texts and images. Analyses of such data often aim to unveil deep patterns, whereas quantitative data are often analyzed using shallow methods, and, unlike quantitative data analyses, typically leave room for interpretation. Unstructured data analyses are, therefore, often enhanced through the incorporation of domain knowledge (Tan and Lai 2000) – a process that is automated in the DoL framework.

1.3.2 Justificatory Knowledge

We provide justificatory knowledge for our design theory by motivating the need for the DoL framework from three different viewpoints, namely the viewpoints of (mathematical) optimization theory, economics, and artificial intelligence. The DoL framework is based on the assumption that complex tasks can be solved more efficiently by subdividing them into less

---

[1] Expository instantiations are presented in studies presented in subsequent chapters.

complex sub-tasks solved by experts. We justify this assumption – from the viewpoint of optimization theory – by using the fact that splitting an optimization problem (i.e., a task) into a set of smaller optimization problems (i.e., sub-tasks) generally reduces the search space of that problem. Although not necessarily the case for all optimization scenarios, in practice, most of them are solved faster once the search space is reduced (Bengio 2009). For an illustration of search space reduction by splitting a problem into sub-problems, consider the following formalization.

Formalization: Search space reduction through task division

Let H be an optimization problem comprising N interdependent optimization problems $\forall_{i=1}^{N}: \mathcal{H}^{(i)}$, all of which, for reasons of simplicity, have a search space of size $\forall_{i=1}^{N}: s(\mathcal{H}^{(i)}) = d$. Solving these optimization problems individually yields a total search space of size

$$s_{individual} = \sum_{i=1}^{N} s(\mathcal{H}^{(i)}) = N \cdot d \qquad (B\text{-}1)$$

On the other hand, solving the whole optimization problem H corresponds to jointly – rather than individually – solving the sub-problems and yields a search space of size

$$s_{joint} = \prod_{i=1}^{N} s(\mathcal{H}^{(i)}) = d^N \qquad (B\text{-}2)$$

One may notice that $s_{individual} < s_{joint}$ for $\forall N > 2, d > 1$. That is, the search space of the overall optimization problem is in virtually all cases larger than the sum of search spaces of the sub-problems.

[2]

From an economist's viewpoint, the concept of "division of labor"[3] states that splitting a task into smaller, yet semantically coherent, sub-tasks allows for a specialization of agents in their respective tasks (Smith and Krueger 2003). Division of labor, as proposed by Smith and Krueger (2003), assumes an economy involving humans and requires agents to be adaptive – that is, being capable of learning through observations. The authors argue that specialization of individuals in different tasks, enabled by the adaptability of these individuals, leads to a faster and more effective processing of these task.

---

[2] The formalization shows that the sum of individual search space sizes is smaller than the size of a joint search space. However, the solutions obtained through these two methods are not necessarily equivalent. Nevertheless, as evidenced by, for example, the Knapsack Problem (Andonov et al. 2000), solutions obtained by searching in individual search spaces can be an approximation to the overall optimal solution that is yielded by an exhaustive search in the joint search space.

[3] Not to be confused with our Division-of-Labor Framework.

While adaptability has also been of interest in the data analysis and ML community, as evidenced by methods developed by Bengio et al. (2013), Bifet and Gavalda (2007), and Vaughan and Bohac (2015), the majority of research is concerned with static data analysis rather than dynamic, time-varying models (Alippi and Roveri 2007); Huang et al. 2011; Quionero-Candela et al. 2009). Common exceptions are embedding methods such asWord2Vec models (Mikolov et al. 2013), which map data into different spaces and can be used in further building blocks of different tasks, and deep learning methods that hierarchically process an input through a number of processing layers (Bengio et al. 2013).

Finally, we motivate our framework from the viewpoint of artificial intelligence. Research in this area has been moving away from symbolic problem representation as part of the so-called "good old-fashioned artificial intelligence" (Pfeifer and Bongard 2006). Harnad (1990, p. 1) defines the Symbol Grounding Problem as the problem of making "semantic interpretation of a formal symbol system...intrinsic to the system, rather than just parasitic on the meanings in our heads" (emphasis in original). That is, symbolic representations are high-level and human-readable, but they do not allow a system to attribute meaning to those representations on their own. They are mainly used for problems that suffer from a low degree of uncertainty. Non-symbolic computation allows an agent to self-govern and interpret information, but at the same time makes it infeasible for outsiders to interpret the computation steps (Harnad 1990). Nowadays, parts of the ML community move towards non-symbolic approaches, but the dependence on symbolic computation still largely remains. The DoL framework encourages researchers to make use of non-symbolic problem representations while maintaining a fair share of symbolic computation steps to allow for domain knowledge incorporation.

1.3.3 Constructs

In this section, we name and describe the constructs, that is, the entities of interest (Gregor and Jones 2007), of our theory (see Table B-2). We use these constructs to structure our framework's form and function in Section 1.3.4.

1.3.4 Principles of Form and Function

The DoL framework comprises two component types – the expert and the central Executive (CE). Each class of tasks is processed by one CE and one or more experts. Experts are specialized in a certain class of sub-tasks, whereas CEs are required to possess general knowledge of the task and be capable of consulting the right expert(s) for an incoming task and handling their responses accordingly. The features of an expert and a CE are described in the following paragraphs.

1.3.4.1 Expert

An expert is an agent that is specialized in a certain kind of tasks, for which it possesses domain knowledge. It receives tasks from the CE, processes them and transmits solutions back to the CE. An expert can also simultaneously play the role of the CE of a sub-task (see Figure B:1).

B.I Distributed Cognitive Expert Systems: Deriving Design Principles from Existing Theory

Specialization. An expert is specialized in a certain domain and class of tasks. Thus, the specialization area of an expert is classified by these two properties. With A and B each denoting an area of specialization consisting of k sets each corresponding to the range of a dimension, we obtain the following implication for the degree of specialization (dos):

$$dos(B) > dos(A) \Leftrightarrow \exists_{1 \leq i \leq k} : |A_i \backslash B_i| > 0) \wedge (\forall_{1 \leq i \leq k} : A_i \supseteq B_i) \tag{B-3}$$

That is, one dos is higher than another dos, only if the area of specialization covers a narrower range in at least one dimension of inputs and goals and an equally as broad range in the rest of the dimensions. An expert's degree of specialization is always at least as high as that of its superordinate CE.

Adaptation. Experts receive new data and feedback from their CEs and use them to improve their performance. An expert updates its statistics and learning models as well as possible data repositories when new input is received. Effective adaptation is achieved through a model-specific definition. That is, adaptation should be specified not as a general-purpose process, but with regard to the base models used in the data analysis system.

Table B-2. Definition of the study's core constructs.

Category	Construct	Description
Problem specification	Task	A task is an instance of a class of data analysis problems. It is concerned with the application of learned models to unseen data.
	Sub-task	A sub-task is a separable unit of one task. A sub-task's solution can be used to facilitate finding a solution to its super-task.
Input	Data	Data enter the system as part of a task or for the purpose of achieving specialization. Data contain relevant information regarding a given or future task(s).
	Data type	Different kinds of data require different kinds of analysis techniques. We distinguish between structured (numerical and categorical) and unstructured data.
	Domain	Data are associated with domains. A domain refers to a data set describing the same class or related classes of objects.
Cognitive system	Intelligent agent	An agent is any entity that perceives its environment through sensors and acts upon it through actuators (Russell and Norvig 2010). "Intelligent agents are characterized on the one hand by the fact that they comply with and exploit their ecological niche, and on the other that they exhibit diverse behavior" (Pfeifer and Bongard 2006, p. 67).
Specialization	Specialization	Specialization, as a concept of division of labor (Smith and Krueger 2003), refers to an increased knowledge of a certain area. An agent's area of specialization is its domain and task of interest.
	Degree of specialization	An agent's degree of specialization is the narrowness of its area of specialization. A degree of specialization can be quantified only in a manner relative to another specialization, provided that one of the areas of specialization is narrower or equal to the other area in all of its dimensions.
	Expert	The expert is an agent and an intrinsic component of the DoL framework. One expert is specialized on one or more domains and processes one class of sub-tasks and data sets.

	General knowledge	General knowledge is knowledge of a variety of domains and/or tasks. As the opposite of specialization, generality is a relative property.
	Task distribution	Tasks can be divided into sub-tasks and distributed among experts. Task distribution comprises dividing tasks into sub-tasks and assigning them to the right experts.
Task distribution	Semantic coherence	Semantic coherence is the connectedness of a set of entities on the semantic level. That is, a semantically coherent set of entities contains entities that are semantically similar.
	Combination of partial solutions	Tasks can be divided into sub-tasks that are treated individually. The solutions to sub-tasks are partial solutions that have to be combined to obtain a solution to the super-task.
	Central executive	The central Executive is an agent and an intrinsic component of the DoL framework. It possesses general knowledge, distributes tasks, and combines partial solutions into an overall solution.
	Feedback	After a task is processed, outside feedback may be given to the system to evaluate its performance.
Performance	Adaptation	Given some outside feedback, the system re-evaluates and improves its analysis steps.
	Sustainability	Sustainability refers to the ability of a system to theoretically sustain itself indefinitely. That is, it is able to continuously learn from new data without suffering a significant increase in computation time.
Interpretation	Explanation	For reasons of interpretability by outsiders, the system's components may provide explanations as to why a task was solved in a particular way.

Sustainability (optional). An expert's models have to be adapted when new data are seen. For reasons of scalability, it is necessary for an expert to update, rather than recompute, its models. That is, with $\mathcal{M}_t$ being an expert's model at time t and x_t being the data point received at time t, the expert has to apply a function $u(\cdot)$ with a finite output size (i.e., independent of the number of data points) to update its model according to (B-4).

$$\mathcal{M}_{t+1} = u(\mathcal{M}_t, x_t) \qquad (B-4)$$

However, for some models such as many non-parametric models and data indexes, it is not possible to apply a function of finite output size because those models require storing all data points. For such models, it is necessary to prune the data set when before the storage capacity or computational limit is exceeded. We label sustainability an optional function because, while scalability problems related to big data are becoming increasingly relevant, there are still many practical scenarios, in which data sets are sufficiently small to neglect scalability problems.

Explanation (optional). Data analysts are faced with the prediction-explanation trade-off (Abbasi et al. 2016). That is, sophisticated data analysis methods such as neural networks may perform well on data analysis tasks, but their solutions are hard to interpret. An expert processes tasks in depth and should communicate the rationale behind its solutions (i.e., which particular circumstances led to these particular solutions). The modular structure of the DoL framework facilitates interpretability of results because a researcher may examine solutions to subtasks of a lower complexity rather than solutions to complex super-tasks. We label explanation an optional function because it does not directly contribute to the performance of the system, but rather provides researchers with insights that may be used to further improve the system or the design theory.

1.3.4.2 Central Executive

The central executive is an agent that processes an incoming task by splitting it into semantically coherent and independent sub-tasks.

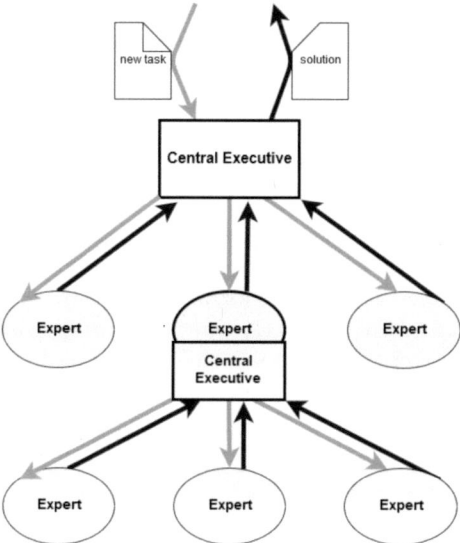

Figure B:1. The Division-of-Labor framework. Gray and black arrows indicate the transmission of (sub-) tasks and their solutions, respectively. Hierarchical re-distribution of tasks is enabled through agents that serve as both experts and central executives.

Semantic coherence and independence are important criteria for the individual sub-tasks because they will be processed independently by subordinate experts. From a set of available experts, the CE then selects the best-suited expert for each sub-task. CEs possess fairly general knowledge regarding their respective tasks such that they can categorize sub-tasks and assign them to the right expert units. After receiving the results for the sub-tasks from the experts, the CE combines them to obtain the result for its main task. A CE, in turn, can be an expert of a super-task, allowing for hierarchies of arbitrary heights. The hierarchy may be either provided by a developer who specifies the number of hierarchy levels and which tasks are solved on each level or automatically inferred by the system by employing an algorithm with each expert that decides whether a task is to be further divided into sub-tasks. This decision may be based on the heterogeneity of a given sub-set of the data.

General knowledge. The CE possesses general knowledge of domains and/or tasks. Each sub-task processed by an expert is also known to its superordinate CE. However, the CE processes tasks at a lower level of depth. That is, it models the overall domain associated to a task using a single model, whereas experts use one model per sub-task, which are typically associated with much smaller domains.

Task distribution and combination of partial solutions. A CE distributes an incoming task according to either of the principles of "division of labor" and "wisdom of the crowds". Distribution according to the division of labor principle occurs by splitting a task or a class of tasks into sub-tasks or classes of sub-tasks that whose domains are disjoint or only partially overlapping. Individual experts then each process a class of sub-tasks and the results are combined by the CE in an adequate manner. Distribution according to the wisdom of the crowds principle occurs by forwarding each task without performing any splitting. The experts then solve that task using their respective models. A combination of individual solutions in this case can often be achieved by computing a (weighted) average or majority vote.

Feedback. CEs may gather feedback from outside of the system. This feedback may assume the shape of "the correct solution" to a task or a quality statement for a solution developed by the system. Let x be a given data point and $\hat{y}$ a solution computed by the system. The feedback may then be the correct solution y – typically available in supervised learning settings – or a real-valued rating $r(\hat{y})$ associated with the solution – observed unsupervised learning settings or supervised settings, in which the outcomes are not directly observable.

Adaptation. In addition to the principles stated for experts, the CE updates its own models and redirects the feedback and the corresponding data to experts involved in the task. In addition to further models used, the CE updates its task distribution and re-combination mechanisms.

Sustainability. The principles described for the sustainability of experts also hold for CEs.

1.3.5 Principles of Implementation

Having described the constructs of our design theory and their respective functions in Sections 1.3.3 and 1.3.4, we now proceed to formulate the principles of implementation. For this purpose, we refer to data analysis systems developed according to the DoL framework as "DoL systems". Given a certain class of data analysis tasks, described by the data specification and the desired information to be extracted from the data, a DoL system is implemented by implementing the CEs and according experts. We describe the implementation steps for experts and CEs in the following paragraphs.

1.3.5.1 Training of Experts

An expert is provided with data (i.e., training examples) over its life cycle. It autonomously processes and learns from these data in accordance with the task(s) that it will solve. The specialization of an expert in a certain task and domain is achieved by the CE's task distribution and does not require additional effort by the expert, other than learning to solve its task based on the provided data. Nevertheless, there are issues that need to be considered.

As previously stated, tasks arrive in a one-at-a-time manner. Consequently, in order to enable adaptability, an expert's learning models have to specify an algorithm for incremental updates, as, for instance, provided by incremental linear regression (Huiwen et al. 2014) and incremental neural networks (Bruzzone and Prieto 1999).

Further constraints arise for an expert due to the DoL framework's aim for sustainability. While incremental learning models address storage capacity and computational limits, methods like clustering and indexing, which, in their standard forms, require access to all previously seen data points, are not in line with sustainability. In order to make these methods sustainable, the number of stored data points has to be restricted and data points are to be removed from the system once the storage capacity is reached. The order of removal is determined by an importance measure, that is, the least important data points are removed first. The importance of a data point may be measured by the recency of its last access.

Finally, an expert may provide explanations for its solutions. Explanations show which features in the data influenced the outcome the most. For models like linear regression, these features can, for instance, be identified looking at the largest products of pairs of weights and features. For multi-layered models such as neural networks, deriving explanations is less straightforward and requires iterative explanations, with explanations of higher-level layers building on explanations of preceding layers.

1.3.5.2 Identification and Assignment of Tasks

As Pfeifer and Bongard (2006) stated in the context of physical agents, it is important that all components of a system are developed in accordance with each other to enable a high synergy. For this reason, we propose that the CE is in charge of managing the training of experts and, thereby, enables their specialization. That is, it selects the data that are used to train each of the experts. For this purpose, the CE has to decide how many experts to create and how to distribute the data among these experts. In order to decide on this matter, the CE has to associate tasks with domains (i.e., perform a categorization of tasks). In the following paragraph, we describe how this decision process can be implemented.

A CE starts without any knowledge of the kind of tasks it will solve. Therefore, each task is initially processed by a single expert. As the number of processed tasks increases, the CE may introduce further experts to cope with the complexity of the data distribution. We consider three kinds of task distribution problems (from most simple to hardest case): (1) Tasks are pre-categorized before entering the system. In this case, the CE simply forwards the task according to its category. (2) Task categories are revealed after the task has been solved. In this case, the CE is faced with a classification problem. A classifier is trained to associate inputs with categories. (3) Task categories are never revealed. In this case, there is no objective notion of categories and the CE has to decide on a categorization without receiving any feedback. We elaborate on this case in more detail: Unsupervised categorization, that is, the problem of dividing the task space into sub-spaces that are each processed by a certain expert, can be treated as a clustering problem. So we refer to these sub-spaces as "clusters". Because tasks are processed one at a time, the CE has to employ an incremental clustering algorithm without a fixed number of clusters. In order for the CE to decide if further experts and, therefore, clusters are needed, it maintains a model of the expected performance of individual experts. The performance can be estimated either in terms of within-cluster homogeneity or, if labeled data are available in the case of classification and regressions tasks, by directly measuring the average accuracy of solutions for past tasks. Once the performance of an expert does not meet a certain requirement, the corresponding cluster is split into two new clusters. This requirement may, for instance, be defined as a function of the performance of the CE or a function of the performance of other experts. More formally, let k be the number of experts and $p(\mathcal{M})$ denote the performance of some model $\mathcal{M}$. Then, cluster i, associated to expert E_i, is split, if the following condition is satisfied:

$$p(E_i) < f(\{\forall_{j \neq i} : p(E_j)\}) \tag{B-5}$$

where $f(\cdot)$ is a user-defined function such as the average function. Clusters are merged, if storage limits are reached or if (B-6) is satisfied, with τ being a certain threshold.

$$p(E_i) > f(\{\forall_{j \neq i} : p(E_j)\}) + \tau \tag{B-6}$$

The sustainability of CEs is achieved through the same principles as used for experts.

1.3.6 Artifact Mutability

The DoL framework offers some room for modifications. Due to the steady development of novel methods in the ML community, the principles of implementations may be considered highly mutable. As new learning algorithms are developed, the implementation steps may be incrementally refined. Moreover, researchers may further develop the principles of form and function of our design, consisting of two components – the CE and the expert –, through minor and major adaptations.

Minor adaptations are additions, removals, and modifications of component properties. They will be required, if certain functions are deemed incomplete or unnecessary or new functions are introduced that can be related to an existing component in a meaningful way. The modification of the CE's function "task distribution and combination of partial solutions" by adding a third task distribution principle is an example of a minor adaptation.

Major adaptations are additions and removals of entire components. Major adaptations should be performed to improve the structure of the framework by attributing related functions to the same component and separating independent functions. An example for a major adaptation is the introduction of an intermediate component between the CE and the expert, which neither plays a role in the task distribution part nor in the specialization part, but deals with input/output transformations between the CE and expert instead. Leveraging the DoL framework's modularity, such a component may be particularly interesting in the context of transfer learning (Pratt et al. 1993).

1.3.7 Testable Propositions

In this section, we propose truth statements (i.e., hypotheses) about products designed according to our theory. These statements may be verified or falsified in future research.

The aim of data analysis algorithms is to automatically extract information from a given data set with respect to a certain task. Algorithms are typically evaluated based on the quality of their solutions to a task and the rapidness of their execution. Based on the property of specialization inherent to experts and the task distribution employed by CEs, we propose a higher accuracy of DoL systems compared to a mere use of shallow ML algorithms. Further, we propose that the adaptation property of experts allows for processing tasks in real time.

i. Data analysis systems developed according to the DoL framework under the use of shallow ML base models produce more accurate solutions than using the same shallow ML models in a stand-alone manner.
ii. Data analysis systems developed according to the DoL framework process tasks in real time.

Furthermore, solutions obtained through data analysis algorithms are preferred to be interpretable (Abbasi et al. 2016). This interpretability is enabled by the optional expert property of explanation emerging from the modularity of the framework and leads us to the following proposition:

iii. Data analysis systems developed according to the DoL framework are positioned at a high level of interpretability, compared to other deep learning architectures, especially in comparison to deep neural networks.

Our final proposition is based on the optional property "sustainability" of experts and relates to scalability issues. We consider an algorithm scalable to big data, if it is able to cope with more data by adding more computing units and the number of required computing units to process the data in a certain time is in linear proportion to the number of data points. We formulate proposition (iv) as follows:

iv. Data analysis systems developed according to the DoL framework scale to big data.

1.4 Conclusion

We developed a design theory – the Division-of-Labor framework – for distributed data analysis. Based on a modular design, the theory leverages specialization of individual components to gain in-depth insights from data. It addresses the need for both new design theories for sophisticated data analysis methods and scalable solutions for the increasingly relevant phenomenon of big data.

Having described the design theory's components in detail and presented principles of its implementation, we made four propositions that can be tested by implementing products according to our theory.

II. Distributed Cognitive Expert Systems in Action: Developing Specific Instantiations of Machine Learning Systems

Having laid the foundation for building ML systems according to a predefined set of requirements, in this chapter, three specific instantiations of the design theory (Gregor and Jones 2007) are developed, contextualized in the area of healthcare (cancer treatment decisions), digitally enabled two-sided platforms (hotel recommendations on a booking website), and autonomous vehicles (real-time decisions on the driving behavior). Through these instantiations, the practical use of the design principles is exemplified to show how different challenges of the given problems (problem complexity, data diversity, and time-critical decisions) can thereby be addressed.

1 Study 2: Distributed Cognitive Expert Systems in Cancer Data Analytics: A Decision Support System for Oral and Maxillofacial Surgery

Table B-3. Fact sheet of Study no. 2.

Title	Distributed Cognitive Expert Systems in Cancer Data Analytics: A Decision Support System for Oral and Maxillofacial Surgery
Authors	Schahin Tofangchi*[a], Andre Hanelt[a], Florian Böhrnsen[b] [a] Chair of Information Management, University of Göttingen, Platz der Göttinger Sieben 5, 37073 Göttingen, Germany [b] Department of Oral and Maxillofacial Surgery, University Medical Center Göttingen, Robert-Koch-Straße 40, 37075 Göttingen, Germany * Corresponding author. Tel.: +49 (0)551 / 39 - 22254. E-mail address: schahin.tofangchi@uni-goettingen.de
Outlet	Proceedings of the Thirty-Eighth International Conference on Information Systems, Seoul (Republic of Korea), 2017
Abstract	Although researchers have uncovered potential positive impacts of digital technologies in healthcare and medical centers have been increasingly making use of technology to digitally store their data, the use of healthcare analytics in clinical practice remains limited. In particular, the application of machine learning (ML) approaches, although holding the potential for providing valuable insights, is mainly restricted to descriptive ML due to the approximate nature of ML, the impact of inaccuracies, and the perceived potential additional efforts in clinical workflows. Taking into account these barriers to healthcare analytics adoption, in this multidisciplinary study, we obtained and jointly analyzed cancer data on 799 cases of cranio-maxillofacial and oral-maxillofacial surgery. We developed a real-time decision support system that predicts optimal treatments and communicates its prediction confidence along with patient attributes that are significant for decision making, thereby providing potentials simultaneously for improving quality of care and for increasing process efficiency for physicians.
Keywords	Healthcare, cancer data, machine learning, online learning, decision support system

1.1 Introduction

Providing excellent and affordable healthcare is one of the grand challenges that contemporary societies face (Agarwal et al. 2010). Due to the increased penetration of digital technologies in several contexts, recent information systems (IS) research has identified healthcare as an important area of inquiry for information technology (IT)-enabled transformations (Lucas et al. 2013). In clinical practice, however, actual usage of health IS by physicians often remains low and progresses slowly (Venkatesh et al. 2011), which significantly harms the realization of the potentials IS offers for improving quality and affordability of healthcare (Kane and Labianca 2011).

Among the diverse research fields that emerge from the beneficial impacts of health IS, data analytics (Cortada et al. 2012) is one key area (Kohli and Tan 2016). It bears the potential for making sense of an increasing amount of data resulting from more and more digitalized clinical processes (Chen et al. 2012) and, thus, supporting medical decision makers such as physicians in yielding better results with increased efficiency (Fichman et al. 2011). Accordingly, initial research has proposed prototypes to realize this potential. For instance, many machine learning models have been suggested and applied to various problems relating to patient treatments (e.g., Lin et al. (2017); Meyer et al. (2014)). However, the majority of conceptual thoughts as well as instances of healthcare analytics that were proposed by prior research build upon the underlying assumption of complete and accurate electronic health records (EHR) (Ghosh and Scott 2011; Kohli and Tan 2016; Kruse et al. 2016). Despite the value of this existing research, we must not forget what these assumptions imply for clinical practice, in terms of maintenance, effort and education (Ward et al. 2014). As described by Romanow et al. (2012), "Physicians appear to be hesitant to adopt the spirit of 'cookbook medicine' inherent in order-set protocols and clinical decision support systems ... and are wary of the potential administrative influence" (p. 6) that may result by these IS. We conclude that medical practice requires solutions that help improve treatment quality and process efficiency for physicians simultaneously.

In this paper we, therefore, present the design of an artifact (Hevner et al. 2004) that recommends treatments on the basis of existing patient data in a spirit that helps recognize the data that is actually necessary to achieve satisfactory predictions. Our research aims to provide improvements to clinical practice by making available potentials of modern machine learning (ML) techniques to recommend treatments, while, at the same time, not producing additional administrative efforts or requiring best-of-breed technical infrastructures, which, due to the heterogeneity of healthcare providers, cannot be taken for granted in the majority of contemporary healthcare organizations (Agarwal et al. 2010). Therefore, this study fits particularly well in IS research and provides important benefits for practice as "growing empirical evidence suggests organizational and data management challenges to be top barriers for health analytics" (Kohli and Tan 2016, p. 564).

Our research is contextualized in the field of oral and maxillofacial surgery. Today, head and neck cancers remain one of the most challenging malignancies in medicine. In this multidisciplinary study, we obtained and jointly analyzed cancer data on 799 cases gathered by the department of cranio-maxillofacial and oral-maxillofacial (OMF) surgery of the University Medical Center Göttingen, Germany. More specifically, in cooperation with physicians who guided the research process and evaluated the outcomes, we designed an evidence-based and contextualized clinical decision support system (DSS) (Zhuang et al. 2013) for the treatment of head and neck cancer patients by using an innovative ML framework – the Division-of-Labor (DoL) framework (Tofangchi, Hanelt and Kolbe 2017). This DSS keeps administrative effort at a low level by being able to function with minimal amounts of input data (i.e., medical staff is not forced to collect a set of mandatory patient attributes in order to receive a treatment suggestion), but at the same time making use of all given inputs to increase its predictive power. The results indicate that our artifact was able to identify a reduced, case-specific number of meaningful attributes that retain sufficient predictive power. Furthermore, our artifact's predictive component – comprising a standard classification model embedded in the DoL framework – outperformed standalone classification models.

With our study, we contribute to the research stream on health IS design by presenting a specific, situated instantiation (thus level 1 contribution type according to Gregor and Hevner (2013)) for advanced decision support that uses timely ML capabilities to aid actual clinical workflows (Agarwal et al. 2010). More specifically, we contribute to the research area of analytics within health IS by following the recent call by Kohli and Tan (2016) to provide new frameworks and techniques and, more importantly, provide insights about "What data need to be acquired ... in order to conduct data analytics and how analytic results are made available to support clinician decision making and patient behaviors" (p. 564-565).

1.2 Background

1.2.1 Data Analytics in Healthcare ISR

With the emergence of big data technologies, researchers have increasingly been developing automated data analysis methods to support decision making processes on both operational and strategic levels in various industries (Lucas Jr et al. 2013; Newell and Marabelli 2015; Woerner and Wixom 2015); the healthcare industry is no exception (Kruse et al. 2016). Describing the potentials of ML in healthcare, Gianchandani (2011) names descriptive analytics for the assessment of process efficiency, recommendation systems and risk identifying tools, computer vision and robotics for surgical assistance, as well as therapy success predictions as contributions of analytics to medical processes.

Many ML models have been proposed and applied to various problems relating to patient treatments. Noteworthy examples are the prediction of stroke risks using support vector machines (Khosla et al. 2010), the use of logistic regression to predict lung cancer (Tammemägi et al. 2013) and detect depression (Kim et al. 2015), the use of prescriptive analytics to avoid high lengths of stay in hospitals through k-Means-based outlier modeling (Gartner and Padman 2016), and the prediction of diabetes-induced hospitalization of patients by using extended Cox models to address the challenge of irregularly spaced data, which are often observed in chronic disease treatment (Lin et al. 2014). Furthermore, Lin et al. (2013) propose an integration of a rule-based method with a conditional random field for modeling patients' clinical timelines from textual data, Meyer et al. (2014) develop a reinforcement-learning-like approach to support decision making in dynamic environments with complex decision chains and demonstrate its performance on treatments of type 2 diabetes patients, and Lin et al. (2017) conduct design science research to construct a model for risk prediction of multiple adverse events for diabetes patients and exploit correlations between these events to achieve higher prediction accuracies.

The mentioned approaches make use of different automated feature selection methods. Some also use various imputation-based techniques for handling missing values. Applying imputation is problematic in general due to the replacement of non-existing values with some assumed values – leading to biased outcomes –, but more importantly, it is particularly questionable in the context of healthcare data because such data often contain large numbers of missing values (Wells et al. 2013). Since many predictive analytics tasks in healthcare are concerned with the prediction of adverse events, the most popular predictive analytics model in healthcare is the Cox proportional hazards model (Lin et al. 2014). As different kinds of analyses gain attention – such as outlier detection and segmentation of patients –, other existing and novel ML models are employed that are particularly suited for such analyses. Despite the development of data analysis methods that are specifically tailored for use in particular medical scenarios, employing such methods in practice poses a challenge due to the great impact of treatment decisions and the uncertainty that comes with machine intelligence. Furthermore, besides skill-shortages and privacy concerns (Angst and Agarwal 2009), the administrative consequences resulting from and required by the implementation of the applications is an important barrier to adoption (Romanow et al. 2012). Especially, Ward et al. (2014) in elaborating the hurdles in practical health analytics adoption, point to the connection between the required data for data analytics and the processes, efforts and costs of data collection, particularly challenging in the context of clinical practice due to the nature of the subject, where "useful data does not necessarily happen as a byproduct of the system" (p. 578). In addition to this practical barrier, the majority of research on healthcare analytics is still concerned with descriptive analytics – and not predictive analytics (Kohli and Tan 2016). That is, researchers use data analytics to gain explanatory information from healthcare data, but do not employ ML models to derive predictions or prescribe decisions. The emergence of the concept of big data has also given rise to the notion of agnostic collection of vast amounts of data – in the sense that data are collected without having a certain purpose in mind (Constantiou and Kallinikos 2015). While such measures may be beneficial in some contexts, they may have negative impacts when employed in medical institutions, in which data collection is often accompanied with high amounts of human labor. In such scenarios, it is more advisable to collect smaller, but more meaningful, sets of data. We label such data sets, collected with a certain purpose in mind, as "significant data", as opposed to big data sets that are collected agnostically with respect to their purpose.

1.2.2 Digitalization of Oral and Maxillofacial Surgery

Head and neck cancers concern tumors of the squamous cells that line the mucosal surfaces inside the mouth, the nose, and the throat. These cancers are often referred to as head and neck squamous cell carcinomas and are associated with risk factors such as smoking and excessive alcohol consumption. Localized near vital structures, the transition of a localized tumor to an invasive systemic carcinoma can rapidly worsen the prognosis for the patient (Bohrnsen et al. 2014). An oncologic treatment plan requires a collaborative effort of surgeons, pathologists, oncologists, researchers and radiologists (Stoekle et al. 2017). Size, stage, histological characterization and clinical status of the patient determine the long-term success of such therapies. Clinical and prognostic data and recent research have generated a more comprehensive understanding of the nature of head and neck cancer (Bohrnsen et al. 2017; Mery et al. 2017; Moy et al. 2017). At the same time, the amount of clinical data, on individual patients and from clinical examinations, has been growing extensively (Yu et al. 2014), posing new challenges as well as opportunities in this field due to the digitalization of medicine and research and advances in diagnostics and complex imaging.

So-called "tumor boards" – a classic, collaborative method for evaluating data on cancer patients and discussing clinical treatment plans – are used to cope with the growing complexity of available information, arising from a higher variety of data. While their primary objective is to improve treatment and care management, they also improve communication and interaction between different specialties, leading to a more personalized treatment approach (Stoekle et al. 2017). However, transaction inefficiencies result in unnecessary testing, excessive administration, and high costs for the implementation of innovative approaches (Schilsky et al. 2014). Efficiency is of importance in the field of head and neck cancer, since recent innovations in 3D-reconstruction (Bosc et al. 2017; Schepers et al. 2013) and oncologic treatment (Ferris and Gillison 2017) have caused an increasing complexity of conjoint therapy. Analyzes of clinical characteristics of different head and neck cancers, along with the interpretation of tumor-related data, are essential for delivering patient-centered, state-of-the-art care. Therefore, it is imperative to identify significant data while at the same time focusing on the volume and breadth of individual and collective data.

While it has been shown that HIT can lead to a more coherent application of guideline-based care, surveillance and monitoring, this benefit is often only achieved in academic research centers that have implemented internally designed solutions that may not be feasible for most institutions (Chaudhry et al. 2006). Recently, complex data bases, such as the head and neck cancer register of the German-Austrian-Swiss head and neck cancer group (DÖSAK), have collected data to facilitate treatment decisions. Founded in 1969 the DÖSAK has also worked together with the Bone Tumor Reference Center in Basel (Switzerland) on establishing a nationally and internationally recognized database for head and neck tumors. Although tumor databases are often growing to accommodate larger amounts of medical information, they remain static in their structure. In addition, the combination of data, treatment and technology results in an unguided complexity of EHR, raising more questions than answers.

Recent attempts have proposed new strategies to assess the problem of static, inconclusive, unavailable or insufficient data to fully inform clinical decisions (Abernethy et al. 2010). To tap into the potential of HIT and EHR, rapid-learning systems for cancer care have been introduced. The goal of this approach is to drive the process of treatment, care, and scientific discovery through routinely collected clinical data (Abernethy et al. 2010). This goal is achieved by collecting and analyzing clinical data, which is in turn used to generate evidence through retrospective analysis along with the information of prospective studies (Abernethy et al. 2010). ASCO's CancerLinQ can be described as one of such rapid learning systems. Implemented in the United States of America, CancerLinQ was launched in 2015 and has more than 1 million patient records. The collected data includes demographics, treatment schedules, billing codes, patient visit and encounter details, medical history as well as physical examination, family and social histories, consult reports, surgery reports, pathology and laboratory data, medication and prescription history (Schilsky et al. 2014). Although there has been a positive acceptance and growing interest concerning big data, evaluating CancerLinQ has shown that issues of data safety and security concerning patient identification, genetic information, informed consent and sharing data remain critical and challenging (Mayo et al. 2017).

While the interest in ML has led to the impression that big data approaches can solve most problems, such approaches often fail to provide conceptual accounts for the processes to which they are applied (Coveney et al. 2016). Medical-driven evaluations of data sets are dependent on the applied algorithms and the data specifications. Higher accuracy is often needed to improve clinical impact, since an incorrect evaluation can put clinicians and investigators on a costly and unsuccessful path (Valdes et al. 2016). To improve the accuracy and in return the clinical impact on oncologic patient care, analytic systems have to represent the oncologic system and be able to identify significant data and correlations while promoting user training by guided data acquisition. Adhering to these guidelines, static data collection processes may be replaced with a dynamic HIT system, substituting big data with significant data to increase efficiency and reduce costs and data complexity.

1.3 Context and Data

The University Medical Center Göttingen (UMG), Germany, is a joint establishment of the University Hospital and the Medical Faculty of the Georg-August-University. The aim of this integrative union is the close cooperation between the University, Medical Faculty, and the University Hospital in health care, teaching and research. With 1500 beds and 40 clinical departments and institutions, the UMG serves more than 60.000 stationary inpatients and 173.000 outpatients per year. The OMF surgery department of the UMG specializes in treating oncology, injuries and defects in the head and neck as well as the hard and soft tissues of the cranio-maxillofacial region. As a surgical specialty, it is internationally recognized as both a specialty of medicine and dentistry; a dual degree in medicine and dentistry is compulsory in Germany, most of Europe and the UK. The department of OMF surgery of the UMG with its 22 beds serves more than 1500 stationary inpatients and 4000 outpatients per year.

The treatment of oncologic patients is carried out in close cooperation with the University Cancer Center (G-CCC: Göttingen Comprehensive Cancer Center) as an interdisciplinary center of all the clinics and institutes of the UMG. The head and neck tumor board coordinates the interdisciplinary individual treatment plan in cooperation with the G-CCC to ensure the application of the latest research and diagnostic and treatment protocols in cancer medicine and the close cooperation between hospitals and institutes in the G-CCC. To provide patients with optimal counseling and excellent treatment options, the G-CCC cooperates with other universities as well as with its own research institutes in the national network of cancer centers. The close association with the German-Austrian-Swiss head and neck cancer group (DÖSAK) constitutes such a cooperation. The DÖSAK database contains more than 44oo international oncologic records, of which 799 were contributed by the OMF surgery department of the UMG. The current registration is carried out according to § 65c BGBl. I S. Maintenance and assessment of the data are performed by technicians under the supervision of physicians involved in the oncologic treatment plan. All data evaluated in this study has been fully anonymized prior to analysis. In the following, we refer to the collection of attributes belonging to an anonymized patient as "data elements". Each data element is described by 248 numerical and categorical attributes – spread over 21 tables – concerning their demographics, illnesses, tumor diagnostics, and therapies. We consider, besides data on treatment decisions, only those attributes that are regularly collected before the treatment decision is made. The given data set comprises 38 such attributes, related to the patients' demography, medical history, and preliminary diagnoses. Therapies are represented by six attributes, indicating the therapy intention (palliative or curative care) and whether or not an operation, radiation therapy, local chemotherapy, systemic chemotherapy, or other therapy kind was carried out or denied by the patient. While the given data set, with 799 elements, cannot be considered "big", we consider each data element as "big" due to the rather large number of attributes that have been collected without a certain purpose in mind. The effect of this data collection process is clearly visible: Many attributes have not been recorded and the ratio of missing values is rather high. The data collection may be enhanced by focusing a set of significant attributes.

Medical treatments have great impacts and need to be considered carefully. The choice of a treatment is prone to errors and may be a matter of life or death (Aron et al. 2011). We, therefore, consider the problem of allowing physicians to make more informed treatment decisions with the help of a DSS. At the same time, one has to consider that a DSS may create a false impression of omniscience and mislead physicians who blindly trust in it. For this reason, we emphasize the importance of human-machine symbiosis, as opposed to machine-only decision making, and consider the problem of estimating the success of therapies in addition to predicting the optimal therapies themselves. Using the information of expected therapy success, the DSS can encourage physicians to look further into uncertain cases rather than blindly follow the DSS' orders. Furthermore, we require the DSS to unveil the most important attributes for an informed treatment decision. This information is valuable because the large number of missing values in the given data set indicates that data collection poses an inconvenience to medical staff. Knowing the most important patient attributes, the DSS may influence medical staff to collect attributes that make the most significant contribution towards the treatment decision. This practice benefits both the medical staff – who now may focus on collecting a small number of significant data rather than big data of low quality – and the DSS – that can resort to important attributes of higher quality to suggest treatments.

1.4 Design of a Real-time Decision Support System

Given a data set comprising various medical attributes on 799 anonymized head and neck cancer patients, we consider the problem of developing an ML-based DSS for the treatment of such patients.

1.4.1 Data Preprocessing

In order to make the data set fit for use in ML tasks, we have to preprocess it in two ways. First, we need to transform the numerical and categorical values into a unified format such that they can be used by vector-based ML methods. We apply the transformation by introducing dummy variables for categorical attributes, representing each possible value with a zero, if the value is absent for a patient, or a one, otherwise. We further scale all numerical values to a range [0, 1] to ensure that all values are on the same scale by applying feature scaling (see (B-7)) to every instance x_i of a numerical attribute X.

$$\hat{x}_i = \frac{x_i - \min(X)}{\max(X) - \min(X)} \tag{B-7}$$

Here, $\min(X)$ and $\max(X)$ denote the smallest and largest possible value for attribute X, respectively.

Second, we need to appropriately handle missing values in the data set because ML algorithms are generally not inherently capable of handling them. There are two popular kinds of techniques for handling missing values: deletion and imputation. Deletion refers to the removal of data – for example, entire data elements or attributes that contain missing values – and is the most straightforward way of handling missing values (Cohen and Cohen 1983). Imputation refers to the insertion of assumed or estimated values as a substitution for missing values; estimates may, for example, be computed as (conditional) means of attributes or through random sampling from an estimated probability distribution of the attribute. However, neither of the methods of deletion and imputation are particularly well-suited for healthcare data, which typically contain large numbers of missing values (Wells et al. 2013). With a missing value ratio of approximately 24 percent, our data set poses no exception to this rule. Deletion of entire data elements is not a viable option because every patient contains multiple missing values. Similarly, the deletion of entire attributes that contain missing values is impractical because almost all attributes are affected. The imputation of values is also inadequate because of the low data quality that would arise from a significant number of inferred values that do not correspond to real-world observations. Due to these limitations, we resort to the method of dummy variable adjustment (Cohen and Cohen 1983), introducing a dummy variable for each attribute in the data, indicating whether the attribute is present in each data element. It is particularly suited for data sets with high ratios of missing values because it neither deletes nor alters any data, but explicitly models the absence of data and, thereby, enables the application of ML models without loss of information in the data set.

Finally, we remove therapies that were denied by the patients because the data does not indicate whether the treatments would have been carried out, if the patients had consented. After transforming our data by introducing dummy variables for categorical values and for representing missing values, our final preprocessed data set contains 786 data elements, described by feature vectors with 160 entries, belonging to patients who received at least one kind of treatment, and labels for each of the six therapy attributes.

1.4.2 Problem Formalization

Our contribution in this paper is threefold: We develop a DSS that (1) finds the most important attributes for treatment decisions, (2) predicts an optimal treatment for a patient based on all available attributes (not restricted to the most important ones), and (3) estimates the accuracy of the prediction. In the following, we formally describe the problems we solve in order to develop the DSS.

Given a set of features $X \in \mathbb{R}^{n \times d}$ and a set of labels $Y \in \mathbb{R}^n$ (here: $n = 786, d = 160$), we formalize the problem of finding the most important attributes in X as the problem of finding a combination of attributes that minimize the generalization error of some classifier that fits a function $f(\cdot)$ such that $f(X) \approx Y$. The generalization error refers to the prediction error for out-of-sample data. In our case we are faced with multiple labels per data element. That is, we have six therapy-related labels that we would like to predict. Therefore, our goal is to find the sets of most important attributes for each of the six classifiers used to fit the functions $f_1(\cdot), f_2(\cdot), \ldots, f_6(\cdot)$ that predict $Y_1, Y_2, \ldots, Y_6$, respectively. We define the label for therapy intention Y_1 as "zero", if the intention is palliative, and "one", if the intention is curative. For the remaining labels, each entry $y_{i,j}, i \in \{2,\ldots,6\}, j \in \{1,\ldots,786\}$ is equal to zero, if the corresponding treatment type was not carried out for the corresponding patient, and equal to one otherwise. The sets of most important attributes are combined to obtain the overall most important attributes.

We formalize the problem of predicting optimal treatments as a set of six classification problems – one for each set of treatment labels. That is, for each set of labels Y_i, we solve a binary optimization problem of the shape shown in (B-8).

$$\underset{\theta}{\mathrm{argmin}}\ err\bigl(f_i^\theta(X), Y_i\bigr) \tag{B-8}$$

subject to classifier-specific constraints

Here, $f_i^\theta \colon \mathbb{R}^{n \times d} \to \{0,1\}^n$ denotes the i-th predictor function with a set of variable parameters θ that we seek to optimize and $err(\cdot, \cdot)$ denotes function measuring the error between a set of predictions and a set of labels. For our problem, we choose the inverted F_1 score as our error measure; that is, $err\bigl(f_i^\theta, Y_i\bigr) = 1 - F_1(f_i^\theta, Y_i)$. The F_1 score is a commonly used measure of accuracy for classifiers that takes into account possibly imbalanced class distributions and allows for direct comparisons between the performance of classifiers by combining the performance indicators "prediction" and "recall" into a single metric (Baeza-Yates and Ribeiro-Neto 1999). A therapy suggestion for a new data element x_{new} is then given by the outputs of all predictor functions $f_1(x_{new}), f_2(x_{new}), \ldots, f_6(x_{new})$.

Finally, we formalize the problem of estimating the accuracy of a treatment prediction as finding the likelihood that a data element belongs to its predicted class. That is, for a data element x_i, we seek to find the probability of x_i belonging to each of the classes predicted by the predictor functions (see (B-9)).

$$\forall_{j=1}^{6}: p\big(C = f_j(x_i) | X = x_i\big) \tag{B-9}$$

1.4.3 Design of a Decision Support System according to the DoL framework

In order to address the problems described in the previous section and cope with the complexity of our analysis tasks, we adopt the DoL framework for the development of durable ML systems (Tofangchi, Hanelt and Kolbe 2017). We briefly introduce this framework and use it to design our DSS.

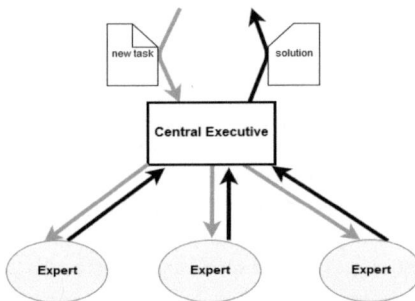

Figure B:2. The Division-of-Labor framework. Gray and black arrows indicate the transmission of (sub-) tasks and their solutions, respectively (Tofangchi, Hanelt and Kolbe 2017).

The process of automatically producing insights from data is often accompanied with great amounts of human labor (Bengio and Lecun 2007). Even so, shallow learning algorithms may still produce results of low quality and Bengio and LeCun (2007) call for more deep-learning-based algorithms, applying models of higher complexity to data. While increasing the models' complexity may improve results of analyses, it simultaneously hinders the interpretation of results – an essential aspect of analyses (Abbasi et al. 2016). We suggest that an effective way of making use of data-driven techniques in medical environments lies in a trade-off between model complexity and interpretability as well as in a modular design of the analysis process – a design comprising reusable data analysis modules – and in fostering human-machine symbiosis – the interplay between physicians and machine-based data analysis. The DoL framework comprises the components of the "expert" and the "central executive" (CE) (see Figure B:2) and is particularly suited for our problem because it treats complex analysis tasks as compositions of less complex sub-tasks (task division) and its architecture resembles the established decision making processes at the UMG's department of OMF surgery, where multiple physicians, specialized in different medical fields, gather different kinds of information on a patient and collaborate to make final treatment decisions. Experts and CEs satisfy a set of properties (see Table B-4).

Table B-4. Properties of experts and central executives in the Division-of-Labor framework (based on Tofangchi, Hanelt and Kolbe (2017)).

				Adaptation	Sustainability (optional)
Expert	Specialization	Explanation (optional)			
Central Executive	General knowledge	Task Distribution	Feedback		

From here on, we refer to an instantiation of a DoL-framework-based system as a "DoL system". We proceed to describe a set of ML models that we will use as building blocks for the development of the DSS that addresses our problems while adhering to the DoL framework's specifications.

1.4.3.1 Base Models

For our DoL system, we make use of three kinds of ML models. First, we employ a feature selection method, namely the least absolute shrinkage and selection operator (LASSO (Tibshirani 1996), to identify the most significant patient attributes. The LASSO is a common method for feature selection that uses regularized regression to identify important features (i.e., perform dimensionality reduction). However, unlike other popular regularization-based regression models that shrink the magnitude of the coefficient vector without performing a dimensionality reduction, such as ridge regression (*Tikhonov 1963*), *the LASSO explicitly sets coefficients corresponding to attributes of low importance to zero.*

Second, we use a binary classification model for the prediction of treatments. The final version of the DoL system employs a single type of classification. However, as part of our research, we try out several classification models – both in a stand-alone manner and as a part of a DoL system – in order to find a model of high quality with respect to our measure of accuracy (i.e., the F_1 score). More specifically, we test the following base models.

1. Random guesser: guesses the class of a data element at random
2. Prior classifier: always predicts the class has the most occurrences in the data set
3. LASSO classifier: LASSO regressor extended to classification problems
   - predicts class 0, if the regressor predicts a value smaller than 0.5
   - predicts class 1 otherwise
4. Logistic regression (Cox 1958)
5. Linear Probability Model (LPM) (Cox and Snell 1989)
6. Decision tree: trained with the CART algorithm (Breiman et al. 1984)
7. Soft-margin support vector machine (SVM) (Cortes and Vapnik 1995)
8. Deep neural network (DNN) (Bengio and LeCun 2007) with four hidden layers

Here, the random guesser and the prior classifier serve as baseline (trivial) solutions, to which we compare the other models in order to find out whether they meet minimum quality requirements.

Third, for the purpose of task division – realized through patient segmentation –, we make use of a clustering algorithm. Clustering the data before applying a predictive model can have a positive influence on the predictive accuracy. We demonstrate this potential by a simple example. Consider the T-classification of tumors, which groups tumors into four categories.

For the sake of simplicity, we disregard the fourth category. The T-classification then groups tumors according to their sizes (see (B-10)).

$$\text{category}(\text{tumor}) = \begin{cases} 1, & if\ size(tumor) \leq 2cm \\ 2, if\ 2cm < size(tumor) \leq 5cm \\ 3, & if\ 5cm < size(tumor) \end{cases} \quad \text{(B-10)}$$

Given a data set containing examples of such categories for a set of tumors, we may now train a linear regression model that learns to predict the T-classification from the tumor size. We consider the following data set consisting of (size, category)-tuples: {(1, 1), (1.7, 1), (1.9, 1), (2.2, 2), (4, 2), (4.6, 2), (5.4, 3), (6, 3), (7.5, 3)}. A single linear regression model, trained on the whole data set, will produce predictions that are subject to errors (see Figure B:3 (a)). However, if we first cluster the data in a meaningful way and then train a linear regression model for each cluster, we can completely eliminate the error in this particular scenario (see Figure B:3 (b)).

Our clustering approach is a variation of x-Means (Pelleg and Moore 2000) – a top-down hierarchical clustering algorithm that iteratively splits clusters, if the split leads to a lower Bayesian (Schwarz 1978) or Akaike (Akaike 1973) information criterion. We modify this algorithm such that a cluster is split, if the corresponding base classifier achieves a higher predictive performance on the new set of clusters. The predictive performance is assessed through threefold cross-validation. From here on, we refer to this method as a "cost-based clustering algorithm".

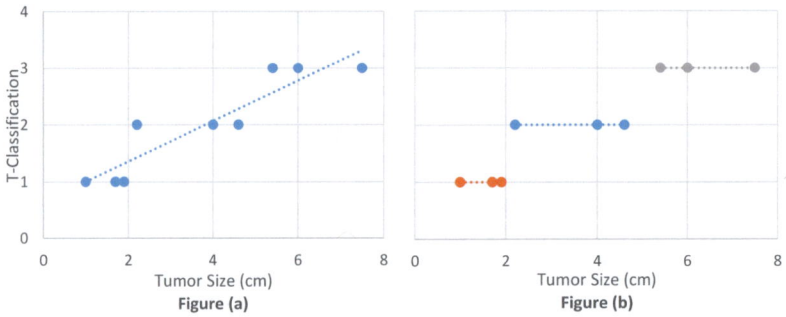

Figure (a)

Figure (b)

Figure B:3. The potential of clustering in prediction tasks. Part (a) depicts a simple regression line and part (b) depicts regression lines that were computed based on three clusters in the original data. All regression lines were computed using the method of least squares (Legendre 1806).

1.4.3.2 Expert

We divide an expert's tasks into learning tasks – performed when the expert receives new labeled data – and analysis tasks – performed when the expert is queried for information. The learning task of an expert is defined as (1) learning attribute importance ratings for each of the six treatment decisions and (2) modeling the relationship between the 160 features and the treatment decisions. Each time an expert is provided with a data element, it updates its learning models for both tasks in an online manner and returns the suggested treatment decisions.

Learning task (1) is solved by a LASSO for each treatment decision that derives a set of non-zero coefficients for attributes that contribute to the predictive power of a classifier. We employ an online version of the group LASSO (Yang et. al 2010) – a generalization of the LASSO to sub-sets of attributes. We define each individual attribute in our data set as such a sub-set in order to obtain a solution to the ordinary LASSO problem. Since all attributes are on the same scale – between zero and one – we may interpret the non-zero coefficients obtained through the LASSOs as importance scores of the attributes. Learning task (2) is solved by a classifier for each treatment decision. As previously stated, we try out different classification models to find the model that performs the best. However, the final system only makes use of a single model type, for which we implement an online learning algorithm. Our analyses (see "Results" section) reveal that logistic regression achieves the best performance. For this reason, we describe the solution to this learning task by the example of logistic regression, which we apply in an online manner by using the method of stochastic gradient ascent (Bottou 1998). Logistic regression predicts class probabilities for a given data point x_i according to (B-11).

$$p(y_i|x_i) = \begin{cases} 1 - \dfrac{1}{1+e^{-\theta^T x_i}}, & if\ y_i = 0 \\ \dfrac{1}{1+e^{-\theta^T x_i}}, & if\ y_i = 1 \end{cases} \qquad (\text{B-11})$$

Here, we denote the set of model parameters as $\theta \in \mathbb{R}^{160}$. We estimate the optimal parameters by making a step towards a local maximum of the natural logarithm of (B-11) (i.e., the "log-likelihood" of y_i given x_i). For this purpose, we compute the gradient of the log-likelihood (B-12).

$$\frac{\partial}{\partial \theta_j} \log(p(y_i|x_i)) = \big(y_i - log(p(y=1|x_i))\big) \cdot x_{i,j} \qquad (\text{B-12})$$

θ_j and $x_{i,j}$ denote the j-th entry of the parameter set and of x_i, respectively. With some small learning rate γ (e.g., $\gamma = 0.01$), the parameters are then updated according to (B-13).

$$\theta_j \leftarrow \theta_j + \gamma \cdot \frac{\partial}{\partial \theta_j} \log(p(y_i|x_i)) \qquad (\text{B-13})$$

An expert's analysis tasks involve (1) identifying the 10 most important attributes and (2) predicting an optimal decision for each treatment type and (3) estimating the accuracy of each prediction.

Analysis task (1) is straightforward and solved by selecting the 10 attributes for each treatment decision, for which the LASSOs computed the largest coefficients. Analysis task (2) is solved by selecting the class of highest probability for each predictor function. For each of the six classifiers $c_m: \forall m \in \{1,\ldots,6\}$, the class associated to a data point x_i is predicted according to (B-14).

$$\hat{y}_i^{(m)} = \underset{y\, \in\, \{0,1\}}{\operatorname{argmax}} p^{(m)}(y|x_i) \qquad (\text{B-14})$$

With classifiers that assign scores to each class, analysis task (3) can be generally solved by computing the normalized score of the predicted class. In the special case of logistic regression, we get $p(y = 0|x_i) = 1 - p(y = 1|x_i)$. The accuracy then reduces to the likelihood of the predicted class; that is:

$$\text{accuracy}(x_i) = \frac{\max_{y \in \{0,1\}} p(y|x_i)}{p(y = 0|x_i) + p(y = 1|x_i)} = \frac{\max_{y \in \{0,1\}} p(y|x_i)}{1 - p(y = 1|x_i) + p(y = 1|x_i)} \quad \text{(B-15)}$$
$$= \max_{y \in \{0,1\}} p(y|x_i).$$

The experts achieve the property of "adaptation" through the learning tasks, the property of "sustainability" through the application of online algorithms, and the property of "explanation" by communicating the most important attributes for decision making. The property of "specialization" is enabled by the CE.

1.4.3.3 Central Executive

Again, we divide the CE's tasks into learning tasks and analysis tasks. The CE has a single learning task whose goal is to perform patient segmentation and create/update an expert for each segment. The analysis tasks involve (1) querying the most suitable expert for a prediction and (2) identifying the most important attributes for decision making.

The learning task is solved by applying a cost-based clustering algorithm and maintaining an expert for each cluster. Initially, the whole data is grouped into a single cluster. Once a new data element (or an arbitrary number of data elements) enters the system, the CE simulates a split for each modified cluster and creates two copies (children) of the respective experts. The models of each new child expert are refined using a random sample of at most 100 data points from its associated cluster. If a pair of newly created experts achieves a better performance (F_1 score) than its parent expert, the new clusters and experts are kept; otherwise, they are discarded and their parent is used.

Analysis task (1) is performed by finding the nearest cluster center to a given data element, using Euclidean distance, and querying the associated expert for a prediction and the respective prediction accuracy. Analysis task (2) is solved by querying all experts for their 10 most important attributes and their scores for each prediction task. The CE aggregates the scores by computing the unsigned average for each attribute and prediction task, weighted by the number of data points in each expert's cluster and proceeds to find the minimum of the fifth largest score for each prediction task; that is:

$$s_{min5} = \min_{i \in \{1,...,6\}} s_5^{(i)}, \quad \text{(B-16)}$$

where $s_j^{(i)}$ denotes the j-th highest score for the i-th prediction task. The sets of attributes and scores are then pruned by discarding attributes with scores smaller than s_{min5}. A set of the five overall most important attributes is then computed by averaging the attribute scores over the prediction tasks and selecting the five attributes with the highest scores.

The CE achieves the property of "adaptation" through its learning task and the property of "sustainability" through the application of an online algorithm. It acquires "general knowledge" of descriptive nature on the data by dividing it into clusters and uses them to perform "task distribution" according to the principle of division of labor, enabling the "specialization" of experts on the respective clusters. It "combines partial solutions" to obtain a set of the overall most important attributes and acquires "feedback" in the shape of treatments that were actually carried out for patients, which it redirects to experts.

1.5 Results

We compare the performance (i.e., the F_1 score) of our approach to the performance of some baseline models and other popular classification methods – with and without the use of the DoL framework. We tune hyper-parameters for the LASSOs, logistic regression models, decision trees, and SVMs – both as standalone models and as base models in a DoL system – and for the DNN – only as a standalone model. For this purpose, we use an exhaustive grid search over reasonable ranges with threefold cross-validation to tune parameters such as regularization constants, kernels, splitting criteria, class weights, hidden layer units, and activation functions. We assess the expected generalization performance by using 10-fold cross-validation with the training set containing 90% and the test set containing 10% of the data in each iteration (see Table B-5). Additionally, we compute true positive and true negative rates, using the same cross-validation method (see Table B-6). We show the attributes that were identified by the system as significant for treatment predictions in Table B-7.

Table B-5. F1 scores of different classifiers for the prediction of therapy intentions and each treatment type. The overall score is the average of the scores for all prediction tasks, weighted by the number of samples in the respective test sets. The best score is highlighted for each prediction task.

	Therapy Intention	Operation	Radiation	Local Chemo-therapy	Systemic Chemo-therapy	Other Therapy	Overall
Random Guesser	0.120	0.610	0.315	0.00752	0.234	0.0153	0.218
Prior Classifier	0	0.961	0	0.286	0	**0.571**	0.308
Prior Classifier DoL	0	0.961	0	0.286	0	**0.571**	0.308
Lasso	0	**0.966**	0.48	0.213	0.240	0	0.320
Lasso DoL	0.434	0.958	0.430	0.259	0.259	0.286	0.439
Logistic Regression	0.452	0.958	0.458	0.285	0.285	**0.571**	0.500
Logistic Regression DoL	**0.649**	0.957	**0.528**	**0.496**	**0.561**	**0.571**	**0.620**
LPM	0.336	0.945	0.457	0.127	0.127	0.146	0.358
LPM DoL	0.526	0.946	0.454	0.139	0.139	0.146	0.392
Decision Tree	0.308	0.932	0.355	0.240	0.22	0.223	0.382
Decision Tree DoL	0.455	0.937	0.448	0.304	0.258	0.242	0.442
SVM	0.260	0.957	0.397	0.286	0.300	**0.571**	0.465
SVM DoL	0.41	0.959	0.513	0.476	0.517	**0.571**	0.577
DNN	0.0317	0.851	0.104	0.143	0.0395	**0.571**	0.316

Generally speaking, the DoL system based on logistic regression achieves the highest performance. Note that this particular model was implemented in an online manner because initial analyses revealed its superior performance, in contrast to other models that were implemented as batch models.

Noteworthy classification tasks are the recommendation of an "operation" and the recommendation of an "other therapy". The former is the only task for which the prior classifier was not (significantly) outperformed by the other models. For the latter task, multiple classifiers were tied in terms of highest accuracy. This outcome can be explained by the fact that these attributes have highly imbalanced values: About 92% of the recorded patients have received an "operation" and about 98% have not received an "other therapy". Classifiers, thus, tend to recommend an operation and no other therapy for every data element. This behavior is confirmed by the true negative rates, which are low for most "operation" classifiers, and the true positive rates, which are 0 for all non-random "other therapy" classifiers (see Table B-6). The DNN generally performed poorly. This poor performance can be explained by a small sample size, which is generally not suitable for highly complex models such as DNNs.

Table B-6. True positive (TP) and true negative (TN) rates of the classifiers for the prediction of therapy intentions and each treatment type. The overall rate is the average of the rates for all prediction tasks, weighted by the number of samples in the respective test sets.

	Therapy Intention		Operation		Radiation		Local Chemo-therapy		Systemic Chemo-therapy		Other Therapy		Overall	
	TP	TN	TP	TN	TP	TN	TP	TN	TP	TN	TP	TN	TP	TN
Random Guesser	50.0%	50.0%	50.0%	50.0%	50.0%	50.0%	50.1%	50.0%	50.0%	50.0%	49.8%	50.0%	50.0%	50.0%
Prior Classifier	0%	100%	100%	0%	0%	100%	0%	100%	0%	100%	0%	100%	17.2%	82.8%
Prior Classifier DoL	0%	100%	100%	0%	0%	100%	0%	100%	0%	100%	0%	100%	17.2%	82.8%
Lasso	0%	100%	99.6%	49.0%	15.7%	50.2%	15.0%	46.2%	15.3%	48.6%	0%	100%	25.4%	63.9%
Lasso DoL	10.9%	50.3%	99.6%	12.3%	10.1%	48.5%	15.1%	48.5%	15.1%	48.5%	0%	100%	26.7%	50.5%
Logistic Regression	10.8%	51.1%	99.6%	11.2%	15.6%	52.9%	15.6%	48.9%	15.6%	48.9%	0%	100%	27.4%	50.9%
Logistic Regression DoL	19.7%	88.5%	99.3%	9.74%	32.6%	60.7%	29.2%	56.8%	34.3%	59.6%	0%	100%	37.0%	59.7%
LPM	9.8%	41.0%	99.4%	0%	15.6%	52.9%	7.66%	30.5%	7.66%	30.5%	0%	100%	24.4%	41.2%
LPM DoL	22.9%	59.3%	99.4%	0%	15.0%	52.9%	14.4%	33.9%	14.4%	33.9%	0%	100%	28.7%	44.9%
Decision Tree	13.1%	39.9%	99.3%	0%	10.2%	44.4%	13.2%	39.4%	13.4%	35.2%	0%	100%	25.9%	42.0%
Decision Tree DoL	12.2%	51.5%	99.3%	0%	10.2%	47.4%	15.2%	41.0%	11.8%	39.5%	0%	100%	25.6%	45.4%
SVM	7.12%	33.6%	99.6%	0%	13.6%	47.4%	13.6%	40.4%	13.5%	43.0%	0%	100%	25.6%	45.0%
SVM DoL	8.45%	50.0%	99.6%	0%	22.9%	57.8%	18.9%	44.7%	18.9%	46.9%	0%	100%	29.2%	48.9%
DNN	1.53%	12.0%	88.5%	0.79%	8.41%	11.4%	4.2%	14.9%	2.10%	4.01%	0%	100%	18.5%	22.3%

Table B-7. Most important attributes and their scores for each prediction task. The scores of the overall most important attributes are their average over all prediction tasks, weighted by the number of samples in the respective test sets.

Decision Category	Attribute	Score	Decision Category	Attribute	Score
Therapy Intention	Lymph node-(N)-classification	0.825	Systemic Chemo-therapy	Tumor-(T)-classification	0.692
	Tumor-(T)-classification	0.438		Diagnosis admission status	0.505
	Metastasis-(M)-classification	0.332		Clinical state	0.441
	Grading of squamous cell carcinoma	0.202		Tumor number	0.357
	Clinical state	0.129		Tumor type	0.337
	Height	0.0714		Reason for visit	0.278
	Tumor number	0.0698		Sex	0.274
	Familial tumor predisposition	0.0648		Height	0.211
	Reason for visit	0.0568		Familial tumor predisposition	0.185
Operation	Metastasis-(M)-classification	0.276		Amount of alcohol	0.169
	Grading of squamous cell carcinoma	0.146	Other Therapy	Clinical state	0.906
	Lymph node-(N)-classification	0.145		Reason for visit	0.358
	Tumor type	0.0592		Duration of precancerous lesions	0.109
	Tumor-(T)-classification	0.0494		Tumor type	0.0811
Radiation	Tumor-(T)-classification	0.366		Tumor-(T)-classification	0.0550
	Lymph node-(N)-classification	0.322	Overall	Tumor-(T)-classification	0.323
	Inflammatory response	0.0789		Clinical state	0.299
	Degree of dysplasia	0.0533		Lymph node-(N)-classification	0.273
	Existing precancerous lesions	0.0430		Reason for visit	0.140
Local Chemotherapy	Heavy heart disease	0.0790		Metastasis-(M)-classification	0.120
	Grading of squamous cell carcinoma	0.0682			
	Lymph node-(N)-classification	0.0675			
	Restricted lung functions	0.0554			
	Existing precancerous lesions	0.0454			

The attributes identified by the DSS were evaluated with respect to their validity by multiple physicians from the University Medical Center Göttingen. On the one hand, many identified attributes confirm existing theory on head and neck cancer treatments and are already used by physicians to make decisions such as the tumor-(T)-classification, lymph node-(N)-classification, and the metastasis-(M)-classification. The TNM classification of malignant tumors, comprising a patient's T-, N-, and M-status, has been developed by the Union for

International Cancer Control (UICC) and is globally recognized as a standard for classifying the extent of spread of cancer. Derived from the TNM-classification, head and neck tumors are grouped into clinical stages – an attribute that our DSS also identified as a significant contributor to the treatment plan. On the other hand, the DSS identified attributes that researchers and practitioners do not typically consider for making treatment plans, such as a patient's reasons for the initial visit to the doctor – an attribute that has limited causal implications, but is of statistical importance for treatment decisions –, as well as attributes that have not yet been introduced into medical guidelines, but have been the focus of ongoing research, such as the inflammatory response of tissues surrounding a tumor: The invasive potential of cancer is dependent on the tumor environment and its interactions at the invasive edge of cancer (Bohrnsen et al. 2014; Bohrnsen et al. 2017; Crusz and Balkwill 2015).

1.6 Discussion of Findings

In their recent research commentary, Kohli and Tan (2016) pointed to the demand for healthcare analytics: "The healthcare industry requires smarter, more informed, decisions to improve health outcomes ... Research to develop the analytics capabilities required to access and derive meaningful insights from data available across the healthcare ecosystem to create better outcomes for patients, customers, and other stakeholders would be timely and imperative" (p. 563). However, besides these potentials, we know from prior empirical work that, in the healthcare industry, actual adoption and usage of new IS is non-trivial to understand and difficult to achieve (Venkatesh et al. 2011). By no means, as we have also learned in this multidisciplinary research project, this is to say that physicians, in general, employ skeptical views on IS per se. Instead, specific factors that relate to the profession of physicians (see Fichman et al. 2011; Romanow et al. 2012) as well as certain factors that relate to the particular design of healthcare IS and their implications for clinical practice require particular attention. A lack thereof is the reason why the use of data analytics in healthcare, in comparison to other contexts, lags behind (Chen et al. 2012). In this study, in order to contribute to the emerging field of healthcare analytics and help fill the void regarding predictive analytics in this regard (Kohli and Tan 2016), we present an innovative approach. Prior instances in the field of healthcare analytics rest on the assumption that these systems require large and sound data elements, in a sense that there is full information available for each patient, as well as additional organizational procedures for their maintenance (Ghosh and Scott 2011). Regarding data quality, we agree on that completeness and correctness are valuable (Kohli and Tan 2016). However, the question arises as to what amount of data these attributes relate to. Ward et al. (2014) state: "Instead of collecting as much data as possible, institutions should actually take the opposite approach, ensuring that they collect on the minimal set of data elements that are required." (p. 578).

While, from a purely analytical viewpoint, a higher amount and variety of data may lead to more informed decisions, collecting these data requires massive investments, either in human labor or in technical infrastructures (Angst and Agarwal 2009; Fichman et al. 2011) or organizational hurdles and capability gaps (Ghosh and Scott 2011). In clinical practice, capacities to handle the amount of data have been exceeded years ago (Weigel et al. 2013). Our findings indicate that one could resolve these contradictions by focusing the analysis to uncover the most meaningful attributes and, building upon this foundation, restrict the data needed for decision support (and thus the effort to collect and maintain them). We developed an intelligent DSS (Arnott and Pervan 2008) that is evidence-based and makes situationally relevant recommendations (Zhuang et al. 2013). It achieved the goal of supporting decision making processes by providing treatment suggestions while, at the same time, not producing additional administrative efforts for medical staff by designing the DSS in a way that allows utilizing all patient attributes provided by the user while being able to function with the smallest sets of inputs. That is, the DSS does not require any input at all in order to function, but its ability to make informed suggestions increases with the number of provided attributes. In combination with the prediction accuracy provided by the DSS, physicians are given sufficient information to decide whether to accept or deny such a suggestion. Furthermore, the DSS provides a list of attributes significant for the decision making process – serving as a hint, rather than an obligation – that can be used by medical staff to focus the data collection process. Thereby, administrative, technical and organizational hurdles can be reduced while analytical and predictive power is retained. At the same time, physicians can derive new insights on the importance of specific factors, thus leading to increased learning based on evidence (Gupta and Sharda 2013) and potential improvements of care through their integration in clinical workflows (Agarwal et al. 2010).

As a result of this approach, our artifact has yielded results that are reasonable and insightful from the viewpoint of clinical practice in oral and maxillofacial surgery. In cancer treatment planning, it is of importance to identify and correlate significant patient attributes while reducing unnecessary information and inefficiencies, to allow cancer centers to offer a fast and successful patient-guided treatment plan. Our DSS identified a set of attributes significant for treatment recommendations, out of which most are aligned with existing guidelines and some have not yet been introduced into medical guidelines, but have been the focus of ongoing research, such as the inflammatory response of tissues surrounding a tumor. Following the initial success of immune- and inflammatory-modulating therapies, it is to be expected that inflammation and immunity will become important targets in patients with cancer in the future. Apart from that, to make use of data analytics in healthcare, it is essential to overcome the challenges of heterogeneous, inaccurate, and incomplete data structures, real-time environments, and the resilience of health care workers to changing technologies and IS techniques (Kruse et al. 2016). Using the DoL framework, we simulated the underlying analytic framework representing the collaborative characteristics of the medical experts involved in the treatment planning session of head and neck tumor boards, thereby reaching a higher degree of contextualization of the artifact (Romanow et al. 2012).

Evaluating the results from a technical point of view, we observe that DoL systems with different base models in most cases lead to an enhanced accuracy compared to the use of the respective base models in a standalone manner. This advantage comes about by the specialization of experts in the DoL framework achieved by a division of the input space such that data points in the resulting sub-spaces are more easily separable (i.e., classifiable). Logistic regression – both as a standalone classifier and as part of the DoL system – demonstrated a superior performance, closely followed by SVMs. Decision trees achieved a mediocre accuracy, which was not greatly improved through the DoL framework. In general, it is reasonable to assume that using a DoL system based on decision trees will only yield insignificant improvements, if at all, because decision trees, by themselves, perform an input space division; further divisions by a DoL system may have counter-productive effects.

1.7 Implications

Big data approaches in healthcare promise to provide solutions for patient and disease management as well as efficiency in care. Recent studies, however, have outlined obstacles in the application of big data. These are often related to inaccuracies in data structure, standardization, and analytics (Kruse et al. 2016; Valdes et al. 2016). Moreover, big data applications often illustrate a gap between IS theory and practical implementation since the underlying structures in care are seldom represented by the data framework (Coveney et al. 2016). This asymmetric divergence results in a resilience of health care workers to constantly evolving IS technologies. Our artifact is designed to reflect the dynamic expert-driven decision process applied in cancer tumor boards. Tumor boards use guidelines and significant diagnostic data to determine the oncologic treatment plan and management of cancer patients. Guidelines of clinical care are routinely published by specialist and international associations in the field. They review and incorporate current research and literature and outline significant information for the clinician to be able to provide the best care for the patient (Gregoire et al. 2010; Nekhlyudov et al. 2017; Wolff et al. 2012). It is, therefore, important to change the perspective on IS health care applications from big data to significant data. Reducing waste of information will result in an increased efficiency, improved health care planning and ease of IS health care application. As shown in our study, the dynamic DSS based on the DoL framework identified guideline-specific data and analytics that was consistent with head and neck cancer guidelines. It was also able to identify correlated features, which are currently under clinical investigation. These findings are of great importance in current health care. In the future, significant data-driven frameworks will have to allow for the dynamic evaluation and correlation of additional research data to improve decision making and the quality of care.

Our results reveal three important implications for IS research on health analytics. First, we advocate for more design-oriented research that identifies and addresses the existing challenges and requirements of clinical practice (Hevner et al. 2004). Design issues are among the key challenges of digital transformation in general (Majchrzak et al. 2016) and, even more so, in the specific case of healthcare, rendering new insights valuable (Agarwal et al. 2010). In engaging in design studies, researchers should build upon the shoulders of prior works following the behavioral paradigm on factors influencing the adoption or resistance of physicians to new health IT (e.g., Venkatesh et al. (2011)) and adapt more to the contextual specifics of healthcare (e.g., Fichman et al. (2011)). Second, when designing health analytics artifacts, we call for a more careful consideration of the consequences that would result in the practical application of the solution. More specifically, we point to the value of using less, yet more meaningful data in order to realize the value of analytics without increasing cognitive and administrative loads, which, in turn, should motivate the use of artifacts and deliver the inputs needed. Third, and in summary, we call for a socio-technical perspective on designing health analytics artifacts (Bostrom and Heinen 1977). Even though a long-established view in IS research, recent findings on failures in health IS adoption point to the value of reinforcing this perspective in the digital transformation of healthcare (Agarwal et al. 2010). Through such a view, the very specifics of healthcare can be considered and the potentials of data analytics can be delivered in a targeted way. However, this is not to say that existing contextual factors in healthcare IS should be taken for granted. Instead, we believe in a symbiotic relationship between humans and machines in healthcare (Döppner et al. 2016) that is beneficial in a sense that artifacts account for the contextual situation and, because of that, humans adapt their behavior for the increased use of the artifacts, leading to more informed decisions and improvements of healthcare quality and efficiency (Kohli and Tan 2016).

Based on our findings, we further derive implications for ML research in general. Guided by the call of Bengio and LeCun (2007) for increased research on deep learning architectures and the call of Abbasi et al. (2016) for interpretable ML models, we performed a trade-off between our model's processing depth and the interpretability of its predictions. By employing a base classification model on top of a clustering layer, our model processes data in more depth and has a higher complexity than standard classification models without reaching the depth of common deep learning models, thereby maintaining both high prediction accuracies and the ability of communicating attributes of highest significance to the decision making process. Applying such a trade-off when designing ML models may, thus, yield predictions with high accuracies and at the same time offer insights into the prediction process, allowing researchers to make informed refinements to their models. Achieving significant gains in predictive performance in comparison to standard classification algorithms, our results indicate that task division has great potential in ML. Without high amounts of incorporated prior knowledge, our system improved the performance of classifiers by dividing the input space, using a clustering algorithm that does not require the specification of hyper-parameters, and fitting a classifier in each sub-space, as proposed by the DoL framework (Tofangchi, Hanelt and Kolbe 2017). The presented DoL system is highly dynamic, applying real-time learning algorithms at each layer of analysis and, thus, anticipating its employment in environments of steady data flows. Using such real-time models is important for ensuring scalability of DSSs – an issue that needs to be considered when developing ML models – that are intended to be used over long periods of time (Tofangchi, Hanelt and Kolbe 2017). Furthermore, considering that each treatment decision is made by a different individual and is ultimately a product of information gathered by several physicians, the proposed model does not only learn to imitate a certain physician's decision making, but implicitly exploits the fact that the data contains decisions by multiple physicians, creating a wisdom-of-the-crowd effect (Yi et al. 2012). For the development of DSSs, this effect underlines the importance of collecting data from various sources to enhance the DSSs' recommendations.

1.8 Limitations

Our artifact – a DSS for the treatment of cancer patients – is subject to certain limitations. First, the artifact addresses a certain class of clinical decision making problems. That is, the artifact is suited for treatment planning in the area of chronic diseases, for which mid-term decision making is required. It is neither favorable for very long-term strategical decisions, for which batch models may produce better results than real-time models, nor for very short-term decisions as required for outpatient treatments. Further limitations that may be addressed in future research are explained in the following. The effectiveness of suggested treatments is limited by the knowledge of physicians. This limitation is partially mitigated by the data set containing decisions by multiple physicians. However, this circumstance has a positive effect, only if the majority of physicians agree upon a favorable treatment, and the inherent limitation of the quality of treatment suggestions being bounded by the quality of the physicians' decisions still remains. This limitation may be addressed by collecting additional information on the success of applied treatments. A further limitation is that, although our artifact identifies important attributes for each treatment type, only the overall important attributes have an effective use in improving data collection steps. Future research may develop a method to make use of the important attributes for each treatment type to improve decision making processes without the loss of efficiency. A related issue is that the set of important attributes may be different for each model type. We refrained from identifying these sets for each individual model in order to keep the Results Section clear. Instead, we used a LASSO – a popular model for feature selection – to obtain important attributes with fairly general validity. However, in practice it can be beneficial to compute model-specific important attributes. For most model types, these can be easily obtained by using L1 regularization (Tibshirani 1996) in the model's cost function and retaining those attributes that are associated with non-zero coefficients. Moreover, finding a way to reduce the cost of acquiring more attributes per patient (i.e., reducing the number of missing values) by improving the means of data collection may be an effective strategy to improve decision support systems. Examining such a strategy is not within the scope of this paper, but can be considered complementary to our proposed artifact because it is capable of utilizing an arbitrary number of attributes known to the system. A limitation that is inherent to the given data set is that the attributes "operation" and "other therapy" have highly imbalanced values. Imbalanced classes are a frequent problem in medical data sets and can, for instance, be addressed by performing over- or undersampling (Rahman and Davis 2013). However, since our data set is relatively small, we are left with too few learning examples for the minority classes of said two attributes. For the same reason, we were not able to adequately assess the performance of DNNs for comparison purposes. These limitations should, thus, be addressed by collecting more data. Finally, while our artifact is designed to be durable and perform real-time learning/analyses and we have addressed the main issue with real-time systems – namely that the employed models need to be updated rather than recomputed when new data is seen –, there remain two issues that may arise in the future, if the artifact is employed over an indefinite time. First, although the clustering model employed by the CE is updated in real time, the performance declines as more data is added – a limitation inherent to clustering algorithms, as stated by Tofangchi, Hanelt and Kolbe

(2017), who suggest a solution by pruning data elements. Future research may develop a pruning strategy that retains the most relevant data elements. Furthermore, not all changes to the input space are anticipated by the artifact. That is, the artifact accounts for a reduction of observed dimensions, but adding new dimensions to the data is not supported. Future research may extend the model to perform updates not only for new data points but also for new input dimensions.

1.9 Conclusion

Healthcare analytics bears the potential to drive efficiency and quality in healthcare. However, compared to other contexts, the advancement and actual adoption in practice lags behind. In our multidisciplinary research, we jointly designed an evidence-based and contextualized clinical DSS for cancer treatments in oral and maxillofacial surgery. The DSS takes into account potential adoption barriers that were identified by physicians participating in our research. We designed an artifact that predicts optimal treatments, but restricts the amount of required data to the most valuable attributes. Thus, with our work, we contribute to healthcare analytics in IS research, proposing an artifact that improves efficiency and quality of decision making in clinical practice.

2 Study 3: Advancing Recommendations on Two-Sided Platforms: A Machine Learning Approach to Context-Aware Profiling

Table B-8. Fact sheet of Study no. 3.

Title	Advancing Recommendations on Two-Sided Platforms: A Machine Learning Approach to Context-Aware Profiling
Authors	Schahin Tofangchi[*a], Andre Hanelt[b], Siyuan Li[c] [a] Chair of Information Management, University of Göttingen, Platz der Göttinger Sieben 5, 37073 Göttingen, Germany [b] Chair of Digital Transformation Management, University of Kassel, Kleine Rosenstraße 3, 34109 Kassel, Germany [c] Mason School of Business, William & Mary, P.O. Box 8795, Williamsburg, Virginia 23187-8795, United States * Corresponding author. Tel.: +49 (0)551 / 39 - 22254. E-mail address: schahin.tofangchi@uni-goettingen.de
Outlet	Proceedings of the Fortieth International Conference on Information Systems, Munich (Germany), 2017 (forthcoming)
Abstract	Digitally enabled two-sided platforms rely on mediating different actors to evoke transactions. Here, the core value-generating mechanisms of these platforms relate to the recommendations that persuade users to make future transactions, thereby driving sales, customer satisfaction, efficiency, and trust. To generate effective recommendations, accurate user profiling is fundamental. Ubiquitous computing provides valuable data to enhance user profiling by uncovering behavioral patterns of individual users. Specifically, through machine learning methods, recommendation systems are able to understand users better by considering both past individual behaviors and their respective contexts. However, state-of-the-art recommendation systems rely either on collaborative or content-based approaches, thereby neglecting a user's time-varying contexts and the dynamics that influence these contexts. We address this shortcoming by developing a context-aware and user-specific hybrid recommendation system using transfer-learning techniques based on (recurrent) neural networks. Evaluating our approach on Expedia's hotel booking data, we demonstrate its enhanced performance compared to common recommendation approaches.
Keywords	Recommendation systems, machine learning, representation learning, transfer learning, time-series analysis, hybrid recommendations, context awareness

2.1 Introduction

Digitally enabled two-sided platforms are among the most indicated phenomena in business practice (Eisenmann et al. 2011; Evans and Schmalensee 2016) and information systems (IS) research alike (Parker et al. 2016; Bharadwaj et al. 2013). We witness a plethora of such platforms emerging and competing in various industry segments such as retail, entertainment, housing and mobility (Parker et al. 2016). A key characteristic of a two-sided platform is that it assembles different types of stakeholders (including both customers and merchants) and facilitates the interactions between them (Rochet and Tirole 2003). Among various platform features, the recommendation system is a decisive factor in the battle between players that vie for dominance in certain contexts (de Reuver et al. 2017) and is considered the key value generator (Parker et al. 2016). Thus, advancing recommendation algorithm and increasing its accuracy are vital to a two-sided platform's success.

To date, most major two-sided platforms (e.g., eBay and Expedia) have used one of the following mechanisms to generate recommendations for their users: *content-based* recommendations, which rely on focal users' historical preferences; *collaborative* recommendations, which are based on other users' preferences who share common interests with the focal user; *knowledge-based* (or rule-based) recommendations, which use expert knowledge and/or respond to users' specified needs; and *hybrid* approaches, which constitute an integration of multiple mechanisms mentioned above (Adomavicius and Tuzhilin 2005). These two types of recommendations have been widely applied in practice and closely examined in prior research (Adomavicius and Tuzhilin 2005; Smith and Linden 2017), but have certain weaknesses that have been addressed by hybrid recommendation systems (Çano and Morisio 2017).

As users' personal data become more accessible, digital platforms evolve towards "benevolent servants extracting and analyzing data, providing new forms of contracting through monitoring, and personalizing and customizing their services to match the changing user-needs" (de Reuver 2017, p. 132). In particular, acquired consumer data enable platforms to personalize customer experiences and thus increase customer affection (Li and Karahanna 2015). Therefore, the way in which automated data analysis of user data is rendered in the recommendation generation process is particularly relevant in the context of two-sided platforms. For this reason, many companies make use of machine learning (ML) methods to develop recommendation systems that help personalize customer experience. Prominent examples are given by Amazon and Netflix, who offer individual product and content recommendations based on customers' past behavior (Arora 2016) as well as similarities among user actions (e.g., users' website usage patterns) (Ricci et al. 2011; Su and Khoshgoftaar 2009). However, the mechanisms underlying the computation of these preferences are static in nature and oversee that a user's preferences may change depending on factors such as the time of the day and the user's mood. This oversimplification may be an important underlying reason behind the reported instability of recommendation system predictions (Adomavicius and Zhang 2015). Providing too many unwanted recommendations may lead to frustration of users and a lack of trust in the platform (Bollen et al. 2010; Wang and Benbasat 2007). Although prior research (e.g., Adomavicius et al. (2011)) has called for more work considering the user context in recommendations, practical approaches and empirical studies are still missing (Li and Karahanna 2015).

To fill the above-mentioned gaps in literature and practice, this study combines content-based, collaborative, and context-aware recommendation mechanisms, allowing recommendations to be generated dynamically and data-driven[4], and presents a new hybrid and context-aware recommendation system design that models user profiles based on their observed actions and their respective contexts. We train neural networks (NNs) to learn the embeddings of users' contexts (Bengio et al. 2013) and subsequently feed these embeddings into a recurrent neural network (RNN) (Elman 1990) that models the relationship between time series of embedded contexts and the respective actions. We follow the call in digital platform research for a "stronger interaction between the IS and computer science research communities, which will facilitate fusion of domain expertise with integration of relevant techniques from data mining, machine learning and visualization" (de Reuver et al. 2017, p. 131). In particular, we present an ML approach that not only draws on usage patterns at a macroscopic level but also considers individual-level behavior and, unlike any existing approaches, models actors' internal states through time-series analyses to provide recommendations that are more user- and context-specific. We explicitly refrain from assuming an actor's observable state at any given time – isolated from their past observable states and actions – to be a sufficient indicator of their future actions. To evaluate the proposed approach, we use it to generate hotel recommendations based on data from Expedia's travel platform, therein assessing its predictive performance regarding users' hotel bookings. Comparing our approach with existing classification models and popular data-driven recommendation techniques, we observe a superior predictive performance of our approach according to three different evaluation criteria.

This study contributes to research on recommendation systems by providing a specific, situated artifact for advanced user profiling that uses timely ML capabilities. Such user profiling mechanism assists actual platform operations by accounting for the *context* of individual digital users (Adomavicius et al. 2011, Brenner et al. 2014, de Reuver et al. 2017). While prior approaches have different advantages and disadvantages, most of them share the same trait: They do not consider time-varying contextual factors while, at the same time, exploiting content-based and collaborative knowledge, although contextual information can significantly enhance the quality of recommendations (Adomavicius et al. 2011). In this paper, we point to the importance of integrating content-based, collaborative, and context-aware recommendation mechanisms and develop a meta-level hybrid recommendation system. Using a combination of NNs and an RNN, the system models user states based not only on the observable contexts when performing actions but also on their past behaviors. Thereby, we enable a more accurate representation of user profiles and, consequently, an improved measure of comparing users and inferring reasonable recommendations.

---

[4] Knowledge-based approaches are not included in this study because they are based on expert knowledge on specific products and are static in nature (Adomavicius and Tuzhilin 2005). It is nearly impossible (or very costly) to implement knowledge-based recommendations in a *dynamic context*, which is the primary focus of this study.

2.2 Background

2.2.1 Recommendations and Two-Sided Platforms

From a socio-technical point of view, digital platforms can be defined as "technical elements (of software and hardware) and associated organizational processes and standards" (de Reuver et al. 2017, p. 126). Parker et al. (2016, p. 5) describe the business rational associated with two-sided platforms:

> A platform is a business based on enabling value-creating interactions between external producers and consumers. The platform provides an open, participative infrastructure for these interactions and sets the governance conditions for them. The platform's overarching purpose: to consummate matches among users and facilitate the exchange of goods, services, or social currency, thereby enabling value creation for all participants.

For instance, two-sided platforms such as Airbnb mediate property owners and travelers, Amazon mediates buyers and sellers, and Uber mediates drivers and passengers. As described above, these platforms, acting as intermediaries, focus on matchmaking different actors and enabling transactions between them, which provide the foundation for profit generation. Apart from that, the platform itself does not create much value on its own (de Reuver et al. 2017). Therefore, providing precise matching is the core business function of digitally enabled two-sided platforms (Parker et al. 2016).

While matchmaking generally pertains to both demand and supply side, in the digital age, we witness firms placing a particular importance on the customer side (i.e., the demand side). As described by Lucas et al. (2013), societal digitalization (Tilson et al. 2010) has empowered customers to be better informed, equipped with more choices, while simultaneously becoming less tolerant for digital shortcomings and failures. To accommodate such changes and satisfy recent customer demands, platforms now need to put more attention to understanding said customers and offer better personalized services (Vodanovich et al. 2010). This stems from a platform's function as a filter, which recommends personalized offerings to specific users on the base of algorithmic, software-based tools. Such filters, together with participants and their exchanged values, form the core interaction and are essential to platform's success (Parker et al. 2016).

From the rich body of knowledge about recommendation systems, we can affirm that valid recommendations made to customers lead to increased satisfaction and drive the propensity for future transactions (Liang et al. 2006; Thongpapanl and Ashraf 2011). From a meta-theoretical perspective, recommendations that match personal preferences provide identity verification, which, in turn, relates to positive behavioral and emotional outcomes for the individual (Carter and Grover 2015). In the platform business, creating a superior customer experience and curating the customer base is of particular importance not only because of the value of single transactions but also because of the network externalities involved (El Sawy and Perreira 2013; de Reuver et al. 2017). In addition, contemporary two-sided platforms aim for long-term relationships with customers, comprising m transactions over time, and exhausting functionality available to customers (e.g., Uber Eats). On this premise, generating context-specific recommendations that suit customers' dynamic preferences over time is critical for two-sided platforms.

On two-sided platforms, in order to enable personalized recommendations, user profiling must consider the "'digital user' ... who performs actions in the digital world and who therefore generates new data or puts existing data to use" (Brenner et al. 2014, p. 55). A user profile can be referred to as "a function that for any item predicts the likelihood that the user is interested in that item" (Pazzani and Billsus 2007, p. 328). More generally, items can be seen as instances of "actions" that the user can perform. Accordingly, user profiling has evolved from only considering users' demographics or simple transaction data to also including information about other digital activities such as social media usage or clickstreams (Arazy et al. 2010; Li and Karahanna 2015; Tang et al. 2013). Another evolutionary step, given the increased computing power in everyday life, is that the possibilities and necessities in considering the individual contexts of users have both substantially risen (Yoo 2010). To date, although research on recommendation systems has described the need for context-aware recommendation systems and conceptualized such approaches (Adomavicius et al. 2011), it has lacked practical and evaluated approaches. With the advanced data analytics and the emergence of big data technologies (e.g., Abbasi et al. (2016)), researchers have increasingly been developing automated data analysis methods to support decision making processes at both operational and strategic levels in various industries (Lucas Jr et al. 2013; Newell and Marabelli 2015; Woerner and Wixom 2015). These potentials have recently been applied in digitally enabled two-sided platforms.

2.2.2 Machine-Learning-Based Recommendation Practices on Two-Sided Platforms

Recommendation systems personalize the user experience and present content in a targeted manner to increase the satisfaction of individuals (Li and Karahanna 2015). Depending on the information sources of recommendations, numerous ML-based recommendation mechanisms exist on the market, which are categorized as content-based, collaborative, or hybrid (content-based and collaborative) (Adomavicius and Tuzhilin 2005). Content-based and collaborative approaches are based on a set of often unjustified assumptions, possibly leading to imprecise recommendations. For instance, most collaborative recommendation algorithms such as matrix factorization (Koren et al. 2009; Zhou et al. 2008) derive recommendations based on the past decisions of all users, but neglect the contexts in which these decisions were made; whereas content-based recommendations mostly rely on the focal user's historical decisions (Pazzani and Billsus 2007), but neglect knowledge contributed through other users' decisions. Researchers have developed hybrid recommendation systems that combine the features of content-based and collaborative recommendation mechanisms to generate personalized recommendations to overcome the individual weaknesses of content-based and collaborative approaches. Existing hybrid recommendation systems, attempting to integrate content-based and collaborative characteristics, rely on weighted combinations of the two respective models, use one model as an input to the other model (meta-level), apply content-based pre- or postfiltering, or employ a single unifying recommendation model (Adomavicius and Tuzhilin 2005). Some even resort back to rule-based adaptations to combine the two approaches, which, as opposed to data-driven approaches, limit the system's knowledge acquisition to dynamics anticipated by the developer (Abbasi et al. 2016) and may lead to unsatisfactory recommendations.

Both content-based features, based on which systems "recommend an item to a user based upon a description of the item and a profile of the user's interests" (Pazzani and Billsus 2007, p. 325), and collaborative features, which allow to "predict the utility of items for a particular user based on the items previously rated by other users" (Adomavicius and Tuzhilin 2005, p. 11), are essential to recommendation systems. For this reason, we focus on hybrid recommendation systems, which combine these features (Adomavicius et al. 2011). Hybrid approaches are developed to address one or more of the following issues encountered in collaborative and content-based approaches (Çano and Morisio 2017). The *cold-start problem* arises when a new user or a new action is introduced to the platform and no data is available to infer direct matches. *Data sparsity* describes the problem of a typical recommendation system in which data is available only for a small portion of the <user, action> pairs. *Accuracy* and *diversity* are two conflicting problems that respectively refer to the relevance of recommendations and a recommendation system's ability to make novel and unexpected recommendations. Finally, *scalability* is concerned with the algorithms' ability to cope with a large user base and set of actions often available to platform owners. The approach we propose in this paper offers a solution to the cold-start problem and, more importantly, enhances the recommendation accuracy in comparison to other approaches. Due to the variety of information involved in hybrid recommendations, they therein become complicated problems and require more sophisticated models to process. Therefore, many recommendation systems are based on rule-based adaptations to enable hybrid recommendations (Adomavicius et al. 2011; Bennett and Lanning 2007; Davidson et al. 2010; Pazzani and Billsus 2007). To get a better understanding of current recommendation practices, we review the recommendation systems of Amazon, Netflix, and YouTube – platforms with large user bases and revenues in which recommendations play a vital role.

Amazon still operates using its Apriori algorithm, which initially rose to popularity in 2003 by constituting an item-to-item collaborative approach, as opposed to user-based collaborative filtering, which was more popular in the 1990s (Smith and Linden 2017). Being an instance of an association rules mining approach, a model created through the Apriori algorithm is intuitive and efficient in making recommendations after having been built.

Netflix provides a mixture of recommendations through a set of different mechanisms. Using several content-based and rule-based methods (Gomez-Uribe and Hunt 2016), as well as its original collaborative approach (Koren et al. 2009), Netflix' recommendation system produces recommendations generated by different methods in isolation (i.e., collaborative information is not involved in generating the content-based recommendations). Technically speaking, Netflix employs a hybrid recommendation system, while each individual recommendation itself is not generated through a hybrid approach.

YouTube employs a simple variant of the Apriori algorithm, together with a number of rule-based adaptations (Davidson et al. 2010) to create a hybrid recommendation system. In particular, they compute association rules of length one for videos watched within a period of approximately 24 hours. For a given video, they define related videos based on the k highest-scored association rules and enrich the set through some content-based mechanisms. They then recommend the highest-scored videos constraining the number of videos recommended in each category to exhibit diversity. Although incorporating collaborative, content-based, and (to some degree) contextual information, the recommendation system is limited in its adaptiveness due to its heavy reliance on rule-based processes.

Collaborative approaches play an important role in contemporary platforms. Amazon, in particular, provides recommendations solely based on a collaborative approach. Nevertheless, we observe platform owners increasingly fighting the perceived lack of user specificity of purely collaborative approaches (Davidson et al. 2010) by developing hybrid approaches. Developing such approaches presents them with a challenge because they have to integrate several models with adversarial goals. This issue is amplified when *context-awareness* is added to the system's requirements. Context awareness is achieved by using information-retrieval-based approaches or predictive ML models that associate a given context to an action (Adomavicius et al. 2011). Such predictive models have also been used in content-based approaches to associate content-specific features of actions with their relevance for a certain user (Adomavicius and Tuzhilin 2005). For this purpose, developers have trained a predictive model for each user, which results in a loss of collaborative knowledge and is particularly problematic if individual users do not interact with the system frequently enough to obtain an effective model of their preferences. In general, it is a strenuous undertaking to combine different kinds of recommendation techniques. While researchers have combined some of their features, there does not exist, to the best of our knowledge, any data-driven approach that successfully unifies collaborative, content-based, and context-aware recommendation systems.

2.3 Designing a Time-Series-Based Machine Learning Approach for Collaborative, Content-Based, and Context-Aware Recommendations

In this study, we develop an approach for recommending actions by taking into account the similarity among users, users' contexts, and the similarity among actions. This approach also considers the history and order of an individual's actions and their contexts. The primary objective is to achieve a higher accuracy than existing recommendation approaches. For this reason, we treat the problem as a classification problem that involves predicting the action that a user actually performs. We require the approach to function in environments in which explicit user ratings are not available. Instead, user preferences are to be determined through observations of actions and their contexts. Furthermore, platform owners are typically interested in making a set of recommendations at any instance, rather than just one. For this reason, we require the approach to be probabilistic in order to rank recommendations based on their relevance.

We face the problem of inferring user preferences based on their past actions, while also exploiting knowledge on their similarity to other users. That is, we wish to model user preferences at a general level and fine-tune this general model to the behavior of individual users. Due to this hierarchical problem setting, we design our approach according to the Division-of-Labor (DoL) framework (Tofangchi, Hanelt and Kolbe 2017), which is suited for ML problems that are decomposed into a general-level problem and a set of sub-problems. In the following, we briefly describe the DoL framework before developing our approach in the next section. The DoL framework is an abstract framework that guides the design of ML systems that address a complex data analysis task by decomposing it into several sub-tasks (Tofangchi, Hanelt and Kolbe 2017). For this purpose, the DoL framework introduces two conceptual components, central executives (CEs) and experts. A basic DoL system (i.e., an ML system that is based on the DoL framework) comprises one CE that applies a rule according to which the analysis task is divided and multiple experts that process the sub-tasks and transmit their solutions back to the CE (see Figure B:4).

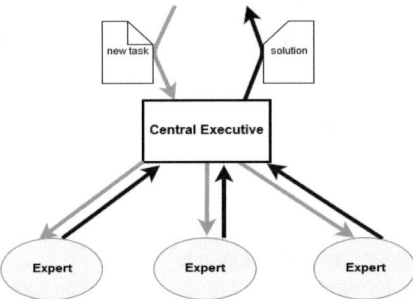

Figure B:4. The Division-of-Labor framework. Gray and black arrows indicate the transmission of (sub-) tasks and their solutions, respectively (Tofangchi, Hanelt and Kolbe 2017).

CEs are required to possess general knowledge of the analysis task. They use this general knowledge in order to perform task division and consult a suitable expert for a given sub-task. They gather feedback from outside of the system and redirect it to the respective experts to enable the adaptation of the models used in the system. Optionally, they perform their learning and analysis procedures in an incremental way, processing one observation at a time, to ensure the system's sustainability and responsiveness. Experts, on the other hand, are specialized on a certain class of sub-tasks determined by their CE. They process these tasks and forward their solutions to the CE along with an optional explanation, demonstrating how the solution was obtained from the given input. Experts use feedback given by the CE to adapt their learning models and acquire their specialization. Comparable to CEs, experts may optionally employ incremental learning models to enable sustainability.

2.3.1 A Division-of-Labor Recommendation System

Before describing the detailed system architecture and the components' functions in the next section, we sketch the design at a conceptual level. We decompose the given problem as the sub-problems of modeling collective behavioral patterns and fine-tuning this model to individual-level behaviors. We develop our solution by using methods from the area of representation learning. That is, experts specialize on individual users by learning embeddings of their time-varying contextual input data. Traditionally, the approach of embedding has been used for dimensionality reduction (van der Maaten and Hinton 2008; Roweis and Saul 2000; Tenenbaum et al. 2000). More recently embedding-based approaches have also proven to be powerful tools for representation learning (Bengio et al. 2013). Popular examples of embedding-based representation learning include Word2Vec (Mikolov et al. 2013) and Doc2Vec (Le and Mikolov 2014) for creating machine-understandable semantic representations of words and sentences, respectively.

We obtain the embeddings through an NN-based approach. Furthermore, the problem we consider involves time series data – sequences of user actions performed in varying contexts. For this reason, we further process the embeddings using Long Short-Term Memory Neural Networks (LSTMs) (Hochreiter and Schmidhuber 1997), which are recurrent NNs that are able to model time-shifted relationships in the data. The proposed system learns to predict a user's action at any given time step t. LSTMs' recurrent nature (see Figure B:5) allows it to also capture information on a user's previous actions and their contexts. As opposed to simple recurrent NNs (Elman 1990) that suffer from the vanishing- and exploding-gradient problem (Hochreiter and Schmidhuber 1997), LSTMs are able to memorize inputs over long periods of time.

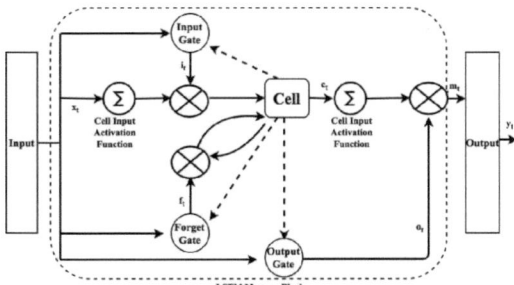

Figure B:5. Long short-term memory neural network (Chauhan and Vig 2015).

2.3.2 Components

Our DoL system comprises one CE and a variable number of experts equal to the number of users in the database. Using the whole data set, the CE trains a feedforward NN to relate contextual data to features of actions. Recommendations can then be inferred by searching the database for actions whose features are most similar to the NN's output. This NN is a model of the average user's preferred action type given a certain context. We refer to it as the average preference model. It can be considered a collaborative, content-based, and context-aware model because it maps from contexts to content-specific features by using collaborative knowledge. However, the average preference model is not user-specific (i.e., it assumes that similar contexts will lead to similar actions irrespective of the user). For this reason, the CE then creates, for each user, an expert that extracts user-specific representations of contexts and returns them to the CE. The CE transmits a copy of the average preference model to each expert. Experts refine their respective models by further training them a small number of instances (e.g., five times) on their respective users' data. Thereby, each expert's model becomes user-specific, being slightly biased towards the respective user's preferences. The pre-training of the NN by the CE ensures that it possesses collaborative qualities and that the experts' individual NNs produce values in similar ranges. While each expert's model is user-specific, it is unable to consider the order and recency of past actions taken. For each contextual input, it thus extracts the hidden layer activation of its NN, which serves as a user-specific context representation, and returns it to the CE. The CE finally trains an LSTM through backpropagation (Linnainmaa 1976) to predict actions from the context representations. The LSTM has an internal state that depends on its past inputs. After having seen all data associated with a user, its internal state is reset to its initial instantiation. With the user-specific, collaborative, content-based, and context-aware NNs serving as inputs to the LSTM, which treats the data as time series, it is able to combine all these traits and further enhance the predictions by taking into account the order of actions and their contexts. Conceptually, the processes involved in the DoL system can be divided in the learning phase, in which the system learns user preferences, and the prediction phase, in which the system is queried for recommendations. The system's function and its overall architecture are depicted in Figure B:6. The employed models each depend on a set of hyperparameters that need to be chosen in accordance with the data set used. We deal with the choice of hyperparameters in the Evaluation Section, where we evaluate the proposed approach using a specific data set.

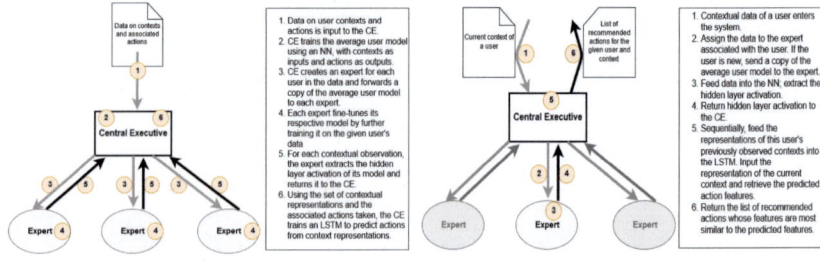

(a) Learning phase   (b) Prediction phase

Figure B:6. The proposed DoL recommendation system.

2.4 Evaluation

In this section, we evaluate the proposed approach by applying it to a data set on hotel bookings submitted on Expedia platforms. Since the goal of our approach is to increase the overall accuracy of recommendations, we evaluate it by measuring its ability to predict the actions that users actually performed. We specifically treat the recommendation process as a classification problem. In the following sections, we introduce and preprocess the data set, define the evaluation setting and baseline approaches with which we compare our DoL system, and finally present the results.

2.4.1 Data and Preprocessing

We evaluate our model using Expedia's publicly available data on hotel bookings from 2013 to 2015[5]. This data set contains 1,198,786 users' viewing and booking data for 100 possible hotel clusters including time-varying attributes of the user and descriptive features of the regions in which the hotels are located. The 100 different hotel clusters are groups of hotels that Expedia created prior to providing the data. In total, there are 37,670,293 viewing records with an average of 31.42 and a maximum of 530 viewings per user. Among these viewing records, we observe N=3,000,693 booking records associated with U=813,985 users, with an average of 3.69 and a maximum of 100 bookings per user. Table B-9 shows the complete set of variables we use. Since we do not have enough features describing a hotel cluster, we treat the hotel cluster itself as the latent variable to be predicted by the recommendation system. We treat all other variables as explanatory variables that are used to carry out the prediction.

Table B-9. Variables of the Expedia hotel booking data set.

	Variable name	Variable description	Variable type
1	date_time	Date and time of the hotel viewing	Custom
2	site_name	ID of the Expedia point of sale	Categorical
3	posa_continent	Continent of the Expedia point of sale	Categorical
4	user_location_country	Country in which the user is located	Categorical
5	user_location_region	Region in which the user is located	Categorical
6	user_location_city	City in which the user is located	Categorical
7	orig_destination_distance	Distance between user and hotel	Numerical
8	is_mobile	Whether accessed through mobile device	Categorical
9	is_package	Whether the user searched for a package	Categorical
10	channel	Marketing channel	Categorical
11	srch_ci	Check-in date	Custom
12	srch_co	Check-out date	Custom
13	srch_adults_cnt	Number of adults specified in search	Numerical
14	srch_children_cnt	Number of children specified in search	Numerical
15	srch_rm_cnt	Number of rooms specified in search	Numerical
16	srch_destination_id	ID of the hotel's location	Categorical
17	srch_destination_type_id	Type of the destination	Categorical
18	hotel_continent	Continent in which the hotel is located	Categorical
19	hotel_country	Country in which the hotel is located	Categorical
20	hotel_cluster	ID of the hotel's associated cluster	Categorical

Our data set contain both content-based (e.g., *orig_distination_distance*, *hotel_country*) and contextual (e.g., *date_time*, *is_mobile*) features. The original data set also includes a user ID that we use to create sequences of data that belong to the same user and 150-dimensional vector embeddings that were created by Expedia according to an undisclosed method for

---

[5] The data set was retrieved from https://www.kaggle.com/c/expedia-hotel-recommendations/ on 15th November 2017.

describing the set of regions in their data set. Although this additional information may enhance the quality of predictions, we discard them from our data set because otherwise these additional vectors would unnecessarily increase the complexity of our data without contributing to understanding our proposed approach and the evaluation of our models. Since we are interested in predicting hotel bookings, we discard the viewing data and use the approximately three million booking records. At this point, we have selected the features that we use in our evaluation, which contain no missing values. We proceed to preprocess these features as follows. We first delete all columns that do not contain any non-zero entries. Then, we distinguish between categorical and numerical features (see Table B-9) and preprocess categorical variables by turning them into dummy vectors representing each possible value with a zero, if the value is absent, or a one, otherwise. We preprocess numerical variables through min-max normalization, scaling them to a range [0,1] according to the following rule:

$$\hat{v}_i = \frac{v_i - \min(v)}{\max(v) - \min(v)} \tag{B-17}$$

, where v denotes an arbitrary numerical variable, $\min(v)$ the smallest possible and $\max(v)$ the greatest possible value of v, v_i a certain value representing an instance of v, and $\hat{v}_i$ the transformed instance of v_i. The variable describing the date and time of the hotel viewing requires special treatment. That is, we first extract the month, the day of the week, and the time of the day from this variable. We treat the month and the day of the week as categorical variables and transform them into dummy vectors. We treat the time of the day as a numerical variable that we rescale based on $\min(time) = 0$ and $\max(time) = 24$. At this point, each data point is described by a 77,505-dimensional vector. We strive to reduce the size of these vectors to allow for an effective use of ML models that are increasingly difficult to train on data with higher dimensionalities. The dimensionality reduction process is described in the next section. Finally, we center the data for our approach (i.e., subtract the sample mean from each dimension) according to (B-18), where $\bar{\hat{v}}$ is the sample mean of $\hat{v}$, n the total number of data points, and $\hat{v}_i^{(C)}$ the centered instance of $\hat{v}_i$.

$$\hat{v}_i^{(C)} = \hat{v}_i - \bar{\hat{v}} = \hat{v}_i - \frac{1}{n} \cdot \sum_{j=1}^{n} \hat{v}_j \tag{B-18}$$

Centering is particularly important for the NNs used in our approach because it enhances the training process (LeCun et al. 2012). We train and test other approaches that we use in this evaluation on un-centered, but min-max-scaled, data.

2.4.1.1 Dimensionality Reduction

The data matrix in its current shape is sparsely populated (i.e., most entries are equal to zero) due to the dummy variables used to represent the data. Reducing the dimensionality through feature selection is, thus, not practicable because most of the 77,505 individual features capture only a tiny share of the overall information available. Instead, we use a feature extraction technique (Khalid et al. 2014) to map the data into a lower-dimensional space through linear or non-linear transformations. In particular, we evaluate three projection-based methods for our purpose, which are increasingly being used because they explore nonlinearities in richer ways than methods based on component analyses such as (kernel) principal component analysis (Sorzano et al. 2014). Namely, we try out locally linear embedding (LLE) (Roweis and Saul 2000), IsoMap (Tenenbaum et al. 2000) and t-distributed stochastic neighbor embedding (t-SNE) (van der Maaten and Hinton 2008).

To select the best method for our problem, we compare the three methods by taking a random sample of size 25,000 from our data set, reducing their dimensionality according to these methods. We evaluate the predictive performance of different classifiers (logistic regression (Cox 1958), decision tree (Breiman et al. 1984), random forest (Ho 1995), and feedforward NN (Cybenko 1989)) on the transformed data sets. For these tests, we choose intuitively reasonable parameters for the methods: a reduced dimensionality of 50, a perplexity of 30 for the t-SNE (determining the neighborhood), and a neighborhood size of 35 for both the IsoMap and the LLE. Using the transformed data, we optimize the hyperparameters of the classifiers with respect to accuracy by trying out all possible combinations in pre-defined, reasonable ranges. Each model, defined by a certain set of hyperparameters, is trained and evaluated on random samples of the data through threefold cross-validation. Table B-10 shows the hyperparameter ranges and Table B-11 the performance of the combinations of classifiers and dimensionality reduction techniques.

Table B-10. Hyperparameters considered for logistic regression, decision tree, random forest, and NN.

Logistic Regression		Decision Tree		Random Forest		Neural Network	
Parameter	Values	Parameter	Values	Parameter	Values	Parameter	Values
Regularization	L_1, L_2	Metric	Gini impurity, Information gain	Metric	Gini impurity, Information gain	Hidden layers	{20,30,40, 50,60,70}
Penalty	{0.1,0.4, 0.7,1,1.3, 1.6,1.9}	Min. impurity decrease	Range [0.05,0.38] with step size 0.03			Activation function	Logistic, Hyperbolic tangent, Rectifier
		Min. sample size	{2, 4, 6, 8, 10}	Number of trees	Range [5,65] with step size 6	Learning rate	{0.001,0.005, 0.01,0.02,0.03}
		Max. ratio of features	{0.1,0.2,0.3,0.4}				

Table B-11. Results of dimensionality reduction (rounded to three significant figures).

	Logistic Regression	Decision Tree	Random Forest	Neural Network
		Accuracy		
IsoMap	**0.084**	0.042	**0.049**	**0.078**
LLE	0.049	0.042	0.041	0.054
t-SNE	0.046	**0.05**	0.034	0.04
		MAP@5		
IsoMap	**0.129**	0.0881	**0.0917**	**0.128**
LLE	0.0993	**0.101**	0.0747	0.101
t-SNE	0.0878	0.0914	0.0684	0.0813
		F_1 Score		
IsoMap	**0.0179**	0.00143	**0.0260**	**0.0235**
LLE	0.00491	0.00155	0.0148	0.00821
t-SNE	0.0132	**0.00277**	0.0208	0.00912

We note that IsoMap outperforms the other dimensionality reduction techniques for almost all classification approaches and quality measures. Only in combination with the decision tree, the IsoMap is inferior to the other techniques. However, we observe that, while other measures indicate a mediocre performance of the decision tree, its F_1 score is particularly low in all instances compared to other classifiers. For this reason, we neglect the performance of the different techniques combined with the decision tree and select the IsoMap to transform our data set. Before moving to this step, we tune its hyperparameters (number of dimensions in the projected space, neighborhood size) by testing out all combinations of numbers of dimensions in the range [10,110] with a step size of 10 and neighborhood sizes in the range [5,155] with a step size of 20. We tune these hyperparameters with respect to the cost function (reconstruction error) that the model seeks to minimize (Tenenbaum et al. 2000). We illustrate the errors for all hyperparameter combinations in Figure B:7. We observe that the error declines rapidly at first with an increasing number of dimensions and neighborhood size. At some point, the error value slightly increases again. We find the optimal hyperparameters as the combination of a number of dimensions of 110 and a neighborhood size of 125. Given this configuration, the model produces a reconstruction error of 8.62.

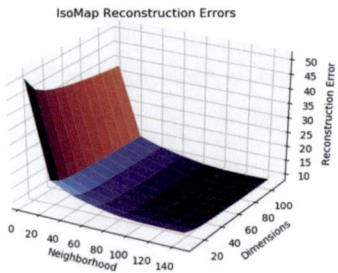

Figure B:7. Reconstruction errors of IsoMap models for different projected dimensions and neighborhood sizes. The highest errors are depicted in dark-red and the lowest in dark-blue.

2.4.2 Basis for Comparison

Being concerned with the accuracy of recommendations, we assess their quality by comparing them to actually made bookings. We use three different measures commonly used for classifications and recommendations: the classification accuracy, the mean average precision, and the F_1 score. The classification accuracy is computed as $accuracy = \frac{true\ predictions}{all\ predictions}$ – the rate of correctly classified bookings. The mean average precision at a certain cutoff k (MAP@k) considers the k highest-ranked predictions for each booking and computes a score depending on the rank of the correct prediction. This measure is particularly suited for recommendation systems, which typically provide not just a single recommendation, but several recommendations at once. We set $k = 5$ and compute MAP@5 according to (B-19), with $Predictions_{i,[1:j]}$ denoting the j highest-ranked predictions for the i-th booking.

$$MAP@5(Bookings, Predictions)$$
$$= \frac{1}{N} \cdot \sum_{i=1}^{N} \sum_{j=1}^{5} Precision(Bookings_i, Predictions_{i,[1:j]}) \quad \text{(B-19)}$$

Being faced with a multiclass classification problem, we compute the F_1 score based on the average precision ($\overline{Prec}$) and average recall ($\overline{Rec}$) over all classes according to (B-20). Although not explicitly used in our evaluation, we also report the precision and recall for each model, for the sake of comprehensibility.

$$F_1(Bookings, Predictions)$$
$$= 2 \cdot \frac{\overline{Prec}(Bookings, Predictions) \cdot \overline{Rec}(Bookings, Predictions)}{\overline{Prec}(Bookings, Predictions) + \overline{Rec}(Bookings, Predictions)} \quad \text{(B-20)}$$

We divide our data into a training set (80% of the data) and a test set (20% of the data), while ensuring that the sets comprise complete sequences (i.e., all bookings associated with one user belong to either the training set or the test set, but not both). The models are trained exclusively based on the training set such that the test set can be used to determine the models' ability to generalize. We compare the proposed approach to a number of baseline approaches, which we describe in the following two sections. We further present the performance of a random guesser, considered a minimum performance threshold, and a naïve model – termed as the "prior classifier" – that always predicts the overall most frequently booked hotels.

2.4.2.1 Baseline Approaches

In addition to the random guesser and the prior classifier, we compare the proposed approach to additional baseline approaches. First, we use all models that were used to evaluate the dimensionality reduction – namely, logistic regression, a decision tree, a random forest, and an NN. Furthermore, we use a plain LSTM, two matrix factorization techniques, singular value decomposition (SVD) and non-negative matrix factorization (NMF). These matrix factorization techniques are not particularly suited for the given problem because they require rated items. Nevertheless, we include them in our evaluation since they are a popular tool for generating recommendations and, most prominently, being a fragment of Netflix' recommendation system (Gomez-Uribe and Hunt 2016), they contribute to an estimated value of US$1 billion per year (Smith and Linden 2017). To enable the use of matrix factorization techniques, we create a proxy for ratings in the range $[-1,1]$ as follows, where -1 corresponds to the worst and 1 to the best possible rating. We assign the value 1 to all <user,hotel> pairs for which the respective hotel was booked by the respective user. We further use the viewing records (i.e., hotels that have been viewed, but not booked, by a user), denoted by $viewings(u_i, h_j)$ to create a further rating $r(u_i, h_j)$ for each user u_i and each hotel h_j according to (B-21), where $\max_{k,l}[viewings(u_k, h_l)]$ denotes the maximum number of times that any hotel has been viewed by any user.

$$r(u_i, h_j) = 2 \cdot \frac{viewings(u_i, h_j)}{\max_{k,l}[viewings(u_k, h_l)]} - 1 \qquad (B\text{-}21)$$

We may apply SVD and NMF to these ratings and obtain predicted ratings for each pair of users and hotels $<u_i, h_j>$ for which h_j has not been previously booked by u_i. The highest-ranking hotels are predicted for each user. For new users, we predict the hotels that have the highest booking frequencies among all users. Furthermore, we use the Apriori algorithm, most prominently used by Amazon (Smith and Linden 2017), to make predictions based on item-to-item association rules. We set the minimum support to zero.

2.4.3 Results

We evaluate the performance of the different models on the original data set and the data set with reduced dimensions. We tune the hyperparameters of the models by performing an exhaustive search over predefined parameter ranges. The parameter ranges for the SVD, NMF, and LSTM are shown in Table B-12. For the logistic regression, decision tree, random forest, and NN, we use the same parameter ranges as before (see Table B-12). Having limited space, we report the optimal hyperparameters only for the NN and the LSTM, which are part of our proposed approach. For the NN, we obtain a hidden layer size of 20, the rectifier activation function, and a learning rate of 0.001. For the LSTM, we get a hidden layer size of 20, the hyperbolic tangent activation, a learning rate of 0.005, a forget gate bias of 1.5, and a batch size of five.

Table B-12. Hyperparameters considered for SVD, NMF, and LSTM.

Singular Value Decomposition		Non-Negative Matrix Factorization		Long Short-Term Memory	
Parameter	Values	Parameter	Values	Parameter	Values
Number of components	{1, ...,35}			Hidden layers	{5, 10, 20, 40, 60, 80}
		Number of components	{1, ...,35}	Activation function	Hyperbolic tangent, Sigmoid
Singular values type	Smallest values, Largest values			Learning rate	{0.001, 0.005, 0.01, 0.02, 0.03}
				Forget gate bias	{0.5, 1, 1.5, 2, 2.5, 3}
				Batch size	{5, 10, 20}

Table B-13 indicates the evaluation results. We do not show the performance on the original data set since it is generally inferior to the performance on the data with reduced dimensions. Among the non-context-aware, collaborative approaches (Apriori, SVD, NMF), we note that the Apriori algorithm performs the best according to all three measures. The poor performance of the SVD and NMF are presumably due to the already-anticipated misfit between the models and the given the problem (i.e., SVD and NMF work well with user-item ratings, while our data includes no ratings). Despite the Apriori algorithm being superior to the SVD and NMF, it does not outperform the prior classifier. This poor performance can be explained by the fact that the Apriori algorithm is typically used with large data sets involving many user interactions (Li and Karahanna 2015), while users in our data set, on average, perform less than four actions.

Table B-13. Prediction scores (rounded to three significant figures).

	Accuracy	MAP@5	F1 Score	Precision	Recall
Random Guesser	0.0101	0.0227	0.00996	0.0101	0.00984
Prior Classifier	0.0410	0.0740	0.000787	0.000410	0.01
Apriori Association Rules Mining	0.0315	0.0614	0.0106	0.00901	0.0129
Singular Value Decomposition	0.0112	0.0257	0.00170	0.000930	0.00988
Non-Negative Matrix Factorization	0.0206	0.0355	0.00800	0.00671	0.009921
Logistic Regression (reduced)	0.0960	0.168	0.0675	0.0667	0.0683
Decision Tree (reduced)	0.0563	0.101	0.00356	0.00192	0.0237
Random Forest (reduced)	0.0747	0.132	0.0573	0.0581	0.0565
Neural Network (reduced)	0.102	0.178	0.0703	0.0714	0.0692
Long Short-Term Memory (reduced)	0.0814	0.143	0.0448	0.0433	0.0464
DoL System (reduced)	**0.108**	**0.199**	**0.0752**	**0.0764**	**0.0741**

The context-aware approaches are clearly superior to the non-context-aware approaches. The proposed DoL system outperforms all baseline approaches according to all evaluation criteria, albeit not by a large margin. This small margin may be explained, similar to the Apriori algorithm, by the small number of actions observed for each user. Performing time-series analyses, LSTMs are likely to produce more accurate predictions if the input sequences contain more observations. Furthermore, we observe that the overall DoL system performs better than its individual sub-components (the NN and the LSTM).

2.5 Limitations

The data collection is limited in the sense that we cannot tell whether a user's selected action actually corresponds to their preferred action. Since Expedia has a large set of hotels, many of which users are unaware of, and their search engine presents users with ranked lists of hotels, we cannot assume that their selection represents the best fit. For the most part, this issue may be mitigated by collecting user ratings.

We realize that there may be approaches that perform better than our proposed approach. However, their superiority is usually limited to a certain data set to which their approach is tailored. They often use rule-based adaptations and extensive feature engineering to exploit the full potential of the data. In this paper, we are concerned with recommendation systems that solve a broader class of problems and dynamically adapt to different contexts. Our evaluation is, thus, limited to purely data-driven approaches.

Researchers develop hybrid recommendation approaches to address different issues with solely collaborative or content-based approaches such as the cold-start problem, data sparsity, and the accuracy, diversity, and scalability of recommendation systems (Çano and Morisio 2017). With our approach, we focus on the cold-start problem and the accuracy of the recommendation system. The approach may be adjusted in future research to address further issues that are beyond the scope of this study.

Furthermore, in practice, employing the proposed approach – and recommendation systems in general – may degrade the quality of recommendations over time. Depending on the willingness of users to accept a recommendation, recommendation systems may increasingly acquire a bias towards their own recommendations. In fact, recommendations may also alter user preferences and bias them towards certain kinds of content, hindering a reliable evaluation of the recommendation accuracy (Adomavicius et al. 2013).

2.6 Implications

2.6.1 Implications for Information Systems Research

Our study has important implications for IS research in the streams of recommendation systems (Xiao and Benbasat 2007; Li and Karahanna 2015) and digital platforms (de Reuver et al. 2017). While prior studies have provided valuable insights and approaches to generating recommendations, they tend to miss a key feature of two-sided platforms. That is, they have not yet considered the changes in customer characteristics that are evoked by ongoing societal digitalization (Tilson et al. 2010). With computing in everyday life (Yoo 2010) and the rise of digital infrastructures (Tilson et al. 2010), first, the option arises for individuals to participate in transactions in everyday life situations mediated by digital platforms; while, second, sound user-information becomes accessible via individual data traces (Brenner et al. 2014).

Therefore, we propose a new approach that accounts for these facts by being consumer-data-driven and adhering to the "mediation of four dimensions of human experiences (time, space, actors, and artifacts) through digital technology" (Yoo 2010, p. 213) by paying particular attention to contexts. The proposed approach does not only learn the influence of context on behavioral patterns at a general level but also at an individual level. In addition, since prior works have not yet produced and evaluated practical approaches for a sophisticated consideration of recommendation contexts (Adomavicius et al. 2011; Li and Karahanna 2015), our study fills this gap by introducing an ML technique that captures the contextual as well as temporal relationships of user states and actions. We also emphasize the benefits of differentiating multiple domains in ML to improve stability (Adomavicius and Zhang 2015) of recommendations and thus contribute to the ongoing value creation for all participants of two-sided digital platforms.

Moreover, unlike prior approaches that deploy a uniformed perspective on users and predict single transactional actions based on the state similarity of the focal user and others, our approach creates a much more complete user profile and accounts for the variances of user internal states. The purpose of doing so is to achieve a precise customer profiling, which enables accurate personalized recommendations and thus enhances customer experience on the digital two-sided platforms. In other words, our new approach profiles users with actual personal characteristics as opposed to simple generalization of user profile from state-action pairs. At a meta level, past approaches followed a collective perspective, where personalization is suppressed and behavioral similarities among collective members are implied (Carter and Grover 2015). These past approaches can occasionally result in either positive or negative identity verification through recommendation depending on the coinciding of the individual and the typical collective preferences in a particular situation. However, in the era of individual IS (Baskerville 2011) when personalization becomes an important design feature of contemporary services (Vodanovich et al. 2010), it is unlikely that past approaches will sustainably lead to strong self-identification or IT identity, i.e., the extent to which an individual views use of an IT as integral to his or her sense of self (Carter and Grover 2015). To emphasize the individual differences during the recommendation generation process, our new approach incorporates users' past actions in various contexts, in addition to the similarities to others in terms of their current state. Finally, this approach may also be beneficiary to other platform designs, given that platforms nowadays focus more on long-term customer relationships than one-time impulsive transactions (Payne and Frow 2017).

2.6.2 Implications for Machine Learning Research

The need for the proposed approach – and hybrid recommendations in general – highlights a fundamental limitation of current ML models. That is, viewing ML models as likelihood estimators, they are able to learn conditional probability distributions, while at the same time unable to learn meta probability distributions (i.e., conditional probability distributions whose posteriors are, in turn, conditional probability distributions). Existing recommendation systems that address this problem do not propose a unifying ML model. Hybrid recommendation systems, including the proposed approach, develop workarounds to mitigate the problem. In particular, we use transfer learning (Pratt 1993) to address this issue, treating the users as individual, but interrelated, ML problems. Although our approach enhances the accuracy of recommendations, we call for increased research in ML theory to enable the development of unifying hybrid recommendation models that can directly account for meta probability distributions.

With the proposed approach, we develop a meta-level, hybrid recommendation system (Çano and Morisio 2017) that can increase the accuracy of recommendations through collaborative, content-based, and context-aware techniques. We follow the call by Bengio et al. (2013) for the use of representation learning and the employment of embedding layers in early stages of predictions tasks. Thereby, we explicitly avoid employing rule-based adaptations that may, at first, be superior to purely data-driven techniques, yet still require continuous adjustments, accompanied with intensive human labor, to accommodate changes to the system. Instead, we integrate collaborative, content-based, context-aware, and user-specific techniques, combined with an LSTM-based time-series prediction. Through the symbiosis of representation learning and transfer learning, we design an approach that outperforms existing data-driven approaches. The contextual representations produced by the NNs in our approach serve as inputs to the LSTM that predicts user actions. The LSTM, in turn, being composed of multiple layers, produces contextual representations of its own. These representations capture sequential information regarding the order of contexts and actions of each user. While we use these more sophisticated contextual representations to predict actions, their value goes beyond this purpose. Namely, they can be used as inputs to further ML models, for example to accurately predict a user's mood from their behavior (Sano et al. 2015) or to cluster users according to their context- and time-sensitive representations.

2.6.3 Practical Implications for Two-Sided Platform Operations

Our work has three particular implications for firms operating two-sided platforms. First, with our approach, we point to the value of considering all four dimensions describing the context of a particular digital user into account when it comes to recommendations. This implies that platform owners should, on the one hand, invest in increasing the number of available data attributes to describe the state of a user. Therefore, platform owners should identify potential partners that could provide additional attributes that could be matched with existing customer data. Here, reciprocal and complementary relationships can be built as these partners might be also interested in additional attributes that the platform owner could provide.

Second, since our approach is able to draw conclusions not only from similar experiences made in the past but also from dissimilar experiences, it is not necessary for platform owners to increase the amount of data to capitalize on the potentials of the presented approach. Thus, no further investments in IT infrastructure are needed and additional value from existing data can be redeemed.

Third, a more differentiated view on individual customers enabled by elaborated customer profiles has potentials beyond improving recommendations made to the users. Platform owners could use the approach to estimate the attractiveness of the given portfolio (e.g., of movies to watch) for customers and use this information to strategically optimize it (e.g., by partnering with providers of new contents). Apart from that, the advanced profiling approach may help detect identity theft as an unusual individual behavior can be promptly identified. This improved security measure may increase trust in the platform owner and further cultivate the sustainability of the platform operations.

3 Study 4: A Machine Learning Approach to the Efficiency-Comfort Trade-Off in Everyday-Life Automation – The Case of Autonomous Vehicles and Sharing Business Models

Table B-14. Fact sheet of Study no. 4.

Title	A Machine Learning Approach to the Efficiency-Comfort Trade-Off in Everyday-Life Automation – The Case of Autonomous Vehicles and Sharing Business Models
Authors	Schahin Tofangchi*[a], Andre Hanelt[b], David Marz[a], Lutz M. Kolbe[a] [a] Chair of Information Management, University of Göttingen, Platz der Göttinger Sieben 5, 37073 Göttingen, Germany [b] Chair of Digital Transformation Management, University of Kassel, Kleine Rosenstraße 3, 34109 Kassel, Germany * Corresponding author. Tel.: +49 (0)551 / 39 - 22254. E-mail address: schahin.tofangchi@uni-goettingen.de
Outlet	-/-
Abstract	Increasingly, we witness the dispersion of digital technologies throughout everyday life circumstances, creating potentials for efficiency gains in important societal contexts such as sustainable mobility by the use of data-driven automation. While such benefits manifest at a systems level (e.g., the efficiency of mobility systems), catering to the individuality of people, on the other hand, is becoming increasingly vital for the acceptance of products and services in the era of digitalization. Personal preferences, in turn, may run against socially important system-level goals such as resource efficiency. Thus, efficiency-comfort trade-offs emerge as a key challenge in contexts that are characterized by both high potentials for overall efficiency gains through data-driven automation and deep involvement with individual everyday practices. For the case of autonomous vehicles, an area growing rapidly in importance, we formalize this trade-off while drawing on a unique data set in order to design and evaluate a machine learning approach to handle it. More specifically, we develop prescriptive models for driving behaviors and user preferences and an application that, based on these two models, resolves the efficiency-comfort trade-off. We consider the real-time dynamics and user interactions that affect the decisions of autonomous vehicles and develop a model extension that allows leveraging the properties of sharing-economy environments to make better-informed decisions. Based on our findings, we derive implications for information systems research as well as business practice.

Keywords	Autonomous vehicles, machine learning, consumer-centric design, real-time computation, sharing economy, sustainability, trade-off learning

3.1 Introduction

The increasing proliferation of digitalization throughout our societies (Tilson et al. 2010) renders big data (BD) and data analytics relevant in more and more areas of life, which bears the potential to drive transformational business model innovation that benefits society across contexts (Loebbecke and Picot 2015) and "is a new yet powerful source for potentially immense economic and social value and for gaining competitive advantage" (Grover et al. 2018, p. 390). However, in the pursuit of these potentials, a central tension between system-level goals (such as efficiency) and individual-level goals (such as comfort) often emerges, since automatized processes optimized for overall performance may run contrary to personal preferences, where they are deeply integrated in people's everyday lives (Yoo 2010).

A specific context in which this very tension becomes salient is in the mobility and transportation sectors. Here, visions for a future sustainable mobility system have been articulated to build upon "an integrated network of driverless, electrical vehicles that are connected, coordinated and shared" (Burns 2013, p. 181). The amount of data generated in connected vehicles (Henfridsson and Lindgren 2005) and the ability to transfer them through ubiquitous digital infrastructures (Tilson et al. 2010), along with the technological possibility to analyze them, pave the way for a continual derivation and application of efficient driving patterns (Loebbecke and Picot 2015). This potential is amplified in sharing economies, where intermediary firms offer on-demand temporary access to valuable goods, thereby being more efficient by using the good to capacity, rather than handing over the goods indefinitely. Without having been fueled by changes in demand-side or supply-side fundamentals, intermediary businesses have generated significant revenue by successfully implementing sharing business models (e.g., carsharing, collaborative housing) (Weber 2014). However, from a business operator's perspective, attractiveness to customers is as important as the potential efficiency gains. Here, research has shown that personalization and customization are of utmost importance for the success of digital business models (El Sawy and Perreira 2013) and ubiquitous information systems (IS) used in everyday life (Vodanovich et al. 2010). Accordingly, fundamentally new mobility applications such as shared electric autonomous vehicles (AVs) that are deeply immersed in personal everyday life (Yoo 2010) require consideration of the specific needs and preferences of individuals (Burns 2013; Waytz et al. 2014). Designs attending to both system-level efficiency and individual comfort may yield a truly transformational impact on mobility systems by unlocking profitable business model innovations (Loebbecke and Picot 2015) that allow high levels of value creation for customers and value capture for operators (Priem et al. 2013). Prior work has illustrated the potentials of IS for sustainable mobility (Teubner and Flath 2015), while the literature remains silent as to how to address the emerging efficiency-comfort trade-offs arising from higher levels of automation. Furthermore, IS research on BD analytics, regardless of the context, has not touched this important topic so far.

In this study, we design an IS artifact (Gregor and Hevner 2013) that is capable of deciding upon a vehicle's configuration to drive both efficiently and according to the consumer's preferences. For this purpose, we draw on a longitudinal dataset, comprising sensor data of approximately 35 thousand drives, with 54 million data points gathered from electric vehicles in carsharing. The artifact comprises (i) a recurrent-neural-network-based (Hochreiter and Schmidhuber 1997) prescriptive model for driving behavior built with the goal of minimizing energy consumption, (ii) a recurrent-neural-network-based model of the consumer's preferred driving behavior, and (iii) a novel machine learning (ML) approach to perform a trade-off between energy-efficient and comfortable driving. We identify the need for a real-time adaptive decision-making application given the dynamic nature of consumer preferences – which may vary depending on factors such as weather and road conditions – in addition to the constant flow of information generated by the vehicles' sensors. Furthermore, to allow for a precise trade-off between energy efficiency and comfort, we add a feedback module that allows the consumer to rate the current driving experience in real time. We adapt our ML models to respond to such feedback. Since AVs are particularly well suited for sharing-based business models (Kornhauser et al. 2013), we extend our models to leverage the potential of sharing economies to accelerate the vehicles' learning process and enable better-informed decisions. We take advantage of the large data sets arising from sharing environments by (i) modeling the dynamics of energy consumption based on the data flow generated by all consumers and (ii) creating a profile for each user that is initialized based on the average user's preferences and adapted over time to reflect individual user preferences.

Our contribution is an artifact that can underpin sustainably profitable operations of sharing business models by addressing relevant decision making problems of AVs related to user comfort as well as driving efficiency using ML methods. Our evaluation shows that the recurrent neural networks converge in a reasonable amount of time and have a significant advantage over existing baseline approaches, being 50 times as accurate as the best baseline approach for efficiency predictions and 4 times as accurate for preference estimations. We study the generalizability of the applied design approach to a broader array of analytics-based decision making problems and derive propositions for the artifact's behavior based on its mathematical formulation. Based on our work, we derive important implications for future IS work in this regard and for managerial practice with regard to both AV design and their operation in sharing-based business models.

3.2 Background

3.2.1 Autonomous Vehicles and the Efficiency-Comfort Trade-Off

AVs can be described as "an entire system at least part of which operates 'autonomously'" (Borenstein et al. 2017, p. 69). Given their characteristics and capabilities, AVs offer potentials for efficiency gains. For example, AVs may enable fuel savings of 20 to 50 percent, which in turn means less dependency on depleting natural resources (Fagnant and Kockelman 2015; Ferreras 2014). Furthermore, one of the most promising opportunities in terms of the advancing vehicle automation is the concept of shared AVs (Fagnant and Kockelman 2018).

Despite their popularity, regular carsharing business models struggle with several key barriers such as their limited accessibility and reliability (e.g., Fagnant and Kockelman (2014); Kornhauser et al. (2013)). Due to the potential capabilities and benefits of AVs, the implementation of shared AVs becomes feasible (Zhang et al. 2015). Possible benefits include a higher utilization of resources (Zhang et al. 2015), reduced parking demand (Fagnant and Kockelman 2015; Hayes 2011; Zhang et al. 2015), or reduced costs (Burns et al. 2013).

These advantages and benefits primarily occur on a system level, e.g., on the level of a fleet of vehicles operated by a mobility provider, which aims to maximize value capture (e.g., Fagnant and Kockelman (2018)). However, value creation in this and similar contexts involves serving human beings, rendering an individual perspective particularly relevant. In the recent past, initial studies on an individual level have been conducted in order to examine the attitude of individuals towards AVs. Mainly, two findings have been obtained. First, perceived trust and safety are likely to play a central role for the acceptance of AVs (e.g., Dennis et al. (2016); Kohl et al. 2017; Lee et al. (2015)). Prior research has shown that the use, misuse, and disuse of automation, especially in the case of complex and sophisticated systems, largely depends on trust (Lee and See 2004). AVs may cause fears regarding traffic safety because using them means that the driver gives up the overall control regarding the vehicle (Ernst and Reinelt 2017; Kohl et al. 2017). One way to alleviate these concerns is offering the driver a high level of comfort during the ride. Previous studies on automation have shown that systems that act in accordance with the user's preferences provide a pleasant and comfortable environment, thereby accomplishing a higher acceptance (e.g., Medhi Thies et al. (2017); Nimavat and Champaneria (2017); Tavanapour and Bittner (2018))). Furthermore, the feeling of personal connection with a system may counteract sources of anxiety and distrust towards non-human technologies such as AVs (Benlian et al. 2019; Waytz et al. 2014).

Second, by applying findings from prior research based on technology acceptance theories (e.g., Davis (1989); Davis et al. (1989)) to the context of AVs, positive impacts can be expected from providing hedonic benefits (e.g., Choi and Ji (2015); Ernst and Reinelt (2017); Kohl et al. (2017)) through personalization (Hong and Tam 2006; Lang et al. 2013; Vodanovich et al. 2010). Digital technologies' status as an everyday component of private lives (Yoo 2010) increasingly demands that new products or services meet individual needs and expectations (Hess et al. 2014; Vodanovich et al. 2010) – emphasizing the importance of personalization.

Following this train of thought, providing drivers a high level of comfort by attending to their personal preferences can have a significant influence on the acceptance of AVs, both in terms of supporting perceived trust and safety as well as providing hedonic benefits. A satisfactory customer experience, in turn, may lead to a high loyalty and increases a firm's revenue. On the other hand, providing the user with the highest possible comfort by configuring AVs in accordance with their preferences may contradict the goal of increased efficiency. For instance, recent research results in sharing economy contexts show that the separation of ownership and use can lead to excessive resource consumption by the users (Hildebrandt et al. 2018). As a consequence, it is necessary to find a solution for the resulting efficiency-comfort trade-off to realize the potential benefits of AVs in terms of their efficiency while providing the user with comfort in order to foster the diffusion of AVs.

3.2.2 Machine Learning in the Context of Autonomous Vehicles and Personalization

The rise of digital infrastructures as well as the internet of things manifests opportunities to target grand challenges and wicked problems such as creating sustainable consumption systems by leveraging BD analytics (Ketter et al. 2016). These potentials also give rise to tensions because, despite "the strategic value of these data... for businesses is unquestionable, the implications for individuals and wider society are less clear" (Newell and Marabelli 2015, p. 2).

In the recent past, researchers have developed various ML approaches to different problems in the context of AVs. Their architecture includes several sub-modules (e.g., human interface, route planning, environment perception and modeling), interconnected with a coordination and control module (Borenstein et al. 2017). These sub-modules are necessary to solve problems on different abstraction levels: While object recognition and trajectory planning modules work on a low level and are essential to the immediate driving task (Levinson et al. 2011), driving behavior optimization and human-machine interaction (e.g., through voice control) can be allocated to a higher level of abstraction as they build upon modules at lower levels to enhance the overall driving performance (Levinson et al. 2011; National Highway Traffic Safety Administration (NHTSA) 2017). All these sub-modules need to be interconnected by the exchange of gathered data and processed information. In this paper, we refer to this interconnected set of sub-modules as an analytical chain, in which data and information are processed and exchanged to ultimately react to a particular scenario.

In the following, we briefly describe a sample of past research using ML in the context of AVs. Recognizing objects in image data is one of the most widely researched problems in autonomous driving. For example, building upon prior research on object recognition for AVs (Dickmanns and Mysliwetz 1992; Masaki 1992), Buluswar and Draper (1998) have introduced a general-purpose, color-based approach for the detection of objects. Other researchers have developed methods for adaptive terrain classification (Bajracharya et al. 2009), road detection through support vector machines (Zhou et al. 2010), lane and optimal driving region detection on structured and unstructured roads (Li et al. 2014), and perception creation from image data (Chen et al. 2015). Equally important, researchers have been concerned with developing trajectory planning algorithms (Hellström and Ringdahl 2006; Wit et al. 2004), not only for AVs but also for robots and other moving agents (Morales et al. 2009). Such algorithms translate a given set of high-level routing instructions (Zhao 1997) into explicit movement execution plans to approximately follow pre-defined paths (Hellström and Ringdahl 2006). Research concerned with high-level vehicle control typically builds upon the aforementioned image detection and trajectory planning modules. Although the practical evaluation of such research is constrained due to the fact autonomous controllers can hardly be tested in real traffic due to the potential dangers associated with machine failures, researchers have developed a series of methods for AV control. Virtually all researchers have resorted to simulation-based evaluation of their approaches. For example, some researchers have developed approaches for basic ML-based control of AVs (Schultz and Grefenstette 1992), safety-warning and driver-assistance applications (Li et al. 2004), autonomous reinforcement-learning-based controllers for ground vehicles (Dai et al. 2005) and underwater vehicles (Carreras et al. 2005). Other applications, analyzing a richer set of features of the vehicles' environments, track trajectories of obstacles and other traffic participants to obtain a comprehensive situational understanding and thus enhance motion planning (e.g., Gindele et al. (2010)).

To the best of our knowledge, there are currently no ML-based solutions that adaptively resolve conflicting interests (trade-offs) between actions preferred by a given user and actions that may be desirable from an objective perspective. Nevertheless, a number of researchers have dealt with personalization of driver assistance systems (i.e., vehicles with a low level of automation) – independent of potential trade-offs – by either employing rule-based approaches (which we neglect in this paper due to their lack of adaptability) or by developing individualized or group-based ML applications that personalize adaptive cruise controls (Rosenfeld et al. 2015; Wang et al. 2013), brake assistance (Muehlfeld et al. 2013; Wang et al. 2016), lane keeping (Lefèvre et al. 2015), and lane changing (Butakov and Ioannou 2015). Some of these approaches have yielded desirable results (e.g., Hasenjäger and Wersing (2017)). However, approaches that are heavily group based may fail to perform an effective personalization because they neglect individual preferences (Adomavicius et al. 2011). Individualized personalization approaches for driver assistance systems do not take into account possible time-varying effects and are, therefore, not effectively applicable to fully autonomous vehicles whose decisions are often based on sequences of observations rather than a single snapshot of a particular situation. Considering the case of fully autonomous vehicles, Kuderer et al. (2015) propose an approach to personalizing the driving experience based on examples. That is, the user is required to manually control the vehicle for a certain amount of time to allow the vehicle to learn their preferred driving behavior. Personalizing the user's driving experience by, in this case, learning their preferred driving behavior, is beneficial to the user's acceptance of the AV (Burns 2013). However, the drawbacks of the approach presented by Kuderer et al. (2015) lie in its static nature (i.e., it neglects the fact that user preferences may vary depending on the situation and time), and in its isolated training of the ML models involved in the AV's analytical chain.

To enable the data-driven optimization of AVs through a coherent system, Bojarski et al. (2016) propose a convolutional-neural-network-based end-to-end approach that learns to directly associate raw camera data to steering commands. While they argue against an explicit problem decomposition and in favor of jointly optimizing an agent's components – an approach that may yield a higher performance (Pfeifer and Bongard 2006) –, their approach has multiple major drawbacks. First, the application requires the user to initially provide training examples by fully controlling the vehicle. This requirement implies that the user has to control the vehicle whenever they enter new environments, which may negatively affect their trust into the application. Second, and more importantly with respect to ML research, the application's decisions are based on just a single ML model. While the, thereby induced, lack of a problem decomposition enables the joint optimization of all application components with respect to the overall task, it also leads to the inability of adding further modules to the application and to a lack of interpretability of the application's behavior. Such generic and non-modular application designs hinder the incorporation of new modules for individual sub-tasks such as object recognition and trajectory planning, calling for approaches that are based on a modular application design, with each module solving a particular task of autonomous driving, and able to intertwine these modules through data-driven techniques.

3.3 Research Setting

ML-based autonomous driving (e.g., using deep neural networks (NNs)) is, on the one hand, associated with enormous efficiency gains compared to manual driving (Vanderbilt 2012). On the other hand, the technology is embedded in social systems that discuss and decide upon its acceptance and utilization. Scholars conducting research on ML-based AVs should thus take into account the interaction between machines and humans and adopt a human-centered design perspective (Gasson 2003) to not only optimize vehicles' capabilities of analyzing their environments and finding efficient driving patterns but also to consider users' preferences to enhance their driving experience and thereby their trust.

We develop an IS artifact that derives driving policies based on energy consumption and user satisfaction. Note that our research is not concerned with low-level processes such as modeling roads and obstacles. Instead, our research focuses on a set of simple, configurable parameters of a vehicle – influencing the driving behavior and contributing to a user's comfort – and derive a data-driven approach to determining a configuration that minimizes energy consumption while maximizing the user's driving experience at the same time. To do so, we require a model relating vehicle configuration to energy efficiency and a model of each individual user's preferences under different conditions. Moreover, we need a method that draws on these models in order to determine a vehicle's configuration in every situation to cater to both the user's preferences and the vehicle's energy efficiency.

Since we are dealing with a distributed, real-time learning problem (i.e. the data are processed by multiple vehicles and produced at a high pace while the vehicles are in use) involving large amounts of data, we adhere to the Division-of-Labor (DoL) framework (Tofangchi, Hanelt, and Kolbe 2017) to develop our ML application. This framework ensures the application's practicability by appropriately handling real-time data and their effectiveness by using distributed analysis modules to improve its analytical capabilities. The DoL framework enables a modular composition of an ML application. Leveraging the concept of task division, it divides analysis tasks into sub-tasks of lower complexity. An application based on the DoL framework – henceforth referred to as a DoL application – solves these sub-tasks to obtain a solution to the overall task. Based on this approach, it may yield results of a higher quality than those obtained without the use of task division. The framework comprises two computational component types: the expert and the central executive (CE) (see Figure B:8).

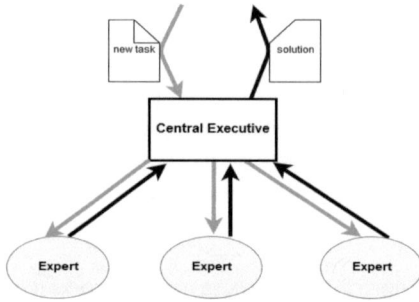

Figure B:8. The Division-of-Labor framework. Gray and black arrows indicate the transmission of (sub-) tasks and their solutions, respectively (Tofangchi, Hanelt and Kolbe 2017).

Apart from handling task division, experts and CEs satisfy a set of additional properties that contribute to the overall usability and comprehensibility of DoL applications (see Table B-15). In order to enable learning, CEs gather feedback from outside the system and redirect it to experts that adapt their models accordingly. Both experts and CEs possess an additional optional property, sustainability, that requires them to adapt their learning models in real time (i.e., updating their models, rather than entirely recomputing them, whenever new data are seen), ensuring the system's scalability.

Table B-15. Properties of experts and central executives in the Division-of-Labor framework (Tofangchi, Hanelt and Böhrnsen 2017).

Expert	Specialization	Explanation (optional)		Adaptation	Sustainability (optional)
Central Executive	General knowledge	Task Distribution	Feedback		

After developing our artifact, we evaluate it using a data set that comprises sensor and booking data provided by a carsharing company. Because the data were not collected in AVs, but in cars entirely controlled by users, we cannot rely on the raw data set to perform the evaluation. Instead, we apply some transformations and restrictions to the data in order to properly evaluate the artifact with respect to its objective in the context of autonomous driving. We describe the details of how we handle these data in the Evaluation Section.

In the next section, we develop the artifact by first defining a set of ML models that we use as building blocks and then describing the processes in which these models are employed to form the ML application. We further define the interaction between the user and the ML application and show how the resulting artifact satisfies the properties of the DoL framework.

3.4 A Division-of-Labor Application for Resolving the Efficiency-Comfort Trade-Off in Autonomous Driving

We design the ML application to learn to make decisions on a predefined set of driving parameters (configuration) of a vehicle with the goal of minimizing energy consumption and maximizing user comfort. The application thus contributes to the analytical capabilities of AVs and is concerned with high-level vehicle configurations such as velocity, acceleration, air conditioning, and gear rather than with lower-level capabilities such as road and road sign detection, obstacle avoidance, or routing. It makes "soft" decisions that are based on the vehicle's sensory input but is ultimately restricted by decisions made at lower levels of the vehicle's analytical chain. Since the application decides on high-level configurations that are required to be adapted frequently throughout a drive, it receives inputs and makes decisions at intervals of seconds or milliseconds. We divide the given inputs into two sets of variables: one set comprising data on the vehicle's environment that are immutable by the application and one set comprising the vehicle's configuration parameters that may be modified by the application. While both of these sets serve as descriptors of the current situation, the application only modifies the latter set to respond to a situation.

The application comprises three ML models. First, we employ a recurrent NN (Elman 1990) – in particular, a long short-term memory network (LSTM) (Hochreiter and Schmidhuber 1997) – to model the relationship between the vehicle configuration and the energy efficiency. Recurrent NNs are supervised learning models that can be applied to time-series data. LSTMs constitute the state of the art in this context and have shown great performance in various learning problems involving time series (Chen, Parada et al. 2015; Ma et al. 2015; Sak et al. 2014). We train this model to learn the energy efficiency of a drive, based on the sequence of inputs received. Second, we use a further LSTM to build a context-sensitive model of user preferences regarding modifiable configurations. We are faced with a paradox because, in order to be able to build such a model to enable autonomous decisions by the application, we require data on configurations set by the user. Acquiring these data requires a violation of the application's autonomy. We address this issue by largely letting the application choose the configuration and allowing the user to manually set individual configurations. Users will use this function to adjust the driving behavior whenever they are dissatisfied with their existing driving experience. We treat the manual adjustments as real-time user feedback that we use to adapt the model of preferences. In contrast to Kuderer et al.'s (2015) approach, our proposed system does not learn to imitate the user's driving behavior, but acts autonomously in a laissez-faire manner until the user intervenes. This way, the system learns to drive according to the user's preferences as a passenger rather than a driver. We compare both our model for energy efficiency and our preference model with a number of baseline models in the Evaluation Section. Third, we develop a method that resolves the trade-off between efficiency and comfort using the aforementioned models to perform a weighted optimization of efficiency and comfort, in pursuance of making a decision on the vehicle's configuration at each time step. In the following two sections, we describe the design of the CE and experts.

3.4.1 Central Executive

The CE is in charge of maintaining a model of energy efficiency and a model of the average user's preferences. Both these models are independent of particular situations and users, satisfying the DoL property of general knowledge. The model of energy efficiency and the model of the average user's preferences are LSTMs with sets of parameters $\theta^{(E)}$ and $\theta^{(P)}$ (i.e., neural weights) that the CE initializes randomly. In this study, we use so-called "vanilla" LSTMs (Greff et al. 2017) without peephole connections. LSTMs possess a set of hyperparameters (hidden layer size, activation function of the hidden layer, forget gate bias, and learning rate) that we specify in accordance with the given data in the Artifact Instantiation Section. Users need to sign up for carsharing prior to using the AVs and are each assigned to a unique expert by the CE. When a previously unseen user starts using a vehicle, the CE creates an expert for this user and initializes it with the current versions of the model of energy efficiency and the average user's preference model. While a vehicle is in use by some user u_i, sensor data retrieved by the vehicle – comprising a set of environmental variables denoted as $e_{u_i,t} \in \mathbb{R}^p$ and a set of configurable variables (the current state of the vehicle's configuration) denoted as $c_{u_i,t} \in \mathbb{R}^q$ – at each time step t are first processed by the according expert who forwards these data to the CE. We stack these two vectors to obtain the whole set of sensor data $s_{u_i,t} = \begin{pmatrix} e_{u_i,t} \\ c_{u_i,t} \end{pmatrix}$.

The size of the time steps is determined by the frequency at which sensor data are retrieved by the vehicle and should generally be in the range of milliseconds to seconds. The expert further transmits information on whether the user has manually set configuration parameters and, therefore, locked them for modifications by the ML application; this information assumes the shape of a scalar that we denote as $l_{u_i,t} \in \{0,1\}$ and is set to 1 if any configurable variable is locked. Upon receiving these three inputs, the CE stores $s_{u_i,t}$ in a list $S_{u_i,d}$ and, if $l_{u_i,t} = 1$, updates the preference model using backpropagation (Linnainmaa 1976) with a small learning rate by feeding it $e_{u_i,t}$ as the input and $c_{u_i,t}$ as the label for the backpropagation process.

Once a drive has concluded (when the user signs out of the car), the expert informs the CE and transmits the overall efficiency of drive d, computed as $E_{u_i,d} = \frac{distance\_travelled_{u_i,d}}{energy\_consumption_{u_i,d}}$. The CE uses this information to update the model of energy efficiency following the afore-mentioned backpropagation process by sequentially feeding the model each entry from the list of sensor data $S_{u_i,d}$ and using $E_{u_i,d}$ as the label. $S_{u_i,d}$ is deleted subsequently.

As stated at the beginning of this section, the CE satisfies the property of general knowledge by maintaining general-purpose models that serve as bases for the experts' analysis tasks. It satisfies the property of task division by treating the drives associated to a particular user as a sub-task that is handled by an expert. It further satisfies the properties of adaptation and sustainability by adapting its efficiency and preference models when new data are seen and updating these models incrementally, allowing the application to discard all data points after a drive is completed. Finally, the CE does not specifically satisfy the feedback property. However, we move this property to the experts for the reason that experts interact with users in real time and need the feedback immediately, whereas the CE has no time-critical functions and can wait for the experts to forward said user feedback.

3.4.2 Expert

The experts are responsible for modeling individual user preferences. Each expert is associated with one user u_i and holds a model (an LSTM) of their preferences, similar to how the CE holds a model of the average user's preferences, which is also used to initialize the expert's user preference model. The expert thus initializes the LSTM weights with the weights stored in the CE's preference model. At each time step, an expert decides upon the vehicle's configuration based on the LSTM that models its efficiency, whose outputs for a certain input vector $s_{u_i,t}$ we denote as $E(s_{u_i,t})$, and the LSTM that models the user's preferences, whose outputs for an input vector $e_{u_i,t}$ we denote as $P(e_{u_i,t})$.

To determine the vehicle configuration at any given time, we query the preference model for the user's expected preferred configuration. We then employ a gradient-based approach that uses said configuration as a starting point, taking a step towards a more efficient configuration. For this purpose, the expert requires the derivative of the efficiency model with respect to its input, denoted as $\frac{\partial E(x)}{\partial x}$ (the formulae along with the derivations of the LSTM output and its derivative are described by Hochreiter and Schmidhuber (1997)). At each time step t, an expert possesses information on the lock state of the configurable parameters, taking on the shape of a vector $L_{u_i,t} \in \mathbb{N}^q$, where $L_{u_i,t,j}$ denotes the number of time steps for which the j-th configurable parameter will remain locked for changes by the expert. Whenever the user manually adjusts the j-th configuration parameter, the expert sets $L_{u_i,t,j} = lock\_time$, where $lock\_time$ is the number of time steps for which a lock remains active. Taking into account the lock state, the expert computes the new sensor data vector $s'_{u_i,t}$ as:

$$\forall_{j=1}^{p}: s'_{u_i,t,j} = s_{u_i,t_j},$$

$$\forall_{j=p+1}^{p+q}: s'_{u_i,t,j} = \begin{cases} s_{u_i,t,j}, & if\ L_{u_i,t,j-p} > 0 \\ P(e_{u_i,t})_{j-p} + \gamma_{u_i} \cdot \frac{\partial E\left(P(e_{u_i,t})_{j-p}\right)}{\partial P(e_{u_i,t})_{j-p}}, & else \end{cases} \quad (B-22)$$

That is, the set of environmental variables, populating the first up to the p-th dimension of $s_{u_i,t}$, remains unchanged and the set of configurable parameters, populating the $(p+1)$-th up to the q-th dimension of $s_{u_i,t}$, is updated through our gradient-based approach, unless they are currently locked. We introduce a trade-off parameter $\gamma_{u_i} > 0$ that determines the size of the step taken toward an efficient configuration. Since we would like the trade-off to dynamically adapt to user preferences, we introduce two further parameters – the trade-off momentum $m_{u_i} \in (0,1)$ and the trade-off momentum extinction $\alpha_m \in (0,1)$. Note that α_m is a static parameter that assumes the same value for all users. With $n^{(L_{u_i,t})}$ denoting the number of locked configurable parameters associated with user u_i at time t, an expert uses the trade-off momentum to adapt the trade-off parameter according to (B-23).

$$\gamma_{u_i} \leftarrow \gamma_{u_i} + \left(0.51 - \frac{n^{(L_{u_i,t})}}{q}\right) \cdot m_{u_i} \qquad (B\text{-}23)$$

Using the trade-off momentum extinction, an expert adapts the trade-off momentum as:

$$m_{u_i} \leftarrow m_{u_i} \cdot \alpha_m \qquad (B\text{-}24)$$

The coefficient $\left(0.51 - \frac{n^{(L_{u_i,t})}}{q}\right)$ assumes values in the range $[-0.49, 0.51]$, being negative only when the number of locked variables exceeds the number of unlocked variables, and is multiplied with the trade-off momentum to determine the magnitude of the change applied to the trade-off parameter. Subtracting the ratio of locked variables from a value of 0.51 rather than 0.5 results in a small bias of the trade-off towards efficiency. For example, if the numbers of locked and unlocked variables are equal, the trade-off parameter will increase in value and slightly favor efficiency. The trade-off momentum extinction gradually slows down the process of adapting the trade-off parameters for a particular user. The requirement of a high rate of adaptation when the user first enters the application and this rate's gradual decrease as the application becomes more acquainted with the user in order to avoid oscillatory behavior of the vehicle is the intuition behind slowing down the adaptation. Apart from the adaptation of the trade-off and the trade-off momentum parameters, the learning processes of experts involve the adaptation of the preference model, which it carries out the same way as the CE. Finally, at the end of a drive, the expert transmits the overall drive efficiency, $E_{u_i,d}$, to the CE. This information is not transmitted at each time step because the energy consumption is usually not accurately measurable with such small time intervals.

The expert satisfies all properties described by Tofangchi, Hanelt, and Kolbe (2017) except for the optional property of explanation that we neglect because the application's modular architecture makes it easily understandable and foregoes an expectation of significant benefits by explicitly providing explanations for each decision. It specializes on a certain sub-task, namely on controlling a vehicle's configurations for one particular user, and adapts its model based on user feedback while adhering to the principle of sustainability by updating all necessary model parameters, rather than entirely recomputing the models when it receives new data. It further takes care of processing feedback, substituting the CE in this regard to reduce latency in the interaction with the vehicle and the user. The shape and functions of the overall DoL application are depicted in Figure B:9.

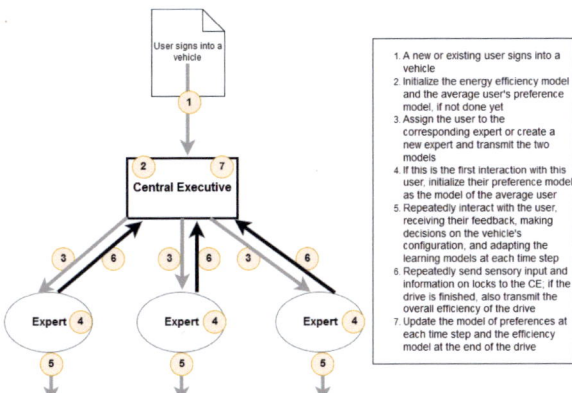

Figure B:9. Architecture of the Division-of-Labor application for autonomous driving based on a trade-off between efficiency and comfort.

3.5 Evaluation

The evaluation is divided into three parts: The evaluation of the overall application is described at the end of this section, whereas detailed evaluations of the two standalone models, based on their adaptability (i.e., decline of undesired behavior over time) on different levels of abstraction (per drive, individual-level adaptability, and overall adaptability), can be found in Appendix C. We evaluate the sub-modules in isolation using the given data set, assuming that a vehicle configuration chosen by the user reflects their true driving preferences. Given the limitation that we may not evaluate the overall system in an actually autonomous setting, we derive statements on its behavior based on a mathematical analysis of the trade-off process. For this purpose, we assume that a vehicle configuration chosen by the user reflects their true preference and that a deviation of a certain magnitude of the vehicle's decision from this preference results in an eventual intervention by the user (i.e., a manual adjustment that we may interpret as user feedback). Whenever such a situation occurs, the application imposes a lock on the affected configuration parameter(s) and sets their values to those that were directly selected by the user. We evaluate our approach using a data set that we collected in cooperation with a German carsharing provider comprising booking and driving data. The carsharing provider operated 97 vehicles, collecting data on 1856 distinct users and 34,987 drives. Details of the data set and the preprocessing are described in Appendix A.

3.5.1 Artifact Instantiation

As an IS artifact addressing a problem in a particular context (Gregor and Hevner 2013), the DoL system developed in this paper is mostly comprised of components that can be used as is. Nevertheless, we introduced a set of parameters to our DoL application that we left uninitialized because they are dependent on the particular user base and the environment in which the application is deployed, although, for many of these parameters, the impact of their initial values is small and diminishes over time. In particular, the artifact instantiation involves a number of experiments to select the LSTM's hyperparameters (see Appendix B) and deals with the instantiation of the following trade-off-related parameters before we may deploy the application: the trade-off parameter, the trade-off momentum, the trade-off momentum extinction, and the lock time. We initialize the trade-off-related parameters as $\gamma_{u_i} = 0.01$ (trade-off parameter), $m_{u_i} = 0.01$ (trade-off momentum), $\alpha_m = 0.99$ (trade-off momentum extinction) and $lock\_time = 60$ (i.e., locks remain active for a duration of one minute at a time). The only constants among these parameters are α_m and $lock\_time$ whose instantiations may be crucial for the application's performance. In general, α_m should be chosen rather large to let the application learn for a large enough period of time. The $lock\_time$ should not be too large since this will lead to extended time periods in which users have to manually interfere, potentially decreasing their satisfaction. However, we designate the $lock\_time$ large enough to let the application learn users' preferred driving behavior from the manual configurations.

3.5.2 Analysis of the Application's Overall Behavior

In this section, we analyze the overall application – a composition of the energy efficiency predictor and the user preference estimator. The evaluation of these standalone models (see Appendix C) reveals that both improve their accuracy over time and, more importantly, outperform all baseline approaches considered in this study. The overall application autonomously makes decisions based on a trade-off module. Since there is no commonly defined, objective way to assess the quality of a performed trade-off, we restrict ourselves to analytically deriving propositions that define the frame of our application's behavior. For this purpose, we abstract from the performance of the efficiency and preference models and make the simplifying assumption that they produce perfect predictions. This assumption allows us to focus the trade-off module and neglect the complexity arising from inaccurate predictions. Given the results of our evaluation of these models in the previous sections, our assumption is close to reality.

The application's most fundamental behavior is the attempt to balance the vehicle's configuration between a preferred and an efficient configuration. More specifically, the chosen configuration will always lie between the preferred configuration and the closest locally optimal configuration regarding the efficiency. The balancing is achieved by taking the preferred configuration as a starting point and making a step towards an efficient solution. The size of this step is determined by the trade-off parameter, whose value is in the long run, determined by the trade-off momentum. While, in the beginning, the chosen configuration is rather biased towards the user's preferences, the term $\left(0.51 - \frac{n^{(L_{u_i,t})}}{q}\right) \cdot m_{u_i}$ in (B-23) makes this bias decline over time and shift towards efficiency, if the user rarely interferes with the vehicle's decisions. We thus arrive at the following two propositions.

Proposition 1a: If the user does not interfere with the vehicle's decisions at all, the vehicle will always choose a configuration that is locally optimal according to its efficiency model.

Proposition 1b: If the user always interferes with the vehicle's decisions, the decisions will become completely biased towards the user's preferences.

Proposition 1a implies that, in the "worst case", in which the user does not provide the system with any data, it neglects user preferences and learns to choose configurations that approximate the optimal efficiency. Thus, the system's behavior in such a case will correspond to that of other already existing solutions that aim to solely optimize efficiency or other system-level goals.

For the following propositions, we build upon the concept of convergence, which refers to the process of reaching a state in which the vehicle's trade-off module no longer adjusts its behavior. This state is reached as described in Proposition 2.

Proposition 2: The trade-off module converges when the trade-off momentum becomes equal to zero.

While Propositions 1a and 1b are concerned with two extreme behavioral patterns, Proposition 3 describes the vehicle's behavior, if the user behaves more moderately with occasional interferences.

Proposition 3: After convergence, with $y_{u_i}^{(0)}$ being the initial value of y_{u_i} and $m_{u_i}^{(0)}$ the initial value of m_{u_i}, the value of the trade-off parameter γ_{u_i} will be given by (B-25) under the assumption that locks have been imposed identically distributed over time.

$$\gamma_{u_i} = \gamma_{u_i}^{(0)} + \left(0.01 \cdot m_{u_i}^{(0)} \cdot a \cdot b^{a_{u_i}}\right) \qquad \text{(B-25)}$$

Here, a and b are operating-system-specific constants that are determined by the floating-point precision[6]. This proposition also implies that, as long as the average ratio of locked variables is smaller or equal to 50 percent, the trade-off variable will be slightly biased towards efficiency.

However, in contrast to the assumption underlying Proposition 3, which suggests a constant resistance of the user against driving patterns that conflict with their preferences, we shall also consider the case in which the user does not constantly interfere with the application's decision after some time has passed. Instead, they may rather try to enforce their preferences at early stages of the learning process and reduce their interferences chronologically. To determine the outcome of such behavior, we make the simplifying assumption that a user applies full locks (i.e., locking all configurable attributes) for k time steps and does not interfere any further afterwards. We thus arrive at Proposition 4.

Proposition 4: After convergence, the value of γ_{u_i} will be given by (B-26) under the assumption that full locks have been imposed for the first k time steps and no further locks have been imposed afterwards.

---

[6] We have empirically determined these constants on a standard 64-bit operating system, approximating them as $a = 0.01028805553494852$ and $b = 4.758349940494463 \cdot 10^{-46}$.

$$\gamma_{u_i} = \gamma_{u_i}^{(0)} + \left(-0.49 \cdot m_{u_i}^{(0)} \cdot \left(\frac{1 - \alpha_{u_i}^{k+1}}{1 - \alpha_{u_i}} - 1 \right) \right) + \left(0.51 \cdot m_{u_i}^{(0)^{\alpha_{u_i}}} \cdot a \cdot b^{\alpha_{u_i}} \right) \qquad \text{(B-26)}$$

3.6 Discussion

3.6.1 Implications for Information Systems Research

Due to advances in digital technology and data analytics (Baesens et al. 2016) leading to increasingly connected people, devices, and sensors and transforming the way that businesses can use data to capture value (Grover et al. 2018), we witness increasing potentials of achieving higher levels of automation in progressively more contexts (Parasuraman et al. 2000). At the same time, however, we are increasingly entering an era of computing in everyday life, in which humans' real-world experiences are digitally mediated (Yoo 2010). This paradigm deviates substantially from representational computing such as using applications for business intelligence purposes (e.g., Lycett (2013)), where the experience of humans interacting with computers was isolated from other aspects of their personal lives. AVs are an instance where both developments – high levels of data-driven automation for system-level optimization as well as deep involvement in the context of human lives spanning time and space – come together.

With the assurance that "humans are not organized like a digital construct" (Mertens and Barbian 2015, p. 401) nor machine-like in general, approaches of data analytics that weave into the fabric of everyday life call for a socio-technical perspective (Gasson 2003). If applications of high levels of data-driven automation fail to incorporate such a perspective, they are likely to risk the acceptance and trust of the surrounding social system (Stilgoe 2017). Therefore, we designed an artifact by building upon human driving behavior and providing human-interaction possibilities to alter the automatized driving process. Our approach makes use of an intermediate level of automation, allowing the computer to act autonomously but granting the opportunity of interventions to the human (Parasuraman et al. 2000). For this purpose, we have employed a multi-model ML application that learns efficient driving patterns and user preferences independently from one another and combines them through a trade-off module. As opposed to single-model ML applications, which in our case may have been achieved, for example, through reinforcement learning (Watkins 1989), that treat a problem as a single, coherent, cognitive task, our application treats the given problem as an array of three sub-problems, out of which we consider learning efficiency and user preferences to be a matter of finding an objectively correct solution (i.e., tasks involving learning hard facts) and deciding which objectives to favor to be a matter of subjective, individual choices. Through this distinction, we accurately model the factors leading to both efficient and preferred outcomes, while isolating the actual decision making process, which is, on an abstract level, solely determined by the trade-off parameter. Thereby, we mitigate the perceived low interpretability of complex ML applications (Shmueli and Koppius 2011) and allow users to understand the decisions of the proposed system. With our approach and its particular design, we add to research that has called for a human-centered perspective in IS design instead of targeting the closure of technology-centered problems (e.g., Gasson (2013)). Moreover, we contribute to emerging research areas that call for designs of ML applications in the spirit of human-machine symbiosis (Döppner et al. 2016; Traumer et al. 2017).

In this study, we follow Newell and Marabelli (2015) in their view that digitalization and algorithmic decision making create trade-offs and tensions by opposing "interests and needs of individuals on the one hand, and the somewhat opportunistic strategic moves of businesses (and governments) on the other" (p. 22). Accordingly, we contend that designing data analytics applications for real world contexts should seek to strike a balance between individual preferences and potential efficiency gains. We develop a novel approach for resolving the trade-off between efficiency and human comfort that arises when vehicles are required to autonomously make decisions on their driving behavior. We deal with one specific high-level decision making problem in the context of AVs. However, other analysis modules of AVs may also be affected by such a trade-off (e.g., routing modules: Which route is the cheapest and which route is preferred by the user under which conditions?). Similarly, our approach is applicable to other contexts of human life that may be subjected to further automation. For instance, in recent years, the employment of robots in nursing or elderly care has been increasingly discussed in relation to the demographic developments, the physical and psychological demands, the societal costs that this type of work involves, and the demographic developments in most developed societies. Here, the trade-off between efficiency and comfort arises as well. On the one hand, data-driven robotic processes can increase the number of patients cared for and extend the service. On the other hand, humans who substantially vary in their preferences and states and are deeply involved in this process reject being treated like the object or resource in a business process. Thus, also in this important context, successful innovation needs to deal with the trade-off of personal needs and the best possible utilization of shared resources (Dussart 2009). An additional example includes energy management in shared living and office spaces, where individual preferences may run against sustainability of the overall consumption. This illustration indicates that finding a balance between efficiency and comfort is a general theme that will increase in importance as digitalization of societies (Tilson et al. 2010) and computing in everyday life (Yoo 2010) progress. Our work contributes a possible solution approach for this important challenge, generalizable to a variety of socio-technical arrangements.

3.6.2 Implications for Developing Autonomous Vehicles and Sharing Business Models

Several contemporary players, including digital born ventures (Tumbas et al. 2017) and industrial-age incumbents (Yoo et al. 2010), have been investing in AVs of late. Depending on the respective strategic agenda, most of their predictions about the large-scale adoption of AVs range between five and ten years. Regardless of the specific time frame, these firms have been undertaking development efforts for self-driving cars and related services. Given the context, gathering individual user preferences and learning from them to increase satisfaction with the driving experience – of utmost importance for vehicle manufacturers – is a key implication. Due to the increased amount of data available to operators of sharing business models, ML models can be trained faster than in single-user environments, allowing users to benefit from other users' participation in the sharing economy. One may observe this phenomenon in the Evaluation Section, in which we show that the predictions of energy efficiency in the first few drives are less reliable or stable in comparison to drives that occurred at later points in time. Note that this discrepancy becomes more prevalent as the number of involved explanatory variables increases; one would then require more training examples to achieve a similar performance. Similarly, one may leverage sharing contexts to build models of average user preferences that serve as reasonable initial guesses for previously unseen users. User satisfaction can thereby be held at a high level, since they will not be forced to drive manually over extended periods of time to provide data on their preferences. Furthermore, managers are not required to make costly investments into researching the relationship between user demographics and their preferences because our proposed approach offers a way to integrate demographic and contextual data to automatically infer preferences. We conclude that sharing business models offer powerful ways to address analytical problems by enabling ML on two levels – on a microscopic level and on a macroscopic level – and, thereby, allowing users to benefit both from information gained through other users and from ML models tailored to individual users. Implemented in practice, the models of average user preferences would not only prevent irrational driving behaviors but also allow for faster adaptations to individual consumers, thereby increasing trust in the application. Thus, the adaptability of vehicles – for instance to varying use cases such as commercial or private use – increases the diversity of users and could help draw larger audiences to self-driving vehicles, potentially increasing their market success. From a managerial perspective, the additional ability of maximizing the AVs' driving efficiency decreases not only operating costs but also environmental pollution, thereby addressing consumers' sustainability concerns – an important task for firms acting in industries that are characterized by consumers' sensitivity to environmental friendliness and wanting to increase their attractiveness (Hu et al. 2016). Although the significance of sustainability and its conflicts with other interests have also received attention in other contexts (e.g., the trade-off between the efficiency and supply reliability of renewable energy (Piel et al. 2017)), our proposed approach is distinct because it is not restricted to trade-offs involving the attributes used in this study (temperature and velocity). Being a data-driven approach, it can also be adapted to other tasks involving trade-offs such as in navigation or other assistance applications. Since we will experience an evolution toward fully autonomous vehicles, the potentials of our approach can also be realized in interim phases on this path.

Moreover, our approach helps improve the performance measures by enabling supra-individual learning, which is particularly relevant for commercial fleet operators as well as firms that aim to develop sharing business models for sustainable mobility. Similarly, today, drivers for car-hailing services such as Uber and Lyft occasionally provide personalized rides by either explicitly querying their customers' preferences or implicitly assuming them and then adapting their driving style accordingly. Since drivers are not inherently motivated to conform to customer preferences, car-hailing services often implement a rating system, which motivates drivers to provide a satisfactory customer experience by attending to individual preferences.

With the proposed approach, such rating systems and the manual querying of customer preferences will become obsolete as providers become increasingly capable of having preferences automatically inferred through the implemented DoL system. From a more technical perspective, these providers need data analytics applications capable of distributed and real-time computations. Such an approach requires widely autonomous processing of individual vehicles (in our case, through experts) as well as a central, remote computation unit (Dean and Ghemawat 2008) that controls these vehicles and takes care of proper synchronization (in our case, through the CE). Besides handling necessary computations, the interaction with the CE, which stores user profiles, ensures that carsharing providers maintain a connection with their consumers. However, it is important to minimize the vehicles' dependency on input from the central unit in order to avoid latency. In our approach, the vehicles only need input from the central unit at the beginning of a drive, henceforth autonomously controlling the vehicle and interacting with the user during the rest of the drive. By employing real-time ML models, we ensure that the application scales to rapid flows of input data. Furthermore, through a distributed design we not only boost the application's processing power but also allow each expert to specialize on an individual user's preferences. Thereby, we increase the application's predictive power (Tofangchi, Hanelt, and Kolbe 2017), enhancing the data-driven personalization of the vehicles.

3.6.3 Limitations and Future Research

Our design has been informed by studies that point to the importance of creating trust in AVs and the value of consumer centrism in this regard. An important effort in the future would be to test the proposed design in real-world settings and assess actual customer feedback in terms of their trust in autonomous driving. Apart from that, with autonomous driving, we focused on one particular mode of personal mobility. However, it is likely that future mobility and transport will comprise a multi-modal mix – for example, involving trains, buses, shared bikes and self-driving cars. Thus, future work should extend our approach by deploying it to such mobility and transport systems. Sustainable mobility and transport, in turn, are just one element of a future smart energy system that dynamically balances distributed sustainable energy generation and consumption (e.g., Watson et al. (2010). In these smart systems, efficient and predictable use of energy by fleets of AVs are an important building block.

Considering the data set we have used, we realize that a larger set of attributes may enable a more meaningful evaluation of our application. While one of our objectives is to model preferred driving patterns, our evaluation only considers velocity and temperature as a matter of preference. In practice, one may identify further attributes whose configurations are subject to user preferences, as shown in Appendix D. Although we have not incorporated all of these attributes in our study, the proposed system – being based on LSTMs, which can automatically unveil temporal relationships in the data – allows for adding these attributes without having to make changes to the system's structure or perform intense feature engineering. Regarding the predictive performance of our application, we note that, on the given data set, the LSTMs achieve high levels of accuracy for both the energy efficiency prediction and the preference estimation. Through these high accuracies, we have laid the foundation for an effective decision making by the trade-off module. We derived testable propositions for this trade-off module based on both reasonable and extreme assumptions. The validation of the application's behavior in a practical setting is thus an important inquiry for future research. Furthermore, the application's modularity allows for easily replaceable individual modules. Future research may, therefore, explore the suitability of other ML models for modeling user preferences and methods for boosting the process of finding a trade-off between energy efficiency and user comfort (e.g., by tuning the trade-off parameters across users rather than individually for each user).

Our research deals with controlling modules situated at high levels of AVs' analytical chain and with intertwining them as part of a coherent application. We propose an approach that resolves a trade-off between two conflicting objectives (i.e., efficiency and comfort). However, we have not considered the interaction of these controlling modules with other modules in a fully functional AV. Their integration and interplay in an autonomous driving system, especially with lower-level modules such as trajectory planning, are important issues to address in future studies. Furthermore, the field of application of our approach is characterized by a meta problem that we have addressed – the trade-off between efficiency and individual comfort as a key concern that goes beyond the field of mobility and transport. Future work may investigate this topic in other contexts in which high levels of data-driven automation can be deployed to raise efficiency but are delicate to implement because there is a need for deep immersion of humans in the respective contexts. For instance, the healthcare sector comprises various areas that are relevant and worth studying in this regard to yield further benefits for the sustainability of society.

3.7 Appendix A: Data and Preprocessing

Here, we describe the carsharing data set and the applied preprocessing. During each drive, the vehicle in use transmitted data describing the vehicle's state and environmental variables in one-second intervals – with few failed transmissions due to connection problems – yielding 54,034,542 entries. We describe the set of variables collected at each time step in Table B-16.

Table B-16. Variables used in the evaluation.

	Category	Variable Name	Description	Variable Type
		Month	Month of the year	Categorical
1	Date	Day	Day of the week	Categorical
		Time	Time of the day in minutes	Numerical
		Lat_deg	Degrees of the north-south position of the vehicle on the earth's surface	Numerical
		Lat_min	Minutes of the north-south position of the vehicle on the earth's surface	Numerical
2	Position	Lat_sec	Seconds of the north-south position of the vehicle on the earth's surface	Numerical
		Lon_deg	Degrees of the east-west position of the vehicle on the earth's surface	Numerical
		Lon_min	Minutes of the east-west position of the vehicle on the earth's surface	Numerical

		Lon_sec	Seconds of the east-west position of the vehicle on the earth's surface	Numerical
		Height	Vehicle's height above sea level in meters	Numerical
3	Temperature	T^{out}	Outside temperature of the vehicle's environment on the Celsius scale	Numerical
		T^{in}	Temperature inside the vehicle on the Celsius scale	Numerical
4	Gear	Gear	State of the gear shift (drive, park, reverse, neutral, engine braking, or unknown)	Categorical
5	Battery Voltage	BatV	Voltage of the vehicle's 12V battery	Numerical
6	Ignition	Ign	State of the engine (turned on/off)	Categorical
7	Odometer	Odo	Distance travelled since the beginning of the drive in kilometers	Numerical
8	Battery State of Charge	SoC	State of charge of the battery (between 0% and 100%)	Numerical

We infer the vehicle's velocity Vel from Odo. At each time step t, we compute $Vel(t) = \frac{Odo(t)-Odo(t-1)}{time(t)-time(t-1)}$, where $Odo(0) = 0\ km$ and $time(t)$ is the number of seconds that have passed at time step t since the 1st January 1970. Furthermore, we compute the overall drive efficiency as $E = \frac{Odo(t_n)}{SoC(0)-SoC(t_n)}$, where t_n is the last time step of the drive. The given variables are divided into environmental variables and configurable variables. For a certain user at a given time point, environmental attributes are given by $e_{u_i,t} = \{Date_{u_i,t}, Position_{u_i,t}, T^{out}_{u_i,t}, BatV_{u_i,t}, Odo_{u_i,t}, SoC_{u_i,t}\}$ and configurable attributes by $c_{u_i,t} = \{T^{in}, Vel\}$. We use the variable *Ign* to determine whether the vehicle is involved in an active drive. Being dependent on the carsharing provider, we were limited in the data that we could collect. In particular, we use only a small set of configurable attributes to provide a proof of concept of our system. In Appendix A, we further discuss the suitability of variables considered in other studies related to the personalization of vehicles.

We preprocess the given variables by introducing dummy values for categorical variables (e.g., if $Month$ assumes the value $July$, we model it as a twelve-dimensional vector with a one in its seventh dimension and zeros elsewhere). We further rescale numerical values to the range [0,1] through min-max normalization. Let X be a numerical variable with a maximum of $\max(X)$ and a minimum of $\min(X)$. Let x be an instance of X. We then compute the normalized (rescaled) value $\hat{x}$ according to (B-27).

$$\hat{x} = \frac{x - min(X)}{max(X) - min(X)} \tag{B-27}$$

Finally, we preprocess drives by retaining those drives that have a minimum duration of five minutes (to avoid canceled drives and drives without any displacement), splitting drives if two consecutive entries are more than 10 seconds apart (i.e., the vehicle's connection was somehow disrupted), and discarding data from vehicles that are not equipped with temperature sensors. After applying these preprocessing and data transformation steps, we obtain 2,732 drives comprising 1,091,605 entries associated with 215 users.

3.8 Appendix B: Tuning LSTM Hyperparameters

We carry out experiments to choose sensible values for the two LSTMs' hyperparameters. Our LSTMs each comprise a recurrent layer (see Figure B:10) – which, in this case, is also the hidden layer of each network – followed by a feedforward layer with a linear activation function that outputs the prediction for a given input. In order to choose the four hyperparameters of the LSTMs, we carry out a number of experiments with smaller portions of the data (see Appendix B) to determine configurations that are likely to yield accurate efficiency predictions.

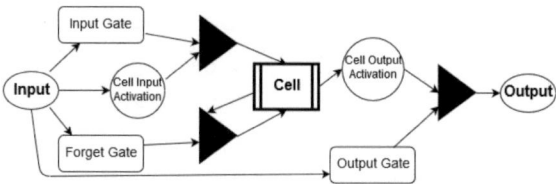

Figure B:10. Architecture of the recurrent layer in an LSTM (non-peephole adaptation based on Chauhan and Vig (2015)). Arrows indicate the propagation of a vector to a recipient. Black triangles indicate that two vectors are added before being forwarded to the recipient.

In each experiment, we optimize for one of the hyperparameters while fixing the rest. Thereby, we approximate the optimal configuration without jointly optimizing for all hyperparameters at once, which would lead to a large search space and an impracticably long runtime. Each experiment is carried out by training and evaluating the LSTM on data belonging to a randomly selected share of 30% of the users (= 71 users). We repeat this experiment five times for each hyperparameter and select the values that produced the lowest average error rate – computed as the mean absolute error – over these five experiments. We start with the optimization of the hidden layer size. We fix the other hyperparameters using reasonable values that are widely used or generally recommended in the literature, namely the activation function as the hyperbolic tangent, the forget gate bias as 1 (Gers et al. 2000), and the learning rate as 0.1. After having optimized the hidden layer size, we proceed to optimize the activation function, the forget gate bias, and the learning rate in this order.

The selected hyperparameters for both the efficiency predictor and the preference estimator are shown in Table B-17. In the following sections, we describe how we arrive at these configurations.

Table B-17. LSTM hyperparameters for efficiency predictions and preference estimations.

	Hidden Layer Size	Activation Function	Forget Gate Bias	Learning Rate
Efficiency Predictions	3	Hyperbolic tangent	2	0.0116
Preference Estimations	70	Hyperbolic tangent	1.23	0.140

3.8.1 LSTM Hyperparameter Tuning for Efficiency Predictions

We try out hidden layer sizes in the range [5,150] with a step size of five. The average errors are presented in Figure B:11.

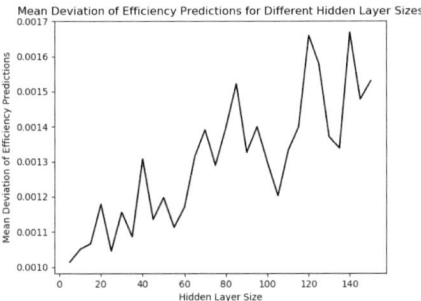

Figure B:11. Mean absolute errors of efficiency predictions (y-axis) for hidden layer sizes in the range [5, 150] (x-axis) averaged over five trials.

We observe that the error generally increases with the hidden layer size and the smallest hidden layer (with a size of five) produces the smallest error. For this reason, we run an additional set of experiments with hidden layer sizes in the range [1,5]. The results indicate that a hidden layer size of 3 produces the smallest error (see Figure B:12).

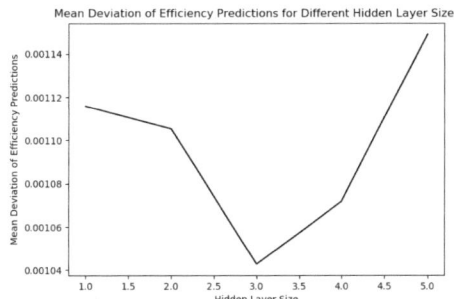

Figure B:12. Mean absolute errors of efficiency predictions (y-axis) for hidden layer sizes in the range [1, 5] (x-axis) averaged over five trials.

Setting the hidden layer size to the newly found optimum and keeping the other hyperparameters as before, we now tune the activation function. The hyperbolic tangent and the sigmoid function have proven to be effective activation functions with LSTMs (Greff et al. 2017). After conducting experiments with these activation functions, we note that the hyperbolic tangent performs better – albeit only slightly – than the sigmoid function (see Figure B:13). This finding is also in line with existing theory that states "convergence is usually faster if the average of each input variable over the training set is close to zero" (LeCun et al. 2012, p. 16) and "this heuristic should be applied at all layers which means that we want the average of the outputs of a node to be close to zero because these outputs are the inputs to the next layer" (LeCun et al. 2012, p. 16). While the sigmoid function is centered around 0.5, the hyperbolic tangent is centered around zero and thus satisfies this heuristic and potentially enables faster learning.

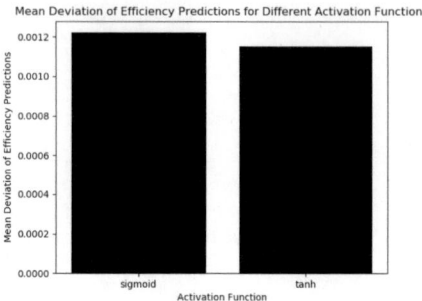

Figure B:13. Mean absolute errors of efficiency predictions (y-axis) for different activation functions (x-axis) averaged over five trials.

We proceed to tune the initial bias of the LSTM's forget gate. Researchers have found that initializing the forget gate bias with a comparably high value (e.g., 1 or 2) improves the training process particularly in the early stages of training (Jozefowicz et al. 2015) because the LSTM "will not explicitly forget anything until it has learned to forget" (Gers et al. 2000, p. 2456). We experiment with 15 evenly spaced values in the range [0.2,2]. The results show that a bias of 2 yields the smallest error (see Figure B:14).

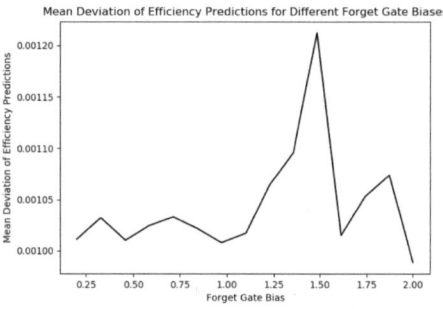

Figure B:14. Mean absolute errors of efficiency predictions (y-axis) for different forget gate biases in the range [0.2, 2] (x-axis) averaged over five trials.

Since the optimal forget gate bias is located at one end of the scale, we run a further set of experiments with values in the range [2,3] with a spacing of 0.1. The results indicate that the error does not significantly change with forget gate biases in the range of [2, 2.2] (see Figure B:15). We, therefore, set the bias to 2.

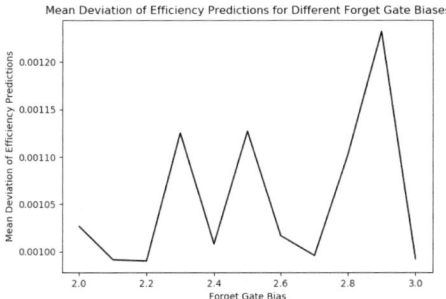

Figure B:15. Mean absolute errors of efficiency predictions (y-axis) for different forget gate biases in the range [0.2, 2] (x-axis) averaged over five trials.

Finally, we tune the LSTM's learning rate. For traditional ML tasks in which the model is tested only after all training steps are done, a smaller learning rate (combined with higher numbers of training epochs) generally leads to lower prediction errors. However, since we train our model in an online setting in which training and testing are performed simultaneously, the model's adaptability is of crucial importance for the overall prediction accuracy. We thus tune the learning rate by experimenting with 15 evenly spaced values in the range [0.001, 0.15].

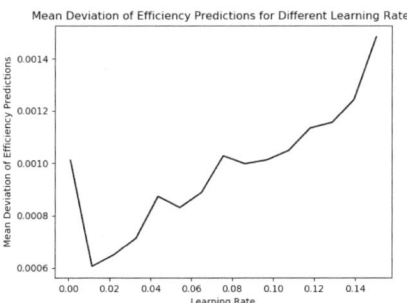

Figure B:16. Mean absolute errors of efficiency predictions (y-axis) for different learning rates in the range [0.001, 0.15] (x-axis) averaged over five trials.

Based on the results of these experiments (see Figure B:16), we set the learning rate to 0.011642857142857142. We observe a particularly large impact of the learning rate on the prediction accuracy: The optimal learning rate yields an average error that is less than half as large as the error obtained with the highest learning rate.

3.8.2 LSTM Hyperparameter Tuning for Preference Estimations

We tune the hyperparameters of the preference model the same way as the energy efficiency model, trying out hidden layer sizes in the range [5,150] with a step size of five. The average errors are presented in Figure B:17.

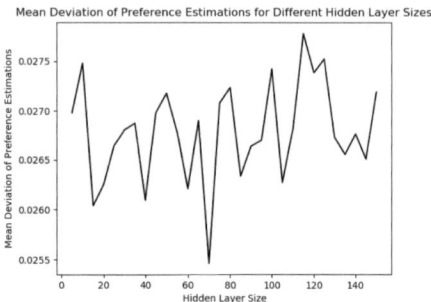

Figure B:17. Mean absolute errors of efficiency predictions (y-axis) for hidden layer sizes in the range [5, 150] (x-axis) averaged over five trials.

Based on these experiments, we set the hidden layer size as 70. Figure B:18 shows that, similar to the case of the efficiency model, the choice of the activation function is insignificant, although the hyperbolic tangent performs slightly better than the sigmoid function.

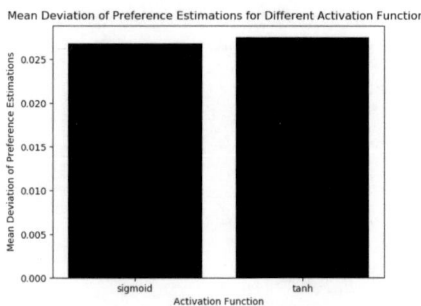

Figure B:18. Mean absolute errors of efficiency predictions (y-axis) for different activation functions (x-axis) averaged over five trials.

Results of the experiments with the LSTM's forget gate show that a bias of 1.2285714285714286 yields the smallest error (see Figure B:19).

B.II Distributed Cognitive Expert Systems in Action

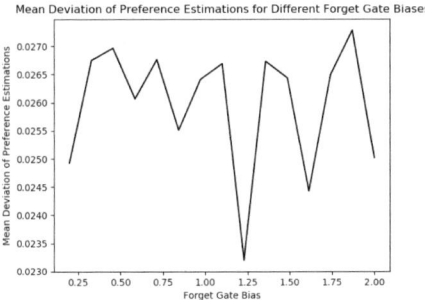

Figure B:19. Mean absolute errors of efficiency predictions (y-axis) for different forget gate biases in the range [0.2, 2] (x-axis) averaged over five trials.

Finally, we tune the LSTM's learning rate and obtain an optimal learning rate of 0.13935714285714287 (see Figure B:20).

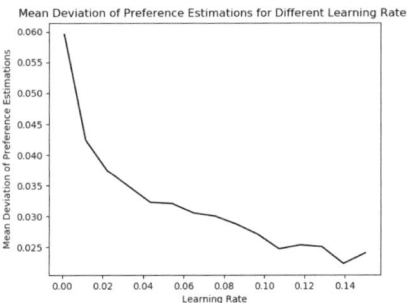

Figure B:20. Mean absolute errors of efficiency predictions (y-axis) for different learning rates in the range [0.001, 0.15] (x-axis) averaged over five trials.

3.9 Appendix C: Evaluation of the Prediction Modules

3.9.1 Evaluation of the Efficiency Prediction

We evaluate the drive efficiency predictions by measuring the corresponding module's error over time. We measure the error at a given point in time as the unsigned difference between the predicted efficiency and the drive's actual efficiency.

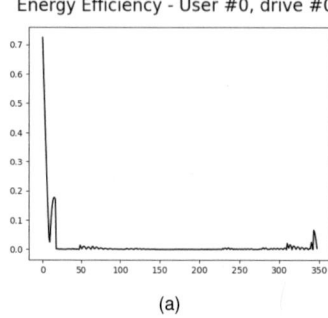 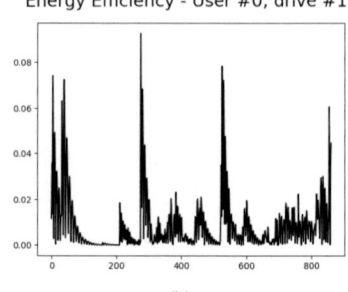

(a)   (b)

Figure B:21. Efficiency prediction errors (y-axis) over time (x-axis) for the first two drives of user #0.

We observe a rapid convergence of the LSTM. While the initial error assumes a high value of 70 percent, it declines to about seven percent at the beginning of the second drive (see Figure B:21). At early phases of the training procedure, the LSTM's predictions oscillate over the course of a drive (see Figure B:21b). These oscillations gradually decrease as the LSTM processes more training examples, eventually vanishing such that it is able to stably predict the energy consumption with a near-perfect accuracy in a short period of time (usually less than two minutes) after the drive commences (see Figure B:22). The error rates are consistently small with minor oscillations over the course of multiple drives (see Figure B:23). After the first drive, the average error over all drives of all users declines to approximately 0.2 percent (see Figure B:24).

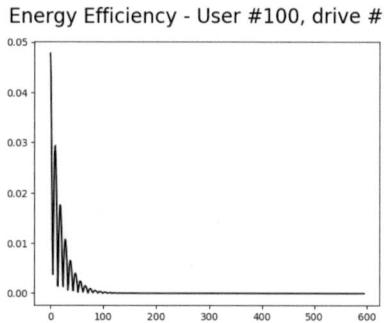

Figure B:22. Efficiency prediction errors (y-axis) over time (x-axis) for the first drive of user #100.

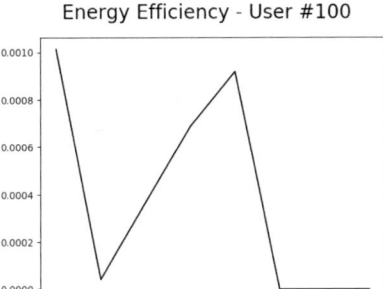

Figure B:23. Average efficiency prediction errors (y-axis) per drive (x-axis) for user #100.

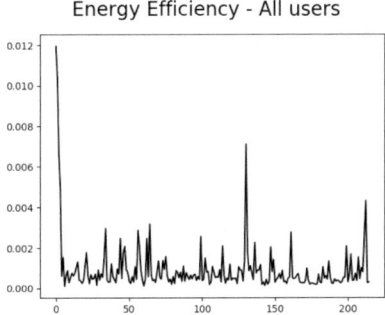

Figure B:24. Average efficiency prediction errors (y-axis) per user (x-axis) for all users.

The error does not vary significantly over different users; the highest average error (neglecting the first user) amounts to 0.7 percent. The model is thus reliably able to predict the overall energy consumption of a drive using only data inputs that are immediately observable during the drive.

Finally, we assess the quality of our approach by comparing it to other existing models that are commonly used for regression. More specifically, we compare it to the following baseline models: random guesser, mean estimator, linear regression (Legendre 1805), decision tree regression (Breiman et al. 1984), random forest regression (Ho 1995), and feedforward NN (Werbos 1974). The random guesser predicts the energy efficiency at random within the range of the lowest value and the highest value observed in the training set and the mean estimator always predicts the average energy efficiency observed in the training set.

We tune the hyperparameters of the baseline models by testing different values and selecting the combination of values that produces the smallest error rate. The following ranges are tested for the given hyperparameters: For the decision tree, the minimum error decrease per split is in the range [0.05, 0.38] with a step of 0.03, the minimum number of samples per split in {2, 4, 6, 8, 10, 14, 18, 22}, and the maximum ratio of attributes to consider in {0.01, 0.1, 0.2, 0.3, 0.4, 0.5, 1}. For the random forest, we tune the number of trees in [5, 65] with a step of 4. For the feedforward NN, the hidden layer size is in the range [10, 15] with a step of 10 and the activation function may be a hyperbolic tangent or a rectified linear unit.

We train the selected models in a batch-processing manner – using 70 percent of the data as the training set and the remaining 30 percent as the test set –, purposely putting them at an advantage over our online LSTM-based approach by allowing them to see the whole training set prior to the testing phase.

Table B-18. Error rates of energy efficiency predictions for different models.

	Predictive Model	Mean Absolute Deviation
1	Random Guesser	0.26387511327321184
2	Mean Estimator	0.029789612329260164
3	Linear Regression	0.030864503090645968
4	Decision Tree	0.029789612328695366
5	Random Forest	0.03056913804624479
6	Feedforward NN	0.029489571866302466
7	Online LSTM	0.0005682773140104865

Our analyses reveal that, despite this advantage, the LSTM outperforms the baseline models (see Table B-18). We illustrate the prediction behavior of the baseline models in Figure B:25, showing the prediction error over time for a randomly sampled drive.

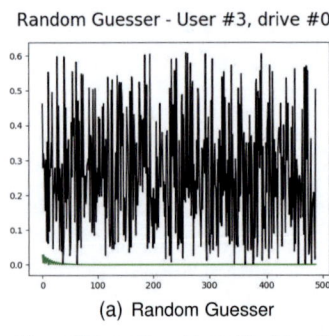

(a) Random Guesser

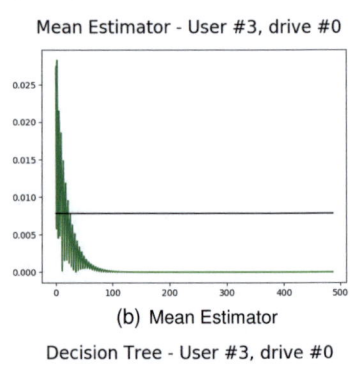

(b) Mean Estimator

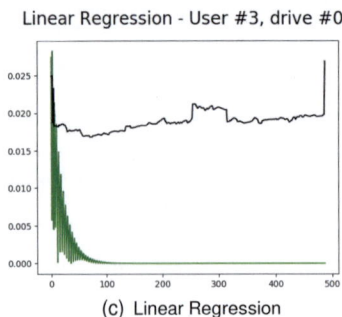

(c) Linear Regression

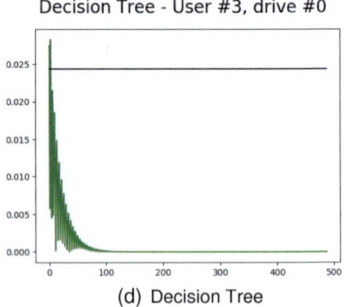

(d) Decision Tree

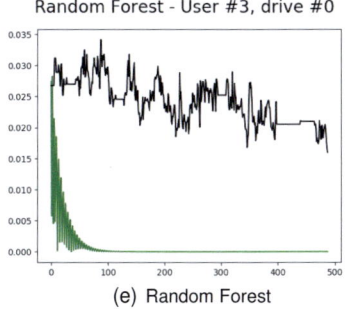 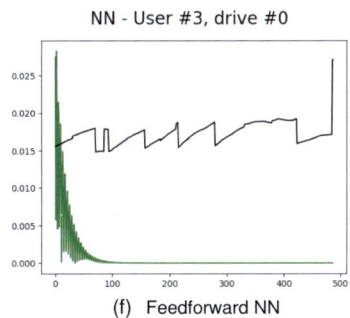

(e) Random Forest　　　　　　　　(f) Feedforward NN

Figure B:25. Efficiency prediction errors (y-axis) over time (x-axis) of baseline models for a random drive, compared to the LSTM's error (green curve).

3.9.2 Evaluation of the Preference Estimation

To assess the quality of the preference estimation module, we assume that the configurations selected by the users and recorded by the carsharing vehicles reflect the users' true preferences, given the corresponding environmental conditions. Under this assumption, we measure the preference estimation error at one point in time as the average absolute deviation of the prediction of each configurable parameter from its true value.

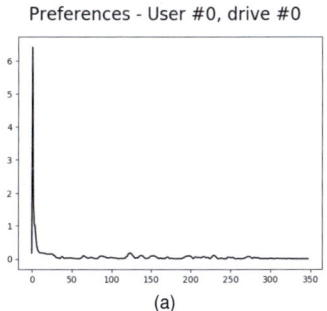 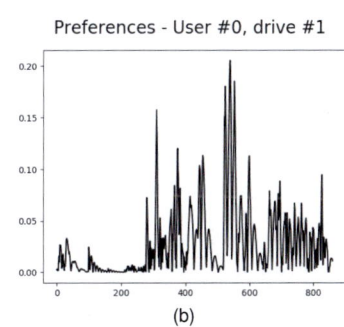

(a)　　　　　　　　　　　　　　　(b)

Figure B:26. Preference estimation errors (y-axis) over time (x-axis) for the first two drives of user #0.

The first drives show that the model gradually learns user preferences with a general downward trend of the error rates (see Figure B:26). We note that the model's error declines within the course of individual drives, but elevates back up periodically when new situations arise that require further adaptations (see Figure B:27 and B:29). Overall, the model produces estimations whose average error is rather low (see Figure B:28 and Figure B:30).

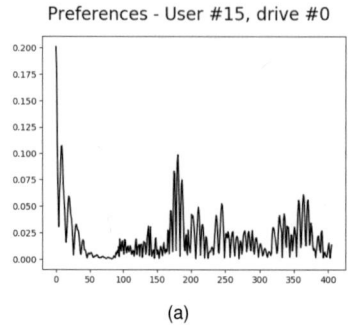 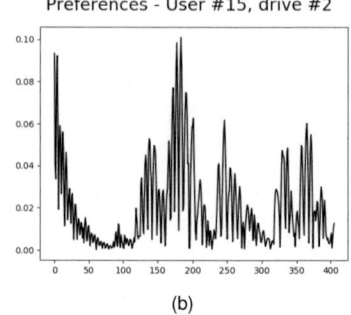

Figure B:27. Preference estimation errors (y-axis) over time (x-axis) for the first and the third drive of user #15.

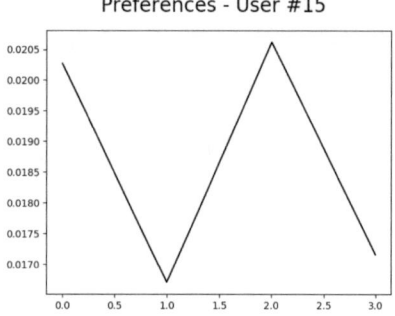

Figure B:28. Average preference estimation errors (y-axis) per drive (x-axis) for user #15.

Figure B:27 has two implications. First, the preference model is able to transfer learned patterns to unseen users: While the error is as high as 600 percent at the beginning of the first drive of User #0, it declines to 20 percent at the beginning of the first drive of User #15; a similar error rate can be observed at the beginning of the first drive of User #100 (see Figure B:29). Second, the model adapts to a particular user and produces lower error rates as time passes: While the maximum error rate amounts to 20 percent in the first drive of User #15, it amounts to only 10 percent in their third drive. This implication is also supported by Figures B:30 and B:31 that show that the average error rate is 2.7 percent (about three percent for users with short drive durations), but the error rate for users with longer drive durations is significantly smaller (close to two percent).

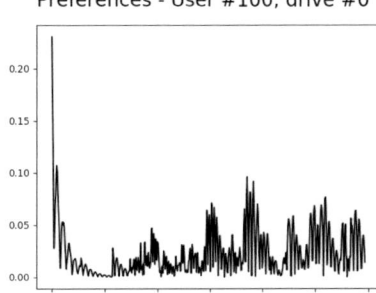

Figure B:29. Preference estimation errors (y-axis) over time (x-axis) for the first drive of user #100.

Although the preference model steadily produces small error rates, its performance is poorer than the performance of the efficiency predictor. We conclude that estimating a user's preferences under different circumstances is more complex than predicting the energy consumption of a drive. Although a vehicle's configuration is subject to dynamic user decisions, the relationship between the set of configurable and environmental variables and the vehicle's energy consumption is entirely determined by the laws of physics and thus static in nature. On the other hand, user preferences are highly dynamic, depending on the current context in which the user is situated (Adomavicius et al. 2011) and varying among users and drives. Despite these challenges, the preference model produces relatively accurate estimates with errors amounting to 2.7 percent on average.

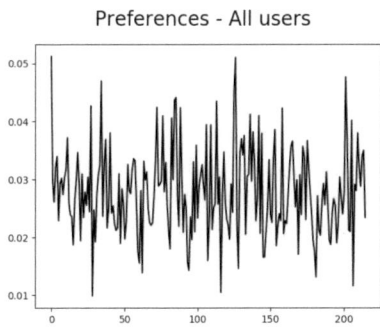

Figure B:30. Average preference estimation errors (y-axis) per user (x-axis) for all users.

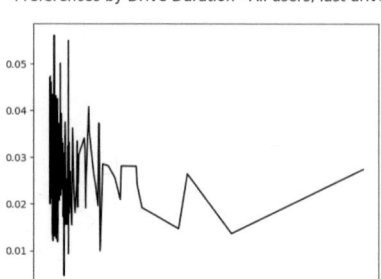

Figure B:31. Average preference estimation errors (y-axis) per drive duration in seconds (x-axis) for the last drive of all users.

We compare the performance of our main approach with a number of baseline approaches, as already done with the efficiency predictor. In addition to using the baseline models used for the efficiency prediction, we further consider some density-based approaches, since they may potentially be well suited to model different levels of preferences. We specifically use a Gaussian probability density function and a kernel density estimator (KDE) (Parzen 1962) with two kernels with desirable analytical properties that have proven to perform well, namely the Gaussian kernel and the Cauchy kernel (Silverman 1986). With these density-based approaches, we predict a user's preferred configuration by taking the vehicle's current configuration and moving to a local maximum according to the respective probability density function. For the Gaussian probability density function, the local maximum is equal to the global maximum.

We tune the hyperparameters of the baseline models the same way as already done for the efficiency predictions. The following ranges are tested for the hyperparameters: For the decision tree, the minimum error decrease per split is in the range $[0.02, 0.38]$ with a step of 0.03, the minimum number of samples per split in $\{2, 4, 6, 8, 10, 14, 18, 22\}$, and the maximum ratio of attributes to consider in $\{0.01, 0.1, 0.2, 0.3, 0.4, 0.5, 1\}$. For the random forest, we tune the number of trees in the range $[5, 65]$ with a step of 4. For the feedforward NN, the hidden layer size is in the range $[10, 15]$ with a step of 10 and the activation function is either a hyperbolic tangent or a rectified linear unit. The Gaussian probability density function has no hyperparameters and for the KDEs we optimize the bandwidth by first computing the analytically optimal solution for the bandwidth $\hat{h}$ for the use of a Gaussian kernel under the assumption of normally distributed data (Silverman 1986). Due to these preconditions not being precisely satisfied, we consider $\hat{h}$ a starting point and test 15 equally spaced values in the range $[\frac{\hat{h}}{4}, 2\hat{h}]$.

B.II Distributed Cognitive Expert Systems in Action

Table B-19. Error rates of preference estimates for different models.

	Predictive Model	Mean Absolute Deviation
1	Random Guesser	0.3236176644863549
2	Mean Estimator	0.1937091976141901
3	Linear Regression	0.10154893676406244
4	Decision Tree	0.14342675394640325
5	Random Forest	0.0948318960532128
6	Feedforward NN	0.09949461584686793
7	Gaussian Distribution	0.14071369488581068
8	KDE (Cauchy Kernel)	0.36844701373480476
9	KDE (Gaussian Kernel)	0.3555353302855647
10	Online LSTM	0.026828600979476376

Again, the LSTM outperforms the baseline models (see Table B-19). Comparatively, the density-based methods produce inaccurate results. In particular, the estimations produced by the KDEs are highly inaccurate due to the high number of local maxima in their probability density functions. We show the baseline models' prediction error over time for a randomly sampled drive in Figure B:32.

Figure B:32. Preference estimation errors (y-axis) over time (x-axis) of baseline models for a random drive, compared to the LSTM's error (green curve).

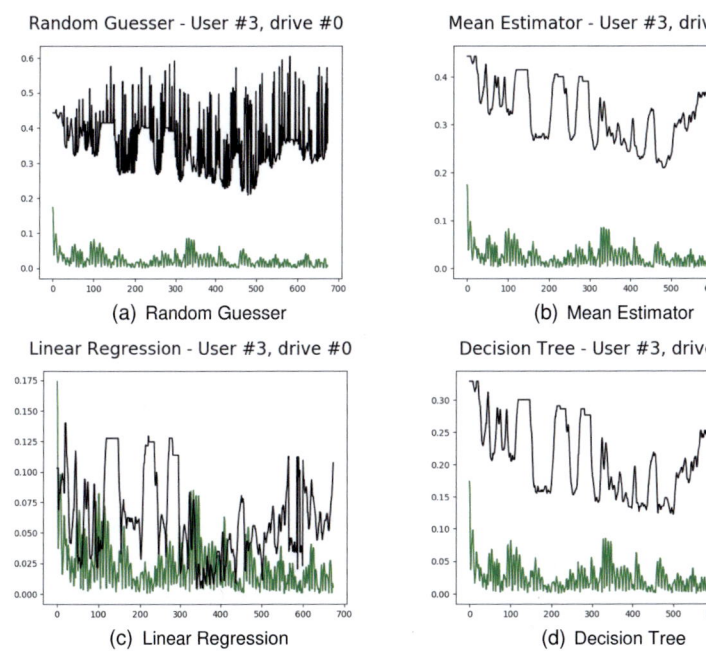

(a) Random Guesser

(b) Mean Estimator

(c) Linear Regression

(d) Decision Tree

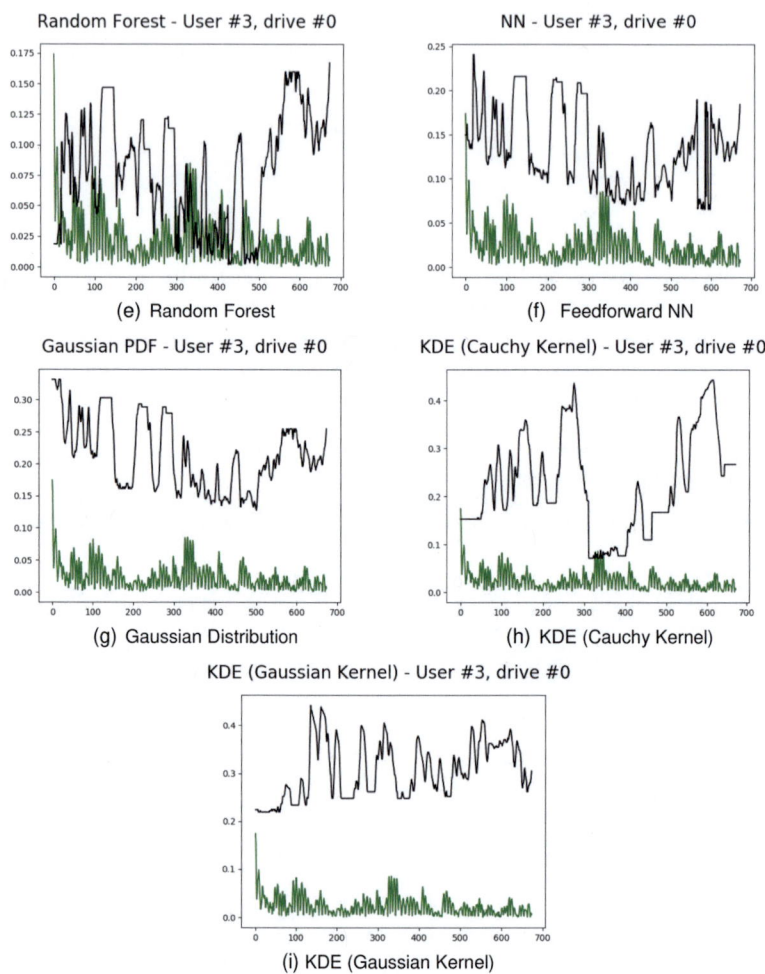

(e) Random Forest
(f) Feedforward NN
(g) Gaussian Distribution
(h) KDE (Cauchy Kernel)
(i) KDE (Gaussian Kernel)

3.10 Appendix D: Variables used for Personalization in Prior Studies

We observe a number of variables (see Table B-20) that have been used in prior studies in which the authors have developed personalization systems for specific problems that autonomous vehicles or driver assistance systems may face (Butakov and Ioannou 2014, Lefèvre et al. 2015, Muehlfeld et al. 2013, Rosenfeld et al. 2015, Wang et al. 2013, Wang et al. 2016).

Table B-20. Variables used in related work.

	Butakov and Ioannou 2014	Lefèvre et al. 2015	Muehlfeld et al. 2013	Rosenfeld et al. 2015	Wang et al. 2013	Wang et al. 2016
System Description						
	Personalized lane change	Lane keeping; learning preferred acceleration	Forward collision warning	Adaptive cruise control	Adaptive cruise control; forward collision warning	Forward collision warning
Configurable Variables						
Velocity	x	x		x	x	
Axial rotation	x	x				
Environmental Variables						
Velocity			x			x
Axial rotation	x		x			
Road type				x		
Road curvature	deemed relevant but not used					
Weather				x		
Distance to neighboring vehicles	x		x	x	x	x
Velocity of neighboring vehicles	x					
Driver age				x		
Driver gender				x		
Driver income				x		
Driver education				x		

The authors of these publications each consider driver behavior in only a single, particular situation rather than modeling the behavior depending on the various contexts. For such purpose, which our proposed system pursues, we deem all environmental and behavioral variables potentially relevant. On the other hand, we consider demographic data such as age, gender, income, and education to be only of minor value for determining exact driver responses in specific situations.

In our study, we have access to only few configurable variables (velocity and inside temperature). However, with our proposed system being based on LSTMs, manual feature engineering can be kept simple because LSTMs are able to extract temporal features from the data (Xu et al. 2015). Thus, adding further variables that represent high-level information – such as road type, road curvature, and the vehicle's axial rotation – is a straightforward process.

C. Contributions

In this part, I summarize the individual studies and explain how they address the goals defined by the research inquiries in Section A.I.2. On a more abstract level, I synthesize the results of the individual findings to show how they relate to the overall aim of this dissertation. I then define the limitations of the research and derive implications for practice and research. Finally, I conclude the dissertation.

I. Findings

This dissertation sets the ultimate goal to develop a design theory for practical ML systems for complex data analysis problems. Pursuing this goal, I define three sub-goals that aim to evaluate the nascent design theory developed in Study 1 by designing situated instantiations (Gregor and Hevner 2013) based on this theory. For a better understanding, I review the contributions of the studies out of order: First, I review the studies presented in Chapter B.II (i.e., the situated instantiations). Afterwards, I synthesize these studies, relating them to Study 1 (i.e., the nascent design theory) and deriving their implications for the design theory.

I.1 Reflections on the Development of a Decision Support System for Cancer Treatments

Study 2 deals with the design of a DSS for treatment decisions for cancer patients diagnosed with cancer in the head and neck region. A summary of its contribution is shown in Table C-1.

Table C-1. Contribution of Study 2.

Distributed Cognitive Expert Systems in Cancer Data Analytics: A Decision Support System for Oral and Maxillofacial Surgery	
Research inquiry	RI 2: Defining the requirements for designing an ML-based decision support system for head and neck cancer treatments; designing the system according to the DoL framework to enhance the decision making process.
Main contribution	An intelligent, DoL-based decision support system for treating patients with cancer in the head and neck region.

Data analytics has the potential to improve treatment processes in healthcare. Study 2 develops a clinical DSS for cancer treatments in oral and maxillofacial surgery that uses ML methods to estimate the most effective treatment for each patient. In the process, it is found that, in the healthcare industry, there are certain adoption barriers for (information) technology (Venkatesh et al. 2011) that need to be addressed. In this study, in cooperation with the department for oral and maxillofacial surgery of the University Medical Center Göttingen, the physicians revealed that one of the factors that hinder the use of ML-based systems is a lack of trust. To address this adoption barrier, the DSS is complemented with two additional features. First, the system automatically identifies patient attributes that the physicians collectively consider significant for decision making and, thereby, allows them to validate the system's understanding of the treatment process. As a side-effect, identifying significant patient attributes allows medical staff to focus their data collection – a time-consuming process, identified as one of the factors hindering the effective use of IT in healthcare. Second, the system estimates the confidence of its own treatment recommendations, based on which physicians can make more diversified judgements and decide, for each individual patient, whether or not to trust the system. Aside from being an intelligent DSS due to its employment of data-driven analyses, the system can also be considered a group DSS (Arnott and Pervan 2005). The treatment process requires the participation of multiple physicians, who can be described not as managers in the traditional sense, but, more abstractly, as decision makers.

The system combines treatment-relevant data and information provided by physicians from different departments to provide physicians with aggregated information that facilitates decision making. Furthermore, this DoL-based DSS, through its modular architecture made up of experts, resembles the decision making practices in cancer treatment where multiple physicians, each specialized on a certain medical field, contribute to the diagnostics based upon which the final decision is made. This resemblance has enabled an increased identification of the physicians with the DSS based on a better understanding of the artifact.

Through these properties, Study 2 provides a level 1 design science artifact (Gregor and Hevner 2013) that constitutes a contribution to healthcare analytics and to the acceptance of IT in healthcare. On a more abstract level, the artifact contributes to evaluating and understanding the nascent design theory surrounding the DoL framework. First, the study shows that a better understanding of ML systems can lead to a higher acceptance of these systems by decision makers (LaValle et al. 2011). The artifact confirms the design theory's postulation that understanding and interpretability can be increased through a modular design of the ML systems. Second, the study shows a way to design a system that learns and carries out a task-division-based data processing fully autonomously by employing a hierarchical clustering algorithm that automatically determines a purposeful number of clusters – in this case, the x-Means algorithm (Pelleg and Moore 2000). Thereby, the artifact exemplifies the implementation of the task distribution principle, which is a central aspect of the DoL framework. Finally, the artifact makes use of an online logistic regression algorithm (Bottou 1998; Cox 1958), which enables frequent updates of the predictive model without performing extensive recomputations of the entire model. Thereby, it showcases the implementation of the principle of sustainability. At the same time, it shows that sustainability cannot be achieved by following a general-purpose cookbook recipe. Rather, each ML model and analysis problem requires special attention and has to be individually incrementalized to accommodate updates to the data.

I.2 Reflections on the Development of a Consumer-Centric Recommendation System for Two-Sided Platforms

Study 3 develops a method for collaborative, content-based, and context-aware profiling of users based on observations of their behavior on two-sided platforms. Applying the DoL framework, a recommendation system is designed, which is tested based on data gathered on the Expedia platform. Table C-2 summarizes this contribution.

Table C-2. Title, research question, and main contribution of Study 3.

Advancing Recommendations on Two-Sided Platforms: A Machine Learning Approach to Context-Aware Profiling	
Research inquiry	RI 3: Determining the specific characteristics of consumer data generated on two-sided platforms; designing an ML system according to the DoL framework that maintains highly individual user profiles to models their preferences in detail.
Main contribution	DoL-based method for dynamic user profiling based on actions performed on two-sided platforms; recommendation system for consumers on two-sided platforms.

Digital two-sided platforms have been used in various contexts to bring together providers and consumers (Parker et al. 2016). Two-sided platforms aim to facilitate their interaction through different approaches (Rochet and Tirole 2003). Netflix has prominently demonstrated that two-sided platforms significantly benefit from an effective recommendation system (de Reuver et al. 2017; Parker et al. 2016) by providing users with desired information and, thereby, increasing their satisfaction (Koren et al. 2016). Study 3 recognizes the importance of high-quality recommendations and describe an approach to providing consumers with more relevant, context-specific recommendations.

The abstract notions of states and actions of users is built upon in order to ensure the applicability of the approach to a wide range of two-sided platforms. Theoretically speaking, a recommendation can be considered accurate if it corresponds to the selected action of a user who possesses complete information on all available actions. Following this notion and given the fact that user states are not directly observable and constitute a highly complex concept (i.e., a decision is based on, among others, the sum of all past experiences (Behling and Eckel 1991)), the accuracy of recommendations is determined by the accuracy of user state models and the amount of detailed data available on the available actions. To achieve a high accuracy, a multi-faceted approach to user profiling is proposed that considers static information on users and actions, time-varying user interactions, and the similarity among users. The contribution is a level 1 design science artifact that uses different kinds of neural networks integrated through the DoL framework to create vectorial representations of user states based upon which recommendations are generated for the user. The artifact is evaluated by training it to make hotel recommendations on the Expedia platform. The results reveal that it outperforms other existing and commonly used approaches.

Through the proposed content-based, collaborative, context-aware (Adomovacius et al. 2011), and user-specific features, an approach to recommendation systems is contributed that more effectively takes advantage of various data gathered on two-sided platforms. Analyzing the sequence of observed actions, it is particularly applicable to platforms characterized by frequent user interactions. The approach makes use of transfer learning (Pratt 1993) by training a general-level neural network to obtain representations of user states, which are fine-tuned by using a further neural network per user. It, thereby, produces user-specific representations of contextual data, which are finally fed into a recurrent neural network to extract features from the sequential order of the observations. The proposed level 1 artifact constitutes a contribution to the design of recommendation systems, showing how platform owners can improve their understanding of their users and, thus, offer more individualized services. The artifact is a further step in the evaluation of the DoL framework. It shows that not only central executives can benefit from experts, but, in turn, also experts can build upon the general knowledge of central executives to obtain their specialization. Moreover, it is shown that the use of unsupervised ML methods in DoL systems goes beyond clustering and the purpose of task division. This study specifically makes use of a dimensionality reduction to facilitate the training of experts. In conclusion, the study exemplifies breaking down the complexity of ML models (i.e., multiple layers of neural computation) through hierarchical task distribution and shows an alternative way of distributing tasks to the learning-based approach proposed by the design theory.

I.3 Reflections on the Development of an Efficiency-Comfort Trade-Off System for Autonomous Vehicles

Study 4 is concerned with a trade-off between the efficiency of and the user preferences regarding the interaction with autonomous systems. The problem is addressed by designing an ML system for the particular case of autonomous vehicles. This ML system consists of an efficiency predictor, an estimator for user preferences, and a module that resolves the trade-off between a driving style that is efficient and one that is preferred by the user. The system the evaluated by creating a simulation environment based on real-world carsharing data and the generalizability of its applied design principles to autonomous systems in general is discussed. The study is summarized in Table C-3 summarizes.

Table C-3. Title, research question, and main contribution of Study 4.

A Machine Learning Approach to the Efficiency-Comfort Trade-Off in Everyday-Life Automation – The Case of Autonomous Vehicles and Sharing Business Models	
Research inquiry	RI 4: Conceptualizing an ML system based on the DoL framework that models driving preferences of users, learns efficient driving patterns, and resolves the trade-off between the preferred and an efficient driving behavior; designing the system as a real-time system that can be used in dynamic situations that occur with autonomous vehicles; evaluating the system in a simulation environment based on real carsharing data.
Main contribution	Design principles for resolving a trade-off between the efficiency and comfort of autonomous agents; a DoL-based ML artifact for autonomous vehicles that addresses a trade-off between efficient and user-friendly driving.

Due to the progressing proliferation of digital technologies and data (Baesens et al. 2016; Galliers et al. 2015), businesses are increasingly given the opportunity to implement data-driven automation (Parasuraman et al. 2000). Autonomous systems are an extreme kind of such automation in which machines are given full control over a particular task. Study 4 considers autonomous systems that interact with human users and whose designs, thus, require special attention. It points out a conflict between system-level and individual-level goals regarding the employment of autonomous systems. In order to address this conflict, the specific case of autonomous vehicles is selected, for which a trade-off situation between the efficiency of drives and users' preferences regarding the driving styles is identified. A system consisting of three ML modules is developed to resolve this trade-off: an efficiency predictor that predicts the efficiency of a drive; a preference estimator that estimates a user's preferred driving behavior; a trade-off module that determines the driving configuration at each instance based on the afore-mentioned models such that both the efficiency and the user's preferences are taken into consideration.

The proposed system uses dynamic vehicle configurations and environmental variables as inputs to determine efficient driving patterns and context-sensitive user preferences. Taking into account that human users, unlike machines, have subjective views and personal preferences (Mertens and Barbian 2015), they may reject a system that solely pursues efficiency. Therefore, I advocate for a socio-technical approach to designing autonomous vehicles that dynamically balances the efficiency and the comfort (measured as preferred driving behavior) of the drive. The system uses recurrent neural networks to predict drive efficiencies and estimate user preferences and provides possibilities for human involvement by allowing them to manually control the vehicle. Thereby, the user implicitly provides the system with feedback on their preferences regarding both the driving pattern as well as the trade-off sensitivity. By inferring these preferences implicitly through observations of the user's behavior, the system facilitates providing feedback, decreasing potential frustration that may arise from requiring too much human input.

With the increasing ubiquitousness of digital devices, which leads to people's everyday lives being accompanied by personal computers (Yoo 2010), we witness increasing potentials for automation and even autonomously acting systems. When developing such systems, it is important to not only strive towards an objective goal but also consider a user's personal preferences in order to drive their acceptance (Stilgoe 2017). Although the artifact is designed for the particular context of autonomous vehicles, its modularity and the genericity of the trade-off module make it applicable to similar problems through minor adaptations in different contexts. The proposed artifact, through its implicit design principles, thus, holds a contribution to trade-off learning in autonomous systems in general.

Similar to the previous study, Study 4 employs transfer learning (Pratt 1993) to refine the model of user preferences created by the central executive. In this case, the general model of average user preferences is used to boost the training of the models for individual user preferences. Furthermore, following the principles of the DoL framework, the proposed artifact shows the benefits of a conceptual distinction between general-level and sub-task-specific learning. While the preferred driving behavior varies among users and is modeled by user-specific experts, the efficiency of driving patterns is independent of the user and can, thus, be determined by the central executive, which applies a general-level model.

I.4 Synthesizing the Artifact Designs: Lessons Learned and Revisitation of the Division-of-Labor Framework

All the artifacts developed in this dissertation constitute individual contributions to research and practice, which I discuss in the previous chapters. These contributions are summarized in Table C-4.

Table C-4. Overview of Studies 2, 3, and 4 and their individual contributions.

No.	Title	Contribution
1	Distributed Cognitive Expert Systems in Cancer Data Analytics: A Decision Support System for Oral and Maxillofacial Surgery	DoL-based method for dynamic user profiling based on actions performed on two-sided platforms; recommendation system for consumers on two-sided platforms.
2	Advancing Recommendations on Two-Sided Platforms: A Machine Learning Approach to Context-Aware Profiling	DoL-based method for dynamic user profiling based on actions performed on two-sided platforms; recommendation system for consumers on two-sided platforms.
3	A Machine Learning Approach to the Efficiency-Comfort Trade-Off in Everyday-Life Automation – The Case of Autonomous Vehicles and Sharing Business Models	Design principles for resolving a trade-off between a system-level goal and an individual goal in autonomous agents; a DoL-based ML artifact for autonomous vehicles that addresses a trade-off between efficient and user-friendly driving.

C.I Findings

However, their main contribution to this work is situated at a more abstract level related to the nascent design theory that is developed in Study 1, which addresses RI 1 (see Table C-5) based on a set of kernel theories (Hevner et al. 2004). As shown in Study 1, the design theory is informed by the theory of mathematical optimization, the principles of economics, and the theory of collective intelligence from the field of AI. More specifically, this dissertation builds upon theories revolving around biological, human, and social entities in the shape of collective intelligence (Wheeler 1911), individual learning behavior (Pfeifer and Bongard 2006), and economies based on a division of labor (Smith and Krueger 2003). These theories are used to develop a design theory that guides the process of creating effective ML systems. The design theory, along with existing domain-specific theory, guides the process of designing the three artifacts, the designs of the artifacts, in turn, have an effect on and implications for the design theory. For a level 2 design theory, developing artifacts, as expository instantiations, is an essential undertaking. Thereby, the principles of the design theory are tested and validated or falsified (Gregor and Hevner 2013). Given this observation that the design of the artifacts is not only guided by the design theory but also by domain-specific theory, and that they, in turn, have implications for the design theory, I present a refined and more concrete research design in Figure C:1.

Table C-5. Title, research question, and main contribution of Study 1.

Towards Distributed Cognitive Expert Systems	
Research inquiry	RI 1: How can ML systems be designed to address complex decision making problems while taking advantage of big data and adequately handling its technical and managerial adoption barriers?
Main contribution	Nascent design theory (DoL framework) for machine learning systems dealing with complex analysis problems. The theory addresses real-time (incremental) machine learning and the benefits of computing machine learning models in a distributed manner.

In this chapter, I revisit the nascent design theory (i.e., the DoL framework) proposed in Study 1. First, I briefly describe the contributions of Study 1 and explain the extent to which the artifacts developed in Studies 2, 3, and 4 are suited to evaluate the design theory. That is, I review the design principles that are applied in the individual studies. Then, based on the development of the artifacts, I discuss some shortcomings of the design theory and potential future refinements that may lead to its enhancement and provide more details on the application of the design principles. Finally, I discuss which principles have so far remained valid.

Study 1 contributes a nascent design theory for designing practical ML systems that address complex decision making problems. It considers problems that are complex in the sense that the factors affecting the decision making process stand in a complex relationship to one another. This design theory further considers challenges and opportunities of big data, requirements for data-analytics-based business intelligence and research, and the self-sufficiency of practical autonomous agents. More specifically, it proposes the principles of hierarchical task division and specialization to take advantage of data volume and variety in order to address the complexity of problems, sustainability to cope with the velocity of large data streams, explanation to create interpretable systems and avoid the typical black-box ML architectures, and adaptation to allow for radical adjustments if the reality to be modeled changes. An overview of the design principles, of which some are considered optional, is given in Table C-6[7].

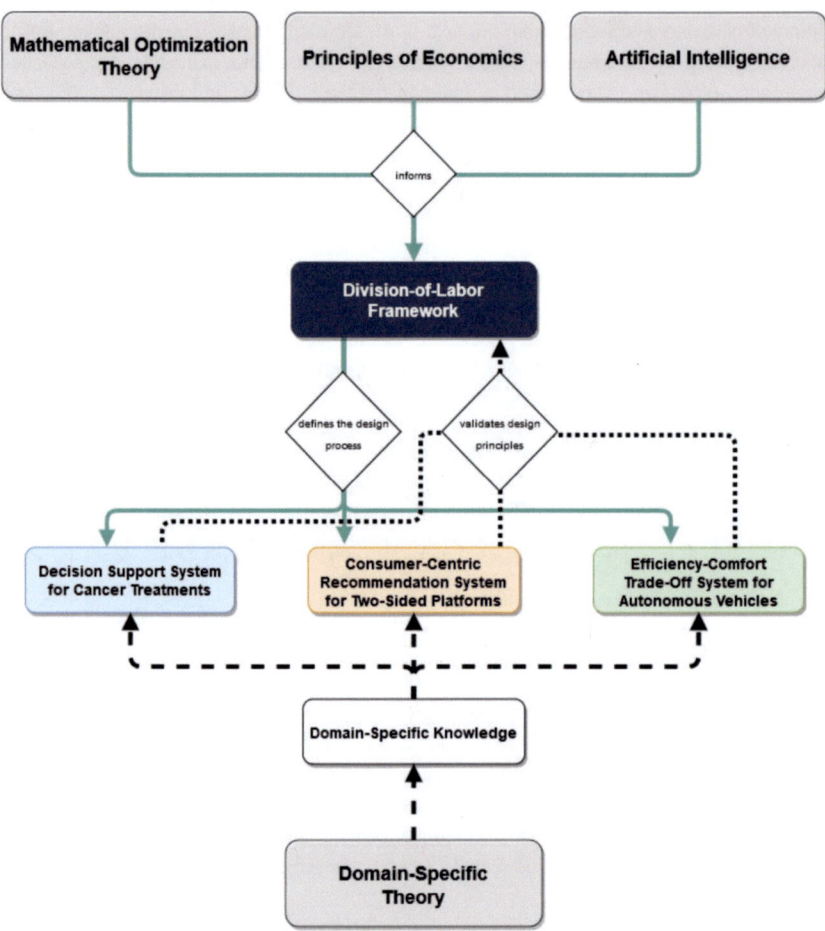

Figure C:1. Revisited research design: the relationship and interactions between the four studies presented in this dissertation.

Table C-6. Properties of experts and central executives in the Division-of-Labor framework.

Expert	Specialization	Explanation (optional)		Adaptation	Sustainability (optional)

---

[7] This table has already been introduced in Study 2.

C.I Findings

Central Executive	General knowledge	Task Distribution	Feedback		

The design theory follows the call of Bengio and LeCun (2007) for increased research on deep learning architectures and the call of Abbasi et al. (2016) for interpretable ML models. It proposes a hierarchical and recursive architecture of ML systems based on central executives and experts, enabling the development of systems of arbitrary depth. However, in contrast to deep neural networks, which also perform in-depth processing of data, it allows for an enhanced interpretability by advocating for a modular architecture. The proposed set of design principles especially addresses predictive ML problems, characterized by a high data relationship complexity, that are to be solved in big data environments, where the user is interested in both obtaining and understanding algorithmically created predictions.

The DoL framework contributes to the effectiveness of the artifacts developed in Studies 2, 3, and 4 and, in turn, benefits from the insights obtained in these studies. Study 2 designs a healthcare DSS that uses task division to make more accurate predictions, incremental logistic regression to achieve sustainability, and explanations of significant patient attributes to increase trust in the system. Study 3 develops a recommendation system for consumers on two-sided platforms that is user-specific and exhibits content-based, collaborative, and context-aware features based on the principles of task division and specialization. Study 4, also by applying the principles of task division and sustainability, designs an autonomous system that balances efficiency and comfort of autonomous vehicles in real time. In designing these artifacts, several design principles of the DoL framework are applied. Specifically, the applied principles of form and function (Gregor and Jones 2007) comprise specialization, general knowledge, task distribution, feedback, and adaptation (Studies 2, 3, and 4), sustainability (Studies 2 and 4), and explanation (Study 2). The applied principles of implementation (Gregor and Jones 2007) comprise adaptability by learning from data, incremental model updating, explanation through the identification of significant features, task distribution through pre-categorization, and learned task distribution (through clustering). The application of these principles proves to enhance the quality of analyses, increase the interpretability of the system, and yield artifacts that foster practical deployment. However, some principles of implementation remain untested for different reasons (e.g., difficulty of implementation or unsuitedness for the given problems). The untested principles comprise sustainable clustering and task distribution through post-categorization.

Most principles of the DoL framework are applied in the design process of at least one of the artifacts. The (lack of) application of the design principles allows me to make more concrete statements regarding their requirements and consequences and adapt the design theory accordingly. First, in Study 1, it is claimed that the design theory is applicable for supervised and unsupervised learning problems. Since none of the artifacts developed in this dissertation primarily address an unsupervised learning problem, this claim requires further analysis. The design theory offers design principles for ML systems that pursue defined goals based on given data sets. There is a mismatch between this objective and the inherent property of unsupervised learning in that it does not aim to solve a problem, but rather extract descriptive information from a data set. For this reason, I reformulate this claim, now stating that, while a DoL system is unsuited for addressing purely unsupervised learning problems, unsupervised learning may be used in DoL systems as a support for analyses, for example to enable self-organization (Hinton et al. 1999).

Furthermore, although the design theory provides two implementation approaches to task distribution, namely division-of-labor and wisdom-of-the-crowds, the developed artifacts exclusively make use of the division-of-labor principle. The lack of attention paid to the wisdom-of-the-crowds principle in these studies does not imply its unsuitedness. The potential of the wisdom of the crowds is well known and has been demonstrated by the example of bagging ML models (Breiman 2001). Nevertheless, the hesitance to adopt this principle may be justified because the division-of-labor principle, in contrast to the wisdom-of-the-crowds principle, enables task division and, thus, the specialization of experts, potentially yielding more accurate results. For this reason, I argue that the division-of-labor principle may be the default principle of the DoL framework, whereas the principle of wisdom-of-the-crowds may serve as a supplement.

The design theory proposes principles for designing distributed, task-division-based ML systems. For a fully autonomous self-organization, it advocates for learning and adapting the process of task division rather than having the developer explicitly define how tasks are to be distributed among experts. Systems pursuing highly complex goals (e.g., biological agents trying to survive in the world) can reduce the complexity of their goals by defining sub-tasks that they solve independently (Margulieux et al. 2012). The ability to define goals for oneself enables a sustainable self-organization without outside interference (Chiu and Soo 2007) and may contribute to being perceived as conscious by outsiders. While, in Study 3 and 4, the principle of learning task division is avoided in favor of assigning an expert to each user, Study 2 employs an x-Means-like clustering algorithm to separate the data space and, thereby, determine the task division. The clusters created through this algorithm and similar algorithms such as k-Means (Lloyd 1982) degrade over time if new data points are merely added to existing clusters without recomputing the entirety of the clusters. Furthermore, while such clustering may enable task division, it is unsuited for the autonomous identification of sub-goals. For these reasons, this design principle, albeit consistent with existing theory, requires further research that provides concrete examples of how task division and sub-goal identification can be achieved for the purpose of self-sustainment. Thereby, the proposed principle can be transformed from a conceptual idea to an implementable process. Moreover, with respect to task distribution, the design theory describes two different principles: division-of-labor and wisdom-of-the-crowds. The former divides a task according to its contents (i.e., different experts are consulted for different sub-parts of the tasks), whereas the latter does not divide individual tasks, but lets all experts solve each task independently and combines their solutions through some mechanism. The originally anticipated principle of division-of-labor, however, does not account for the task distribution employed in Studies 2, 3, and 4. In these studies, experts were trained to each solve different kinds of tasks rather than different parts of the same task.

C.I Findings

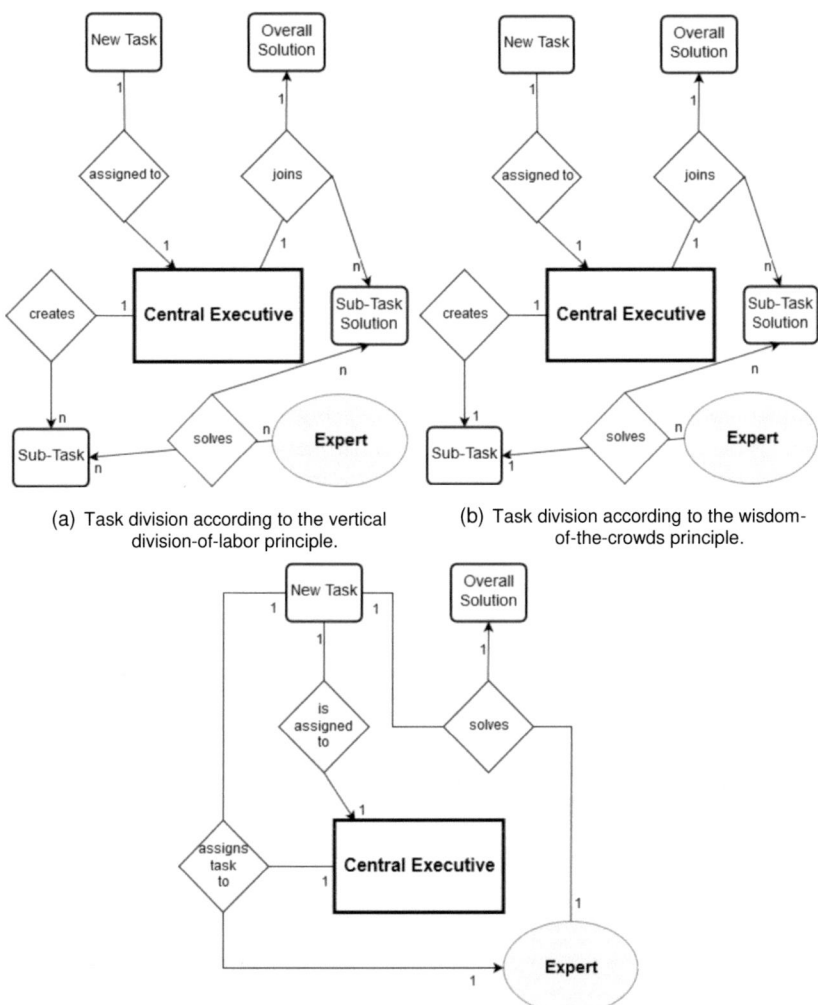

Figure C:2. Entity-relationship models describing potential ways of *task division and recombination in the DoL framework.*

The original principle, which I now term *vertical division-of-labor*, while promising more accurate and possibly efficient analyses, is difficult to implement because it requires the design of a rule that decomposes a task into several sub-tasks. For this reason, I propose adding the more easily implementable principle of *horizontal division-of-labor* to the design theory as a principle of implementation. The design theory then comprises three ways of implementing task division. I formally describe the roles of the CEs and experts through entity-relationship models in Figure C:2.

Finally, the acquisition of general knowledge to perform task division (i.e., learning how to distribute tasks), as desired by the original formulation of the design theory, requires further assessment. In Studies 3 and 4, task division is not learned but rather predefined by the designers because specializing on individual users is an obvious and effective approach to modeling their preferences. Therefore, although the rule that task division is to be learned by the central executive may lead to an enhanced self-organization of DoL systems, it should be loosened to allow for developer-defined task division, which facilitates the design of practical ML systems. Furthermore, although the artifact designed in Study 2 benefits from a learned task division, the clustering method it uses to achieve this goal stands in conflict with the desired sustainability because the computational complexity of updating the clustering model rises with the number of data points added. This issue, not mitigating the fact that the design principle itself promises an increased autonomy of DoL system and, thus, decreased manual (human) labor, calls for further research regarding the implementation of self-organized task division.

Study 1 provides testable propositions that can be used to evaluate whether the design theory is appropriate to achieve its objectives. Based on the critical evaluations of the last paragraphs, Table C-7 shows the degree to which the testable propositions have been verified. In conclusion, I note that several design principles have shown their effectiveness, namely task division (and general knowledge and specialization), feedback (and adaptation), explanation, which increases physicians' trust in DSSs, and sustainability (e.g., through incremental ML models, which can cope with high-velocity data). However, some design principles require further investigation – especially the principle of task distribution, which is the central concept of the proposed design theory.

Table C-7. Overview of Studies 2, 3, and 4 and their individual contributions.

No.	Testable Proposition	Level of Validation: 1 (low) – 5 (high)
i	Data analysis systems developed according to the DoL framework under the use of shallow ML base models produce more accurate solutions than using the same shallow ML models in a stand-alone manner.	4: Verified by all three artifacts in this dissertation, but requires further evaluation.
ii	Data analysis systems developed according to the DoL framework process tasks in real time.	3: Only valid if one complies with the optional sustainability principle (as seen in Studies 2 and 4). Further evaluation required regarding the feasibility of incremental ML for different problems.
iii	Data analysis systems developed according to the DoL framework are positioned at a high level of interpretability, compared to other deep learning architectures, especially in comparison to deep neural networks.	2: Study 2 shows that decision makers can understand the mechanisms underlying the DoL system's recommendations and relate to its findings. However, Studies 3 and 4 lack an evaluation of the systems' interpretability.
iv	Data analysis systems developed according to the DoL framework scale to big data.	5: If task division is applicable (as seen in Studies 2, 3, and 4), the computations can be performed in a distributed manner, which forms the basis for the scalability of big data systems (Dean and Ghemawat 2008).

II. Limitations and Implications

Considering the research conducted in the previous parts, in this chapter, I discuss its limitations and its implications for practice and research in the fields of ML, AI, and IS. Regarding IS research, which is often concerned with interdisciplinary issues (Banker and Kauffman 2004), I derive implications mainly for business intelligence, ML and big data analytics, and design science research.

II.1 Limitations

Each of the individual studies has its own set of limitations. Study 1 proposes a theory for designing ML systems for complex data analysis problems. Although the design theory is primarily intended for big data, it is also applicable to data sets that are not characterized by an extraordinarily large volume, as shown by Study 2, which uses merely 786 data elements. However, it shall be noted that an effective application of the proposed design principles requires a certain number of data elements – similar to the data sizes required by shallow (one hidden layer) neural networks.

Despite Study 1 claiming otherwise, the design theory is not suited for purely unsupervised learning problems. It requires a well defined problem formulation that allows for potential solutions to be objectively assessed regarding the extent to which they solve the problem. For this reason, the main objective of the design theory is limited to supervised or semi-supervised learning problems, while unsupervised learning methods may be used to support the data analyses. A limitation regarding the development of the design theory arises from the top-down design science approach (Iivari 2015) of this dissertation. Using existing theory to derive the design principles rather than solving practical problems to form the design theory in a bottom-up manner, the emerging theory may have flaws, which go undetected because it is not practically evaluated. To mitigate the effects of this limitation in the future, the design theory intentionally leaves room for adaptations by adding, removing, or altering design principles. Thus, further studies are conducted in which three expository instantiations are created that serve as bases of evaluation for and modification of the design theory. These studies have limitations of their own, which I reiterate in the following, as well as limitations regarding their purpose of evaluating the nascent design theory.

Study 2 is concerned with the design of a DSS for treatments of head and neck cancer. The applied principles are specifically intended for intelligent DSSs. While they can be generalized to other kinds of treatment problems, they are not suited for some chronic diseases that require consideration of long-term factors (i.e., the patients' development over long periods of times). On the other hand, they are also unfit for situations in which rapid decision making is required (e.g., in the emergency room). Rather, the design principles are suited for mid-term treatment planning where a significant amount of patient data can be collected, but detailed information regarding the patients' historical treatments can be neglected. Furthermore, due to the artifact treating physicians' decisions as infallible, treatment recommendations are limited by the knowledge of physicians, although this limitation is partially mitigated by the data set containing decisions by multiple physicians. The intention to use this artifact as a real-time system gives rise to a limitation that complicates the incorporation of new patient attributes over time – a process that is essential for the constantly evolving clinical practice. This limitation, albeit unaddressed by the proposed artifact, is not a precondition of employing real-time ML in healthcare, but can be resolved in future research. Finally, the artifact's sustainability is limited. While both the logistic regression model and the clustering model can be incrementally updated, the computational complexity of updating the clustering model steadily increases as more data enters the system. If the system were to be deployed for a large number of hospitals (i.e., a single instance of the system shared by all hospitals), one might observe a gradual decline of the update speed. However, in the single-hospital scenario that is studied, the system will likely not reach its computational capacity due to the typically low number of patients with a certain type of cancer.

Study 3 improves the quality of recommendations on two-sided digital platforms and specifically addresses the cold-start problem and the accuracy of recommendations (Çano and Morisio 2017). It is limited to ML-based (as opposed to knowledge-based) recommendation systems (Adomavicius and Tuzhilin 2005) and relies on the assumption that a user's selected action (under uncomplete information) reflects their preferred action. This assumption does not entirely hold true and, thus, limits the validity of the findings, and yet it is not too far from reality. While their selected action would most likely be different if they had complete information about all possible actions and, therefore, does not always correspond to their most favorable action, it can still be considered to be among the user's top choices because they selected it among all actions that are *known* to them.

Study 4 deals with resolving the increasingly relevant conflict between the efficiency (and system-level goals in general) of autonomous systems and the personal preferences of users of such systems. The study is limited to modeling high-level, behavioral characteristics of the vehicle and is, thus, not concerned with low-level processes such as road and road sign detection and steering control. The evaluation of the proposed artifact is limited to the particular context of autonomous vehicles relies on a simulation environment. Future research may test the applicability of the artifact to further contexts and also focus on testing the artifact in real-world situations, where actual user feedback could be obtained in real time. Furthermore, only a single kind of mobility is considered, whereas, in practice, people may use a combination of several transportation modes such as trains, buses, and bikes to reach their destination. Finally, a minimal data set is used for the evaluation, modeling user preferences only based on the velocity and the inside temperate of the vehicle. Using further variables, future research may show whether the artifact is suited to model all kinds of behavioral preferences.

Considering the artifacts as means of increasing the maturity of the nascent design theory, I identify the following limitations. First, not all design principles are applied in the design of the situated artifacts either because they are inapplicable in the given situation (e.g., task distribution through post-categorization), their application is time-consuming (e.g., wisdom-of-the-crowds task distribution), or a viable way of implementing them has not been found yet (e.g., sustainable clustering for continuous updates to general knowledge). Other principles may have been applied in one or more of the presented studies. However, a principle may be realized in many different ways. For example, acquiring general knowledge can be achieved through various methods of descriptive analysis such as clustering, dimensionality reduction, and density estimation. Even with the relatively small number of studies conducted to evaluate the design theory, I observe both principles of form and function and principles of implementation that are not fully adequate for practical ML problems and, thus, require reformulation. In general, I note that Studies 2, 3, and 4 are a first step towards the maturation of the design theory proposed in Study 1 and future research may pursue further practical inquiries to validate and add to the design theory.

II.2 Implications for Practice

The practical implications of this work are divided into implications of the artifacts and the implications of the overall design theory. Regarding the artifact-level implications, the healthcare DSS developed in Study 2 has multiple implications. It allows for improving data collection in clinical practice, which is often observed to be of low quality (Kruse et al. 2016), for example, due to the large ratio of missing values (Wells et al. 2013). By pointing out patient attributes that are significant for making treatment decisions, the artifact allows medical staff to shift the focus of their data collection – a process that may be perceived as disrupting core clinical processes (Yarbrough and Smith 2007) – to the most important attributes, thereby enhancing the quality of necessary data. Furthermore, data analytics applications for clinical practice rarely reflect the processes to which they intend to be applied (Coveney et al. 2016). By using the DoL framework, a system is developed that reflects the structure of the processes involved in making a decision for the treatment of head and neck cancer patients. Therefore, besides being an intelligent DSS, the system is also considered a group DSS (Arnott and Pervan 2005). It integrates not only the information provided on a certain patient by multiple physicians but also their implicit knowledge that manifests in their historical treatment decisions. This very reflection of the processes familiar to medical staff along with the identification of treatment-relevant data, leading to an increased trust of physicians in the DSS, enables the transfer of data-driven findings from clinical practice to medical research. ML offers appropriate methods that allow not only for capturing the knowledge that is implicit in the physicians' decisions but also for improving on this knowledge by optimizing for a desired outcome. However, despite its great potential this development has to be treated with caution and under consideration of ethical implications. On the one hand, the proposed approach can be considered a step towards ethical data analytics because it employs real-time data analytics that yield desirable insights into the effectiveness of treatments without having to store personal data. On the other hand, while the optimization of treatments through DSSs can provide patients with better healthcare (Chen et al. 2012), an unconstrained algorithmic optimization may result in valuing the reduction of expenditures above saving lives, possibly leading to inhumane practices.

The consumer-centric profiling technique and recommendation system developed in Study 3 has implications not only for the practical implementation of recommendation systems for consumers on two-sided platforms, for which it promises more relatable and contextualized

(Adomavicius et al. 2011) recommendations, which can drive user satisfaction (Carter and Grover 2015). Additionally, platform owners may build upon the profiling technique to assess and improve their product or service portfolio and their customer relationship management in general by developing a better understanding of their customer base, which is a major concern in marketing research (e.g., Montoya-Weiss et al. (2003); Puccinelli et al. (2009); Verhoef et al. (2009)). Apart from that, the ability to predict human behavior under various conditions allows the identification of anonymous users based on their behavioral patterns. For example, platform owners may associate multiple account of the same user by identifying the similar usage patterns. Similarly, this approach can be used to detect identity theft as a sequence of unusual behavioral patterns behavior and, thus, contribute to IT security, increasing users' trust in the platform. More abstractly speaking, profiling techniques combined with the increasing ubiquitousness of IT can yield highly accurate models of individual user behavior that may allow for personal devices to act autonomously, serving as an extension of the user's personality (Carter and Grover 2015). While such personal assistants can immensely improve consumers' quality of life, they also expose them to increased risks. They are built upon models of a users' entire personalities. Limiting the great potential of such models to ethical purposes (i.e., individualized everyday automation) and countering the theft of such sensitive information are non-trivial tasks. Future research will necessarily be required to develop new laws and means to accommodate these developments.

For the efficiency-comfort trade-off system for autonomous vehicles developed in Study 4, I identify several significant practical implications. First, through data-driven personalization the users' self-identification with the IT system is enabled (Carter and Grover 2015), despite its autonomous way of acting, and, thereby, contribute to improving the customer experience (Verhoef et al. 2009). Second, the study provides evidence that the increased data available in sharing businesses can be leveraged to accelerate training of ML models. One may not only use the data generated by the whole user base to learn system-level phenomena but also apply transfer learning to more easily infer new users' preferences with the help of models created for other users' preferences. Third, the trade-off module, which constantly aims to move towards an efficient behavior as long as the real-time user feedback does not indicate a dissatisfaction, contributes a new approach to nudging – the art of influencing the decisions of humans towards a desirable outcome (Thaler and Sunstein 2008). Understanding the user is a fundamental step for designing a nudge (Schneider et al. 2018). By automating this step, a highly individualized nudging of users is enabled. More importantly, the trade-off module gradually and subconsciously introduces the user to a more desirable behavior and adjusts the extent of the nudge on the fly to match the user's pace of adaptation. Thus, this approach may be considered, in the broadest sense, a nudge through a default option (Weinmann et al. 2016). Thereby, the user will be pushed towards a not only less costly but also more ecological behavior without impacting travel times (Gilman et al. 2015; Jamson et al. 2015). Fourth and finally, autonomous vehicles are predicted to be an important transportation modality in the future (Burns 2013). Their potential is particularly high in the carsharing industry. Currently, providers are forced to use designated drivers or pay consumers to move their vehicles to where they are needed the most; this problem is commonly referred to as the vehicle relocation problem (Wagner et al. 2015). On the consumer side, although being offered the benefit of flexible transportation, their comfort is limited because they cannot be picked up and dropped off at arbitrary locations. Users have to pick up vehicles at their current locations and often drop them off at predefined locations near their destinations. Carsharing providers and users are faced with a compromise that results in a two-sided dissatisfaction. This problem can be mitigated using autonomous vehicles that can be called to custom locations based on current demand. Providers can, thereby, offer consumers a more pleasant experience. In combination with an ML-based personalization of the vehicles, consumers can feel as comfortable as in their own personal vehicle while taking advantage of the benefits of carsharing at the same time.

Moreover, the design theory itself has certain implications for the use of data analytics in practice. It can be used to develop ML systems for complex data analysis problems including DSSs and recommendation systems as well as autonomous systems. Through its modular architecture and the design principle of explanation, it helps ML systems become interpretable. Thereby, it contributes to removing adoption barriers for business intelligence intelligent DSSs in managerial (and generally, in decision making) practice, for which a lack of understanding is viewed as a common cause (LaValle et al. 2011). Top management's understanding of analyses provided by business intelligence systems may help them inspire employees to pursue evidence-based decision making and, thereby, foster the development of business intelligence capability (Kulkarni et al. 2017). Furthermore, big data analytics is widely considered to generate value for a firm (Chen et al. 2012; Erevelles et al. 2016; Günther et al. 2017) by leveraging the high variety of big data sets to draw more sophisticated insights from a variety of data from different sources (Goes 2014; Yoo 2015) and their high volume to carry out analyses of increasingly granular relationships (Martens et al. 2016). However, to reach this goal, one first has to address the challenges associated mainly with the volume, velocity, and variety of big data. The proposed design theory helps coping with the volume through distributed data analysis, the velocity through incremental formulations of ML methods, and the variety through a modular architecture in which each component specializes on a particular share of the data. Thereby, it enables the practical employment of big data systems by following a structured design process. Aside from these implications for the performance of data analytics systems, the design theory also holds a set of societal implications. Through an incremental learning process, systems adhering to this design theory achieve an enhanced protection of user data. In the era of digitalization, efforts to improve privacy are becoming increasingly relevant (Galliers et al. 2017) and may be a determining factor for a company's public image and societal value (Günther et al. 2017). Through the design theory's sustainability principle, inducing incremental (i.e., real-time) model updates, data may leave the system (i.e., be deleted) soon after entering it. That is, the data can be used to compute aggregated models without having to store these potentially sensitive data for extended periods of time. Taking this thought a step further, a DoL system can be designed to completely avoid transmission of individual user data to a service provider. Employing computational experts on the user side, one may perform partial analyses of data locally and aggregate the outputs of many users. Leveraging such peer-to-peer settings, data privacy can be enhanced and analyses can be carried out efficiently in a distributed manner. Finally, an implication emerging from the design theory's modular architecture is the increased potential for interactions between humans and ML systems. While, traditionally, humans have been treated as users of ML systems, providing inputs and receiving outputs, the design theory offers interfaces for a higher involvement of humans throughout the analysis processes. Thereby, it contributes to research on human-machine symbiosis (Döppner et al. 2016) and to the futuristic vision of a society in which machines act as full employees and coworkers alongside humans, who both function autonomously striving to reach a common goal.

I provide an overview of the practical implications in Figure C:3.

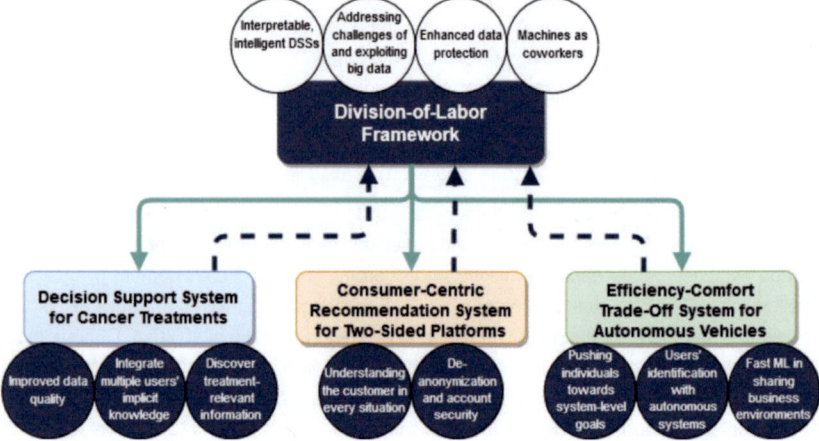

Figure C:3. Overview of the practical implications of this dissertation.

II.3 Implications for Research

This dissertation has a plethora of implications for different areas of research. On a concrete level, I discuss the implications of the artifacts developed in this work, each on its own. Afterwards, I consider their implications for the maturation of the nascent design theory. On a more abstract level, I discuss implications of my coauthors' and my research, taken together, for design science research and, finally, for IS research in general.

The Studies 2, 3, and 4 address problems that are relevant in different areas of research. The DoL framework provides principles for the development of recursive, self-sufficient multi-agent systems. They are recursive in the sense that each layer of modules is based on another layer of modules that are similarly structured. While each module is an agent that pursues a certain objective, the whole system also constitutes an agent following an overall objective. Following these principles, the situated artifacts show the potential of collective intelligence, through which complex behavior may emerge as a composition of multiple agents exhibiting simpler behaviors (Pfeifer and Bongard 2006). More specifically, Study 2 and Study 3 perform a task division based on user accounts and Study 1 uses a data input space division to enable the specialization of individual system components on different sub-tasks. The specialized modules, thereby, each solve a comparatively simple sub-task (e.g., behavioral analyses of a single user) and collectively address the overall, more complex problem. Related to this task division, Study 2 in particular showcases an example of self-organizing systems by proposing an artifact that autonomously learns not only to solve sub-tasks but also to identify coherent groups of sub-tasks. Here, the notion of sub-tasks (or sub-goals) does not exclusively refer to a sequential series of steps necessary to solve an overall task, but more abstractly includes the division of tasks into conceptual elements that have no particular order. Thus, this notion of sub-goals significantly differs from the sub-goal identification employed in reinforcement learning (Morimoto and Doya 2001). Through an effective sub-goal identification – in the aforementioned abstract sense – and the resulting self-organization (Drachen et al. 2009; Verschure et al. 1992), AI systems may reach a level of autonomy that raises their status from machines used for dirty jobs to sophisticated agents that more consciously understand the steps necessary to solve a task.

From the perspective of business intelligence, I identify three implications, which I describe in the following. Study 2 has two important implications in this regard. First, it contributes to the research stream on intelligent DSSs (Arnott and Pervan 2005), which is concerned with data-driven techniques for intelligent analyses that support decision making. Rather than isolating human decision makers from machine-based analyses, it adopts a socio-technical perspective to allow humans to understand the system's outputs at different stages of the analysis process. Thereby, Study 2 adds to emerging research on interpretable ML models (Abbasi et al. 2016; Shmueli 2010) driving the acceptance of technology (Venkatesh et al. 2003), particularly data analytics technology in managerial decision making (LaValle et al. 2011; Yarbrough and Smith 2007). In addition to DSSs providing humans with decision-relevant information, they may influence humans at intermediate stages of the analysis process to enable a targeted collection of data that enhances the quality of analyses. Finally, the Studies 3 and 4 enable an enhanced catering to individual preferences and automated, context-sensitive personalization of products and services. With ubiquitous digital technologies (Yoo 2010) turning users into endless sources of data (McAfee and Brynjolfsson 2012), researchers and practitioners alike can pervasively acquire knowledge in real time. For example, taking into account the individuality of users and acknowledging that they cannot be treated like machines (Mertens and Barbian 2015), the high availability of data to businesses enables the automated extraction of information regarding users' personal preferences, a more targeted, individualized marketing (Erevelles et al. 2016), and the immediate adaptation of products and services to customer expectations and response to unsatisfactory experiences. Consequently, we witness a paradigm shift in customer relationship management, through which the importance of the provider's manual involvement declines in favor of data-driven, automated approaches (Payne and Frow 2017). Given this potential, decision making and forecasting can experience a rapid acceleration (Abbasi et al. 2016). However, in order to exploit this potential, one has to consider the consequences of the high velocity of knowledge acquisition. That is, research has to deal with the questions as to how the velocity of making decisions and performing actions can be matched with the pace of knowledge acquisitions and the value that can be added through IT investments (Boonstra 2003) that enable such high-velocity decision making.

The implications for ML and big data analytics are threefold. The systems employed in Studies 3 and 4, which are composed of a combination of group-level and individual-level behavioral predictive models, contribute to research on transfer learning (Pratt 1993). More specifically, they treat users as individual, but interrelated, ML problems. Based on this problem formulation, an ML model is trained for each individual user by fine-tuning a previously trained general-level ML model. While such transfer learning approaches have already achieved considerable success in the area of automated image analysis (Shin et al. 2016), I advocate for the use of transfer learning in all situations in which a large number of data sources can be represented as minor deviations from a general-level data source – for example, in sharing business models as indicated by Study 3. Study 3 further contributes to trade-off learning – an often neglected approach to integrating conflicting goals. Entities that pursue multiple goals at the same time always have to address a trade-off between these goals. Essentially, a trade-off situation can be reduced to finding weights for the different goals that determine the attention they receive. Resolving a trade-off is often a subjective and objective-specific undertaking and data-driven techniques can help resolving trade-off in a structured way. However, contributions to trade-off learning are highly scarce in the literature and usually address a trade-off in very specific contexts (e.g., Li et al. (1999); Varma and Ray (2007)). With the conducted research, a more general framework is contributed that builds upon two abstractly defined models that indicate the degree to which two conflicting goals are fulfilled in order to learn weightings of the goals through user feedback. The proposed trade-off framework is, thus, suited for autonomous systems that interact with consumers and are continuously faced with a trade-off between their own goal and the consumer's goal. While this approach constitutes a first step towards generalized trade-off learning, I call for further research on different formulations of trade-off learning frameworks for further application scenarios (e.g., autonomous systems pursuing conflicting goals without receiving human feedback), which may ultimately serve as building blocks in fully autonomous, self-organizing artificial agents. Finally, all situated artifacts developed in this work showcase the value of a large volume of data in combination with task distribution in data analysis tasks. While some researchers argue that the volume of big data is a challenge to address and its actual value stems from its variety (Goes 2014; Yoo 2015), this dissertation shows that volume, in itself, is also an important factor. Distributed data analysis has already been deemed an effective way to cope with large data sets (Dean and Ghemawat 2008). Though this dissertation follows the same path, the task distribution proposed in this work substantially differs from a mere division of programming logic. The proposed approach advocates for the division of tasks based on their semantics, which – as evident in Studies 2, 3, and 4 – can lead to more accurate predictions. The data volume is the main enabler of the proposed task division because it provides the computational experts with samples large enough for them to each specialize on different subsamples of the data.

Reflecting on the design principles proposed by the original formulation of the design theory in Study 1, I note several aspects that require further investigation. As already stated in the

C.II Limitations and Implications

Limitations Section, despite the initial proposal of the design theory claiming otherwise, it is not suited for purely unsupervised ML applications. However, unsupervised ML can play a supporting role in DoL systems that intend to solve a particular task. The extent to which unsupervised ML can enhance the structure of DoL systems and enhance analyses (e.g., by enabling task division and building meaningful representations of data (Bengio et al. 2013)) has to be subjected to further research. Furthermore, although the identification of subsets of similar data points for the purpose of creating sub-tasks is addressed in the design theory, the highly related identification of sub-goals, going beyond a mere division of the data input space, is neglected. This aspect requires further consideration and concrete application examples to enable an increased self-organization of DoL systems. Being specific instantiations of the proposed nascent design theory, the situated artifacts have additional implications for the validation and maturation of the DoL framework (Gregor and Hevner 2013; Iivari 2015). They show that different approaches to task division can be useful in different scenarios. In Study 2 a central executive is designed that learns task division. Despite having a high predictive performance, the proposed artifact indicates that the specific implementation of task division learning requires further research to ensure its sustainability. Sustainability of self-organized systems is essential because it allows them to work autonomously without interferences by human developers. Studies 2 and 4 show that sustainability enables real-time data analytics. However, they also show that achieving sustainability using incremental ML models requires careful consideration of the particularities of the systems and its employed models, which change from context to context and, thus, need to be subjected to further practice-oriented research. Moreover, Studies 3 and 4 show that task division can be performed in alternative ways, in this case, with respect to users, which is a straightforward way. This example of rule-based task division based on the domain knowledge of human developers shows that the principle of task division requires further insights regarding alternative task division approaches and the integration of rule-based and data-driven task division to allow for increased human involvement. Apart from pointing to potentials for further investigation, Studies 2, 3, and 4 also contribute to the validation of design principles, as I briefly show in the previous chapter. Specifically, they emphasize the importance of sustainability for big data systems and show how sustainability arises from incremental ML. They show the relevance of the principle of explanation, in particular for DSSs, and how it can be achieved, apart from explicitly using descriptive ML techniques, through a modular system architecture. Finally, they also demonstrate performance gains resulting from the specialization of individual modules, which they achieve by performing task division.

From a design science perspective, beyond the particularities of the proposed nascent design theory, one may distinguish three levels of contributions according to Gregor and Hevner (2013). This dissertation proposes a nascent (level 2) design theory for ML systems that address complex decision making problems. The distinction between a level 2 and a level 3 design theory lies in their level of abstractness (does the theory address a single instance of a problem or a broader class of problems?), their completeness (are all propositions adequately justified?), and their level of maturity (has the knowledge undergone sufficient testing?) (Gregor and Hevner 2013). Although it is important to note that the theory proposed in this dissertation cannot yet be considered a level 3 design theory, the first steps are taken towards achieving this goal. First, the design theory can be applied not just to a particular, materially existing problem, but to the broad and abstract class of problems concerning the development of complex and practically applicable ML systems. Second, justificatory knowledge (Gregor and Jones 2007) has been provided for both the individual problems addressed and the design principles proposed. Third, through situated implementations based on the design theory, the proposed design principles are tested and validated. While they constitute knowledge contributions on their own (Gregor and Hevner 2013), the situated implementations, thereby, collectively contribute to the maturity of the design theory. However, since some design principles may not be applicable to all problems or be mutually exclusive, not all of them can be evaluated in this work. Furthermore, in Chapter C.IV, I identify problems that are out of scope of the design theory that have initially not been recognized as a limitation and I extend design principles to accommodate processes that had previously not been anticipated by the design theory. These findings emphasize the importance of testing the design theory in practical scenarios and anticipating the incorporation of changes to the design theory (artifact mutability (Gregor and Jones 2007)). Since the current state of the nascent design theory satisfies the requirements of abstractness and completeness and has reached an advanced state of maturity, yet still has to be subjected to further testing to validate its effectiveness, one may consider it to be at an intermediate level between a level 2 and a level 3 design theory. Although the artifacts developed in Studies 2, 3, and 4 constitute level 1 design science contributions, cementing the nascent design theory, the fact that they are ML-based systems has to be considered when describing their implications for design science research. While level 1 artifacts generally address a particular problem in a particular context, ML-based level 1 artifacts are, by design, suited for either a certain class of problems or a range of contexts. This potential comes about by ML systems' inherent property of adapting to different situations and learning to solve particular kinds of problems. Therefore, the artifacts developed not only hold implications for the proposed design theory but also provide design principles for similar problems and may be partially applicable to general problem classes (e.g., the general domains of chronic diseases, digital two-sided platforms, and autonomous systems).

One may generally distinguish two different ways of developing a design theory: the bottom-up and the top-down strategies (Iivari 2015). This work follows the top-down approach. That is, it derives the design theory from existing kernel theories rather than solving particular practical problems and distilling the findings into generalizable design principles (Sein et al. 2011). It holds an important implication for design science research, showing that effective and practically relevant design principles do not necessarily have to emerge from the same practical environment for which the principles are intended. On the contrary, when developing design theories for a broad range of problem classes, findings from studies conducted in highly situated environments – often serving as inspirations rather than concrete evidence for more abstract design theories (Iivari 2015) – may be too specific and their potential for generalizability too low. On the other hand, for a narrowly defined problem class, it may be beneficial to start with specific, situated artifact to identify design principles. Although the initial design theory proposed in this work is evidently not perfect, it undergoes constant adaptations,

C.II Limitations and Implications 145

especially in this early stage of its maturation, and moves towards the ultimate goal of becoming a valid and practically relevant design theory. For this reason, I advocate for overcoming the uncertainties regarding the validity of design theories (Iivari 2015) that are intended for a broad range of problem classes and for using a top-down strategy in such cases along with a subsequent series of validations through practical applications to maintain a high generality of the theory.

Apart from design science research, I further identify a number of implications for different areas of IS research in addition to those that have already been described in the previous paragraphs. Study 2 deals with developing a DSS for cancer treatments in the head and neck area and emphasizes the value of data-driven analyses for enhancing research processes. As shown, the DoL-based DSS identifies patient attributes that are significant for decision making. Many decisions in medical practice are based on the experiences that physicians make over the course of many years. By observing the physicians' decisions and identifying the attributes determining them, a DSS may contribute to carrying insights from data that is readily available in clinical environments to research. Thereby, one may reduce additional efforts for carrying out medical experiments. Furthermore, through the modular architecture of DoL systems and their explanation power, they are capable of self-reflective learning, meaning that they not only make predictions regarding a phenomenon of interest but also provide information as to *why* certain predictions are made. This opportunity calls for increased design science research inquiries as to the precise ways of implementation for different kinds of ML models and in different contexts to provide IS scholars with tools that assist in resolving the prediction-explanation trade-off (Müller et al. 2016). They can, thereby, be given the ability to contribute to research by providing predictive knowledge (Shmueli and Koppius 2011) enriched with explanatory insights or vice-versa (Rai 2016). Generally speaking, ML and big data analytics can enable significant progress with regard to computationally assisted research. First, the massive amounts of fine-grained data available to researchers (Martens et al. 2016; Rai 2016) can yield an IT-enabled transformation (Lucas et al. 2013) of behavioral research (Goes 2014). The resulting new opportunity to study individual-level behavior in highly specific situations calls for appropriate tools that allow gaining insights from such data (Abbasi et al. 2016). The design theory responds to this call by providing the means to take advantage of high-variety and high-volume data based on computational experts that extract diverse information from said data. Furthermore, contributors to research have to be aware of the vast body of available literature in order to ensure the novelty and validity of their contributions and the appropriateness of their research methods (vom Brocke et al. 2012). "IS research is a highly diverse discipline" (vom Brocke et al. 2012, p. 206) and requires researchers to "venture across disciplinary boundaries" (vom Brocke et al. 2012, p. 206), making the literature search particularly difficult. A similar problem can be observed in grounded theory research – a common approach in the social sciences –, which involves large amounts of unstructured data and requires the integration of existing theory through constant comparisons with the literature base (Glaser and Strauss 1967). The potential of computer-assisted analyses has already been recognized for grounded theory research and unstructured data analysis in general (Crowston et al. 2012; Berente and Seidel 2014; Rai 2016). However, the automated analysis of unstructured data is a challenging undertaking due to their complexity and typical subjectively interpretable meanings (Rai 2016), as opposed to quantitative data, which are usually considered objective and can be used more readily by automated data analysis tools (Kitchin 2014; Shmueli and Koppius 2011). The proposed design theory addresses complex data analysis problems and, thus, has the potential to cope with the variety and make sense of unstructured data (Constantiou and Kallinikos 2015) and enable the development of tools that serve as effective knowledge seekers in large unstructured data sets. The maturity of data analysis tools notwithstanding, their application has been restricted in qualitative research and has required a high involvement of human actors, who are more capable of generative thinking (Grimmer and Stewart 2013). The abstractness of the DoL framework, employing intelligent agents as individual modules of a system, allows for incorporating both humans and machines that cooperate to solve given tasks. By allowing such human-machine symbioses (Döppner et al. 2016), DoL systems can enable the effective use of big data analytics in research and in other scenarios in which "full automation is not feasible or desirable" (Döppner et al. 2016, p. 2). This dissertation adds to emerging research on the development of ML-based systems that follow the call for an increased human-machine symbiosis (Traumer et al. 2017).

Figure C:4 depicts an overview of the most significant theoretical implications.

C.II Limitations and Implications

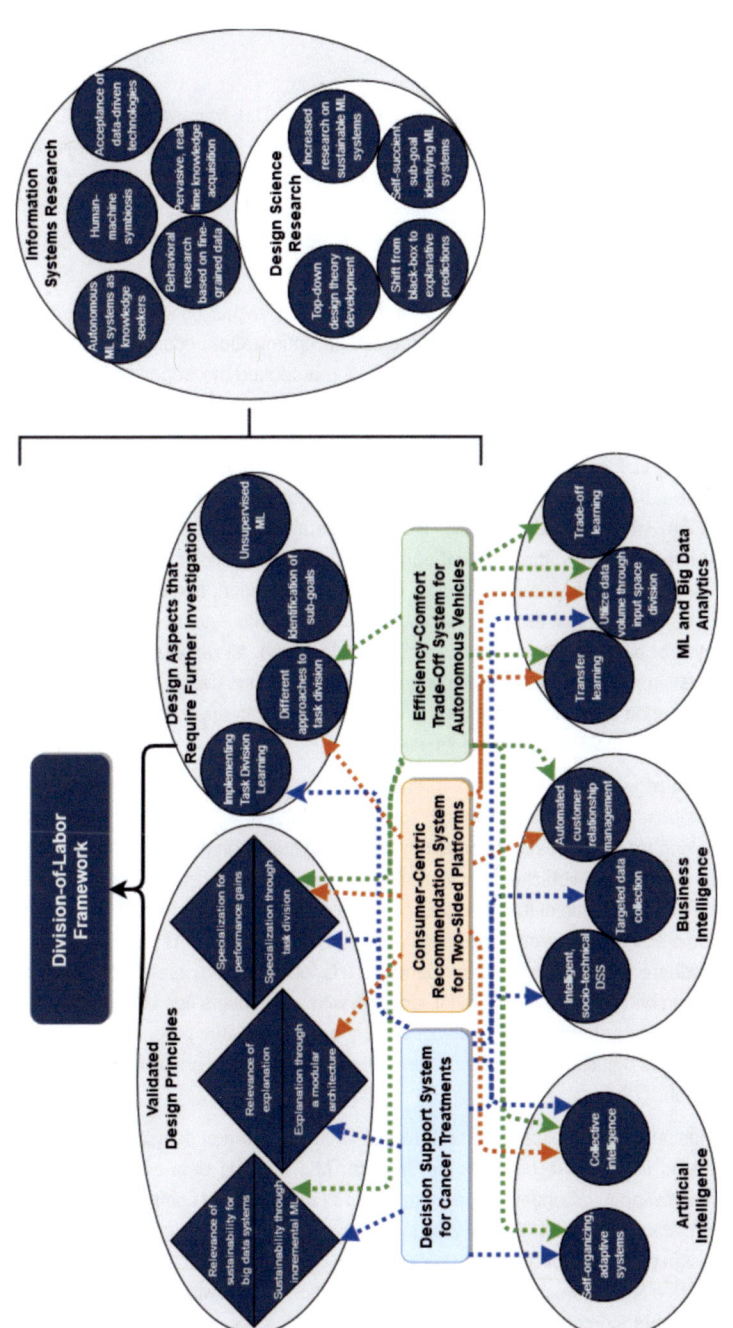

Figure C.4. Overview of the theoretical implications of this dissertation.

III. Conclusion and Outlook

The cumulative dissertation proposes a design theory – the DoL framework – for ML systems that address complex decision making problems – intended for both ML systems used by humans and for autonomous systems. Showcasing the application of the design theory and evaluating its principles in practical settings, three expository instantiations for different contexts are designed. To achieve these goals, Chapters B.I and B.II carry out four different research inquiries.

Chapter B.I proposes an initial formulation of the nascent, level 2 design theory by building upon existing theory from the fields of mathematical optimization, economics, and AI. The design theory is developed according to the approach proposed by Gregor and Jones (2007). However, it is entirely based on existing theory and expository instantiations based on the theory are introduced in Chapter B.II. The design theory offers justificatory knowledge (i.e., reasoning for its validity based on a set on kernel theories), principles of form and function, which describe the prescriptive knowledge in a conceptual manner, and principles of implementation, which provide specific, technical details of implementing the conceptual principles. More specifically, the design theory introduces the principles of general knowledge, specialization, explanation, task distribution, feedback, adaptation, and sustainability to guide the design of ML systems towards being able to cope with and take advantage of the characteristics of big data (i.e., volume, velocity, and variety), all while being interpretable by human analysts and enhancing their predictive power. Finally, the design theory offers testable propositions, stating observable benefits that one may gain from applying its design principles and allow for an effective evaluation of its validity.

Chapter B.II designs situated, level 1 artifacts for specific practical problems. It uses the principles proposed by the design theory to address data analytics problems in treatment decision making for cancer patients, recommendation systems on digital two-sided platforms, and training autonomous vehicles to drive both efficiently and according to users' preferences. It shows that the application of the principles of the design theory yielded artifacts that exhibited an enhanced predictive performance and suitability for big data problems compared to artifacts that do not adhere to said principles. Furthermore, it is found that the application of the design theory results in better understandable ML artifacts with which users can identify. The artifacts helped validate the principles of the design theory and its testable propositions to a certain degree, while also pointing to particular aspects that require further practice-oriented and ML-based research.

This work has important implications for IS research, its sub-area of design science research, and the related fields of AI, business intelligence, ML, and big data analytics. It provides prescriptive knowledge grounded in theory that guides the design of complex ML and big data systems, providing evidence that a top-down development of design theories can yield effective design principles for highly abstract problem classes, which may be further refined by studying its relevance through practical implementations. Following the proposed design theory and further contributing to its maturity, research may move towards increasingly

C.III Conclusion and Outlook

conscious, self-organized, autonomous systems that maintain a high level of interpretability by providing human analysts with information on their own previously acquired knowledge while simultaneously adhering to a modular architecture.

With respect to the further development of the proposed nascent design theory, there is a plethora of diverse opportunities for future research inquiries. Contributions may address either principles of form and function or principles of implementation. For example, the principle of task division can become more concrete through additional research on methods for clustering and sub-goal identification, the effectiveness of the different task division principles can be evaluated in different contexts, the value of unsupervised learning for DoL systems can be re-evaluated, incremental formulations of ML models can be developed, and approaches for self-reflective learning can be studied. The designs of the situated artifacts' proposed in Studies 2, 3, and 4 serve as examples of applying the design theory to real-world problems. They aim to effectively solve those problems loosely guided by the design theory, thereby telling their own stories about the practicability of each design principle. Although these artifacts demonstrate the validity of the nascent design theory to some extent, it still has a long way to go in order to reach a high level of maturity.

References

Abbasi, A., Albrecht, C., Vance, A., and Hansen, J. 2012. "Metafraud: A meta-learning framework for detecting financial fraud," *Management Information Systems Quarterly* (36:4), pp. 1293-1327.

Abbasi, A., Sarker, S., and Chiang, R. H. L. 2016. "Big data research in information systems: Toward an inclusive research agenda," *Journal of the Association for Information Systems* (17:2), pp. 1-32.

Abernethy, A. P., Etheredge, L. M., Ganz, P. A., Wallace, P., German, R. R., Neti, C., Bach, P. B., and Murphy, S. B. 2010. "Rapid-Learning System for Cancer Care," *Journal of Clinical Oncology* (28:27), pp. 4268-4274.

Adomavicius, G., Bockstedt, J. C., Curley, S. P., and Zhang, J. 2013. "Do recommender systems manipulate consumer preferences? A study of anchoring effects," *Information Systems Research* (24:4), pp. 956-975.

Adomavicius, G., Mobasher, B., Ricci, F., and Tuzhilin, A. 2011. "Context-Aware Recommender Systems," *AI Magazine* (32:3), pp. 67-80.

Adomavicius, G., and Tuzhilin, A. 2005. "Toward the next generation of recommender systems: A survey of the state-of-the-art and possible extensions," *IEEE transactions on knowledge and data engineering* (17:6), pp. 734-749.

Adomavicius, G., and Zhang, J. 2015. "Improving stability of recommender systems: A meta-algorithmic approach," *IEEE Transactions on Knowledge and Data Engineering* (27:6), pp. 1573-1587.

Agarwal, R., and Dhar, V. 2014. "Editorial—big data, data science, and analytics: The opportunity and challenge for is research," *Information Systems Research* (25:3), pp. 443-448.

Agarwal, R., Gao, G., DesRoches, C., and Jha, A. K. 2010. "Research Commentary—the Digital Transformation of Healthcare: Current Status and the Road Ahead," *Information Systems Research* (21:4), pp. 796-809.

Akaike, H. 1973. "Information theory and an extension of the maximum likelihood principle," in Petrov, B. N.; Csáki, F., in *Proceedings of the 2nd International Symposium on Information Theory*, pp. 267–281.

al-Rifaie, M. M., Bishop, J. M., and Caines, S. 2012. "Creativity and autonomy in swarm intelligence systems," *Cognitive Computation* (4:3), pp. 320-331.

Alippi, C., and Roveri, M. 2007. "Just-in-time adaptive classifiers in nonstationary conditions," in *Proceedings of the 2007 International Joint Conference on Neural Networks*, pp. 1014-1019.

Andonov, R., Poirriez, V., and Rajopadhye, S. 2000. "Unbounded knapsack problem: Dynamic programming revisited," *European Journal of Operational Research* (123:2), pp. 394-407.

Angst, C. M., and Agarwal, R. 2009. "Adoption of Electronic Health Records in the Presence of Privacy Concerns: The Elaboration Likelihood Model and Individual Persuasion," *Management Information Systems Quarterly* (33:2), pp. 339-370.

Arazy, O., Kumar, N., and Shapira, B. 2010. "A theory-driven design framework for social recommender systems," *Journal of the Association for Information Systems* (11:9), 455.

Arnott, D., and Pervan, G. 2005. "A critical analysis of Decision Support Systems research," *Journal of Information Technology* (20:2), pp. 67-87.

Arnott, D., and Pervan, G. 2008. "Eight key issues for the decision support systems discipline," *Decision Support Systems* (44:3), pp. 657-672.

Arnott, D., and Pervan, G. 2012. "Design science in decision support systems research: An assessment using the Hevner, March, Park, and Ram Guidelines," *Journal of the Association for Information Systems* (13:11), pp. 923-949.

Aron, R., Dutta, S., Janakiraman, R., Pathak, P. A. 2011. "The Impact of Automation of Systems on Medical Errors: Evidence from Field Research," *Information Systems Research* (22:3), pp. 429-446.

Arora, S. 2016. "Recommendation Engines: How Amazon And Netflix Are Winning The Personalization Battle," (https://www.martechadvisor.com/articles/customer-experience-2/recommendation-engines-how-amazon-and-netflix-are-winning-the-personalization-battle, accessed April 30, 2019).

ASCO 2013. "Shaping the Future of Oncology: Envisioning Cancer Care in 2030: Outcomes of the Asco Board of Derectors Strategic Planning and Visioning Process, 2011-2012," (https://www.asco.org/sites/default/files/shapingfuture-lowres.pdf, accessed March 03, 2017).

Atahan, P., and Sarkar, S. 2011. "Accelerated learning of user profiles," *Management Science* (57:2), pp. 215-239.

Babshet, M., Nandimath, K., Pervatikar, S., and Naikmasur, V. 2011. "Efficacy of Oral Brush Cytology in the Evaluation of the Oral Premalignant and Malignant Lesions," *Journal of Cytology* (28:4), pp. 165-172.

Baesens, B., Bapna, R., Marsden, J. R., Vanthienen, J., and Zhao, J. L. 2016. "Transformational issues of big data and analytics in networked Business," *Management Information Systems Quarterly* (40:4), pp. 807-818.

Baeza-Yates, R., Ribeiro-Neto, B. 1999. *Modern Information Retrieval*, Harlow (UK): Addison-Wesley Longman Publishing Co..

Bajracharya, M., Howard, A., Matthies, L. H., Tang, B., and Turmon, M. 2009. "Autonomous off-road navigation with end-to-end learning for the LAGR program," *Journal of Field Robotics* (26:1), pp. 3-25.

Banker, R. D., and Kauffman, R. J. 2004. "50th anniversary article: The evolution of research on information systems: A fiftieth-year survey of the literature in management science," *Management Science* (50:3), pp. 281-298.

Bardhan, I., Oh, J. H., Zheng, Z., and Kirksey, K. 2014. "Predictive analytics for readmission of patients with congestive heart failure," *Information Systems Research* (26:1), pp. 19-39.

Behling, O., and Eckel, N. L. 1991. "Making sense out of intuition," *Academy of Management Perspectives* (5:1), pp. 46-54.

Bengio, Y. 2009. "Learning deep architectures for AI," *Foundations and Trends® in Machine Learning* (2:1), pp. 1-127.

Bengio, Y., and Lecun, Y. 2007. "Scaling learning algorithms towards AI," in *Large-Scale Kernel Machines*, L. Bottou, O. Chapelle, D. DeCoste, J. Weston (eds.), MIT Press, pp. 321-360.

Bengio, Y., Courville, A., and Vincent, P. 2013. "Representation learning: A review and new perspectives," *IEEE transactions on pattern analysis and machine intelligence* (35:8), pp. 1798-1828.

Beni, G., and Wang, J. 1993. "Swarm Intelligence in Cellular Robotic Systems," in *Proceedings of the NATO Advanced Workshop on Robots and Biological Systems*, Tuscany, Italy, pp. 703-712.

Benlian, A., Klumpe, J., and Hinz, O. 2019. "Mitigating the intrusive effects of smart home assistants by using anthropomorphic design features: A multi-method investigation," *Information Systems Journal*, forthcoming.

Bennett, J., and Lanning, S. 2007. "The netflix prize," in *Proceedings of the 2007 KDD cup and workshop*, pp. 35-38.

Berente, N., and Seidel, S. 2014. "Big Data & Inductive Theory Development: Towards Computational Grounded Theory?," in *Proceedings of the Twentieth Americas Conference on Information Systems*, pp. 1-11.

Bharadwaj, A., El Sawy, O. A., Pavlou, P. A., and Venkatraman, N. 2013. "Digital business strategy: toward a next generation of insights," *Management Information Systems Quarterly (37:2)*, pp. 471-482.

Bhaskar, R. 1998. "The Possibility of Naturalism," London (UK): Routledge.

Bifet, A., and Gavalda, R. 2007. "Learning from time-changing data with adaptive windowing," in *Proceedings of the 2007 SIAM International Conference on Data Mining*, pp. 443-448.

Binet, A., and Simon, T. 1905. "Methodes nouvelles por le diagnostic du niveau intellectual des anormaux," *L'Année Psychologique* (11:1), pp. 191-244.

Böhrnsen, F., Fricke, M., Sander, C., Leha, A., Schliephake, H., and Kramer, F. J. 2014. "Interactions of Human Msc with Head and Neck Squamous Cell Carcinoma Cell Line Pci-13 Reduce Markers of Epithelia-Mesenchymal Transition," *Clininical Oral Investigations* (19:5), pp. 1121-1128.

Böhrnsen, F., Godek, F., Kiesel, J., Kramer, F. J., Brockmeyer, P., and Schliephake, H. 2017. "Influence of Tgf-Beta1 on Tumor Transition in Oral Cancer Cell and Bmsc Co-Cultures," *Journal of Cranio-Maxillofacial Surgery* (45:5), pp. 731-740.

Bojarski, M., Del Testa, D., Dworakowski, D., Firner, B., Flepp, B., Goyal, P., Jackel, L. D., Monfort, M., Muller, U., Zhang, J., Zhang, X., Zhao, J., Zieba, K. 2016. "End to end learning for self-driving cars," (available at arxiv.org/abs/1604.07316, accessed July 18, 2019).

Bollen, D., Knijnenburg, B. P., Willemsen, M. C., and Graus, M. 2010. "Understanding choice overload in recommender systems," in *Proceedings of the 4th ACM conference on Recommender systems*, pp. 63-70.

Boonstra, A. 2003. "Structure and analysis of IS decision-making processes," *European Journal of Information Systems* (12:3), pp. 195-209.

Borenstein, J., Herkert, J., and Miller, K. 2017. "Self-driving cars: Ethical responsibilities of design engineers," *IEEE Technology and Society Magazine* (36:2), pp. 67-75.

Bosc, R., Hersant, B., Carloni, R., Niddam, J., Bouhassira, J., De Kermadec, H., Bequignon, E., Wojcik, T., Julieron, M., and Meningaud, J. P. 2017. "Mandibular Reconstruction after Cancer: An in-House Approach to Manufacturing Cutting Guides," *International Journal of Oral and Maxillofacial Surgery* (46:1), pp. 24-31.

Bostrom, R. P., and Heinen, J. S. 1977. "MIS Problems and Failures: A Socio-Technical Perspective, Part Ii: The Application of Socio-Technical Theory," *Management Information Systems Quarterly* (1:4), pp. 11-28.

Bottou, L. 1998. "Online learning and stochastic approximations," *On-line Learning in Neural Networks* (17:9), pp. 9-42.

Breiman, L. 2001. "Random forests," *Machine Learning* (45:1), pp. 5-32.

Breiman, L., Friedman, J. H., Olshen, R. A., and Stone, C. J. 1984. *Classification and regression trees*, Monterey (USA): Wadsworth & Brooks/Cole Advanced Books & Software.

Brenner, W., Karagiannis, D., Kolbe, L., Krüger, J., Leifer, L., Lamberti, H.-J., Leimeister, J. M., Österle, H., Petrie, C., Plattner, H., Schwabe, G., Uebernickel, F., Winter, R., and Zarnekow, R. 2014. "User, use & utility research," *Wirtschaftsinformatik* (56:1), pp. 65-72.

Bruzzone, L., and Prieto, D. F. 1999. "An incremental-learning neural network for the classification of remote-sensing images," *Pattern Recognition Letters* (20:11), pp. 1241-1248.

Buluswar, S. D., and Draper, B. A. 1998. "Color machine vision for autonomous vehicles," *Engineering Applications of Artificial Intelligence* (11:2), pp. 245-256.

Butakov, V. A., and Ioannou, P. 2015. "Personalized driver/vehicle lane change models for ADAS," *IEEE Transactions on Vehicular Technology* (64:10), pp. 4422-4431.

Burns, L. D., 2013. "A vision of our transport future," *Nature* (497:7448), pp. 181-182.

Burns, L. D., Jordan, W. C., and Scarborough, B. A. 2013. *Transforming personal mobility*, New York (USA): The Earth Institute.

Çano, E., and Morisio, M. 2017. "Hybrid recommender systems: A systematic literature review," *Intelligent Data Analysis* (21:6), pp. 1487-1524.

Carreras, M., Yuh, J., Batlle, J., and Ridao, P. 2005. "A behavior-based scheme using reinforcement learning for autonomous underwater vehicles," *IEEE Journal of Oceanic Engineering* (30:2), pp. 416-427.

Carter, M., and Grover, V. 2015. "Me, My Self, and I (T): Conceptualizing Information Technology Identity and its Implications," *Management Information Systems Quarterly* (39:4), pp. 931-957.

Chaudhry, B., Wang, J., Wu, S., Maglione, M., Mojica, W., Roth, E., Morton, S. C., and Shekelle, P. G. 2006. "Systematic Review: Impact of Health Information Technology on Quality, Efficiency, and Costs of Medical Care," *Annals of Internal Medicine* (144:10), pp. 742-752.

Chauhan, S., and Vig, L. 2015. "Anomaly detection in ECG time signals via deep long short-term memory networks," in *Proceedings of the 2015 IEEE International Conference on Data Science and Advanced Analytics (DSAA)*, pp. 1-7.

Chen, H., Chiang, R. H., and Storey, V. C. 2012. "Business Intelligence and Analytics: From Big Data to Big Impact," *Management Information Systems Quarterly* (36:4), pp. 1165-1188.

Chen, G., Parada, C., and Sainath, T. N. 2015. "Query-by-example keyword spotting using long short-term memory networks," in *Proceedings of the IEEE International Conference on Acoustics, Speech and Signal Processing*, pp. 5236-5240.

Chen, C., Seff, A., Kornhauser, A., and Xiao, J. 2015. "DeepDriving: Learning affordance for direct perception in autonomous driving," in *Proceedings of 15th IEEE International Conference on Computer Vision*, pp. 1-9.

Chiu, C. C., and Soo, V. W. 2007. "Subgoal identification for reinforcement learning and planning in multiagent problem solving," In *Proceedings of the 2007 German Conference on Multiagent System Technologies*, pp. 37-48.

Cohen, J., and Cohen, P. 1983. *Applied Multiple regression /correlation analysis for behavioral sciences*, Hillsdale (USA): New Jersey Lawrence Erlbaum Associates.

Constantiou, I. D., and Kallinikos, J. 2015. "New games, new rules: big data and the changing context of strategy," *Journal of Information Technology* (30:1), pp. 44-57.

Cortada, J. W., Gordon, D., and Lenihan, B. 2012. "The Value of Analytics in Healthcare: From Insights to Outcomes," IBM Global Business Services, Life Sciences and Healthcare, Executive Report (http://www-935.ibm.com/services/us/gbs/thoughtleadership/ibv-healthcare-analytics.html, accessed July 29, 2019).

Cortes, C., and Vapnik, V. 1995. "Support-Vector Networks," *Machine Learning* (20), pp. 273-297.

Coveney, P. V., Dougherty, E. R., and Highfield, R. R. 2016. "Big Data Need Big Theory Too," *Philosophical Transactions of the Royal Society A: Mathematical, Physical and Engineering Sciences* (374:2080), pp. 1-11.

Cox, D. R. 1958. "The Regression Analysis of Binary Sequences," *Journal of the Royal Statistical Society. Series B (Methodological)* (20:2), pp. 215-242

Cox, D. R., and Snell, E. J. 1989. *Analysis of binary data, 2nd Edition*, London (UK): Chapman & Hall.

Crowston, K., Allen, E., and Heckman, R. 2012. "Using natural language processing technology for qualitative data analysis," *International Journal of Social Research Methodology* (15:6), pp. 523–543.

Crusz, S. M., and Balkwill, F. R. 2015. "Inflammation and Cancer: Advances and New Agents," *Nature Reviews Clinical Oncology* (12:10), pp. 584-596.

Cybenko, G. 1989. "Approximation by superpositions of a sigmoidal function," *Mathematics of control, signals and systems* (2:4), pp. 303-314.

Dahl, G. E., Yu, D., Deng, L., and Acero, A. 2012. "Context-Dependent Pre-Trained Deep Neural Networks for Large-Vocabulary Speech Recognition," *IEEE Transactions on Audio, Speech, and Language Processing* (20:1), pp. 30-42.

Dai, X., Li, C. K., and Rad, A. B. 2005. "An approach to tune fuzzy controllers based on reinforcement learning for autonomous vehicle control," *IEEE Transactions on Intelligent Transportation Systems* (6:3), pp. 285-293.

Davis, F. D. 1989. "Perceived usefulness, perceived ease of use, and user acceptance of information technology," *Management Information Systems Quarterly* (13:2), pp. 319-340.

Davidson, J., Liebald, B., Liu, J., Nandy, P., and Van Vleet, T. 2010. "The YouTube video recommendation system," in *Proceedings of the 4th ACM Conference on Recommender Systems*, pp. 293-296.

Davis, F. D., Bagozzi, R. P., and Warshaw, P. R. 1989. "User acceptance of computer technology: A comparison of two theoretical models," *Management Science* (35:8), pp. 982-1003.

de Reuver, M., Sørensen, C., and Basole, R. C. 2017. "The digital platform: a research agenda," *Journal of Information Technology* (33:2), pp. 1-12.

Dean, J., and Ghemawat, S. 2008. "MapReduce: simplified data processing on large clusters," *Communications of the ACM* (51:1), pp. 107-113.

Deng, L., and Yu, D. 2014. "Deep learning: Methods and applications," *Foundations and Trends® in Signal Processing* (7:3-4), pp. 197-387.

Dennis, L., Fisher, M., Slavkovik, M., and Webster, M. 2016. "Formal verification of ethical choices in autonomous systems," *Robotics and Autonomous Systems* (77), pp. 1-14.

Devlin, J., Chang, M. W., Lee, K., and Toutanova, K. 2018. "Bert: Pre-training of deep bidirectional transformers for language understanding," (available at arxiv.org/abs/1810.04805, accessed December 8, 2019).

Dickmanns, E. D., and Mysliwetz, B. D. 1992. "Recursive 3-D road and relative ego-state recognition," *IEEE Transactions on Pattern Analysis and Machine Intelligence* (14:2), pp. 199-213.

Döppner, D. A., Gregory, R. W., Schoder, D., and Siejka, H. 2016. "Exploring Design Principles for Human-Machine Symbiosis: Insights from Constructing an Air Transportation Logistics Artifact," in *Proceedings of the Thirty Seventh International Conference on Information Systems*, pp. 1-21.

Dorigo, M. 1992. *Optimization, Learning and Natural Algorithms* (Doctoral dissertation), Politecnico di Milano, Italy.

Drachen, A., Canossa, A., and Yannakakis, G. N. 2009. "Player modeling using self-organization in Tomb Raider: Underworld," In *Proceedings of the 2009 IEEE Symposium on Computational Intelligence and Games*, pp. 1-8.

Drever, J. 1952. *A Dictionary of Psychology*, Harmondsworth (UK): PenguinBooks.

Dussart, F. 2009. "Diet, diabetes and relatedness in a central Australian Aboriginal settlement: some qualitative recommendations to facilitate the creation of culturally sensitive health promotion initiatives," *Health Promotion Journal of Australia* (20:3), pp. 202-206.

Eisenmann, T., Parker, G., and Van Alstyne, M. 2011. "Platform envelopment," *Strategic Management Journal* (32:12), pp. 1270-1285.

El Sawy, O. A., and Pereira, F. 2013. *Business modeling in the dynamic digital space: An ecosystem approach*, Heidelberg (Germany): Springer.

Elman, J. L. 1990. "Finding structure in time," *Cognitive science* (14:2), pp. 179-211.

Erevelles, S., Fukawa, N., and Swayne, L. 2016. "Big Data consumer analytics and the transformation of marketing," *Journal of Business Research* (69:2), pp. 897-904.

Ernst, C. P. H., and Reinelt, P. 2017. "Autonomous car acceptance: Safety vs. personal driving enjoyment," in *Proceedings of the Twenty-Third Americas Conference on Information Systems*, pp. 1-8.

Evans, D. S., and Schmalensee, R. 2016. *Matchmakers: The new economics of multisided platforms*, Boston (USA): Harvard Business Review Press.

Fagnant, D. J., and Kockelman, K. M. 2014. "The travel and environmental implications of shared autonomous vehicles, using agent-based model scenarios," *Transportation Research Part C* (40), pp. 1-13.

Fagnant, D. J., and Kockelman, K. M. 2015. "Preparing a nation for autonomous vehicles: opportunities, barriers and policy recommendations," *Transportation Research Part A: Policy and Practice* (77), pp. 167-181.

Fagnant, D. J., and Kockelman, K. M. 2018. "Dynamic ride-sharing and fleet sizing for a system of shared autonomous vehicles in Austin, Texas," *Transportation* (45:1), pp. 143-158.

Ferranti, J. M., Langman, M. K., Tanaka, D., McCall, J. Ahmad, A. 2010. "Bridging the gap: leveraging business intelligence tools in support of patient safety and financial effectiveness," *Journal of the American Medical Informatics Association* (17:2), pp. 136-143.

Ferreras, L. E. 2014. "The driverless city," *Civil Engineering* (84:3), pp. 52-55.

Ferris, R., and Gillison, M. L. 2017. "Nivolumab for Squamous-Cell Cancer of Head and Neck," *New England Journal of Medice* (376:6), pp. 595-596.

Fichman, R. G., Kohli, R., and Krishnan, R. 2011. "Editorial Overview—the Role of Information Systems in Healthcare: Current Research and Future Trends," *Information Systems Research* (22:3), pp. 419-428.

Frisk, J. E., Lindgren, R., and Mathiassen, L. 2014. "Design matters for decision makers: Discovering IT investment alternatives," *European Journal of Information Systems* (23:4), pp. 442-461.

Galliers, R. D., Newell, S., Shanks, G., and Topi, H. 2015. "The Challenges and Opportunities of 'Datification' – Strategic Impacts of 'Big' (and 'Small') and Real Time Data – for Society and for Organizational Decision Makers," *The Journal of Strategic Information Systems* (24:1), pp. II-III.

Galliers, R. D., Newell, S., Shanks, G., and Topi, H. 2017. "Datification and its human, organizational and societal effects," The Journal of Strategic Information Systems (26:3), pp. 185-190.

Gandomi, A., and Haider, M. 2015. "Beyond the hype: Big data concepts, methods, and analytics," *International Journal of Information Management* (35:2), pp. 137-144.

Gartner, D., and Padman, R. 2016. "Mathematical Modelling and Cluster Analysis in Healthcare Analytics – The Case of Length of Stay Management," in *Proceedings of the Thirty Seventh International Conference on Information Systems*, pp. 1-9.

Gasson, S. 2003. "Human-centered vs. user-centered approaches to information system design," *Journal of Information Technology Theory and Application* (5:2), pp. 29-46.

Gers, F. A., Schmidhuber, J., and Cummins, F. 2000. "Learning to forget: Continual prediction with LSTM," *Neural Computation* (12:10), pp. 2451-2471.

Ghosh, B., and Scott, J. E. 2011. "Antecedents and Catalysts for Developing a Healthcare Analytic Capability," *Communications of the Association for Information Systems* (29:1), pp. 395-409.

Gianchandani, E. P. 2011. "Toward smarter health and well-being: an implicit role for networking and information technology," *Journal of Information Technology* (26:2), pp. 120-128.

Gilman, E., Keskinarkaus, A., Tamminen, S., Pirttikangas, S., Röning, J., and Riekki, J. 2015. "Personalised assistance for fuel-efficient driving," *Transportation Research Part C: Emerging Technologies* (58), pp. 681-705.

Gindele, T., Brechtel, S., and Dillmann, R. 2010. "A probabilistic model for estimating driver behaviors and vehicle trajectories in traffic environments," in *Proceedings of the IEEE International Conference on Intelligent Transportation Systems,* pp. 1625-1631.

Glaser, B. G., and Strauss, A. L. 1967. T*he Discovery of Grounded Theory. Strategies for Qualitative Research*, Chicago (USA): Aldine Publishing Company.

Goes, P. B. 2014. "Editor's comments: big data and is research," *Management Information Systems Quarterly* (38:3), pp. iii–viii.

Gomez-Uribe, C. A., and Hunt, N. 2016. "The Netflix Recommender System: Algorithms, Business value, and Innovation," *ACM Transactions on Management Information Systems* (6:4), pp. 1-19.

Goodfellow, I., Bengio, Y., and Courville, A. 2016. *Deep Learning*, Cambridge (USA), London (UK): MIT Press.

Greff, K., Srivastava, R. K., Koutník, J., Steunebrink, B. R., and Schmidhuber, J. 2017. "LSTM: A search space odyssey," *IEEE transactions on neural networks and learning systems (*28:10), pp. 2222-2232.

Gregoire, V., Lefebvre, J. L., Licitra, L., Felip, E. 2010. "Squamous Cell Carcinoma of the Head and Neck: Ehns-Esmo-Estro Clinical Practice Guidelines for Diagnosis, Treatment and Follow-Up," *Annals of Oncology* (21:5), pp. 184-186.

Gregor, S. 2006. "The nature of theory in information systems," *Management Information Systems Quarterly* (30:3), pp. 611-642.

Gregor, S. 2009. "Building theory in the sciences of the artificial," In *Proceedings of the 4th International Conference on Design Science Research in Information Systems and Technology,* pp. 1-10.

Gregor, S., and Hevner, A. R. 2013. "Positioning and Presenting Design Science Research for Maximum Impact," *Management Information Systems Quarterly* (37:2), pp. 337-355.

Gregor, S., and Jones, D. 2007. "The Anatomy of a Design Theory," *Journal of the Association for Information Systems* (8:5), pp. 312-335.

Gregor, S., Martin, M., Fernandez, W., Stern, S., and Vitale, M. 2006. "The transformational dimension in the realization of business value from information technology," Journal of Strategic Information Systems (15:3), pp. 249-270.

Grimmer, J., and Stewart, B. M. 2013. "Text as data: The promise and pitfalls of automatic content analysis methods for political texts," *Political Analysis* (21:3), pp. 267-297.

Grolinger, K., Hayes, M., Higashino, W. A., L'Heureux, A., Allison, D. S., and Capretz, M. A. 2014. "Challenges for MapReduce in Big Data," in *Proceedings of the 2014 IEEE World Congress on Services*, pp. 182-189.

Grover, V., Chiang, R. H., Liang, T. P., and Zhang, D. 2018. "Creating strategic business value from big data analytics: A research framework," *Journal of Management Information Systems* (35:2), pp. 388-423.

Günther, W. A., Mehrizi, M. H. R., Huysman, M., and Feldberg, F. 2017. "Debating big data: A literature review on realizing value from big data," The Journal of Strategic Information Systems (26:3), pp. 191-209.

Gupta, A., and Sharda, R. 2013. "Improving the Science of Healthcare Delivery and Informatics Using Modeling Approaches," *Decision Support Systems* (55:2), pp. 423-427.

Han, J., Pei, J., and Kamber, M. 2012. *Data mining: concepts and techniques, Third Edition*, Waltham (USA): Morgan Kaufmann Publishers..

Harnad, S. 1990. "The symbol grounding problem," *Physica D: Nonlinear Phenomena* (42:1-3), pp. 335-346.

Hasenjäger, M., and Wersing, H. 2017. "Personalization in advanced driver assistance systems and autonomous vehicles: A review," in *Proceedings of the IEEE 20th International Conference on Intelligent Transportation Systems*, pp. 1-7.

Hayes, B. 2011. "Leaving the driving to it," *American Scientist* (99), pp. 362-366.

Hellström, T., and Ringdahl, O. 2006. "Follow the Past: a path-tracking algorithm for autonomous vehicles," *International journal of vehicle autonomous systems* (4:2), pp. 216-224.

Henfridsson, O., and Lindgren, R. 2005. "Multi-contextuality in ubiquitous computing: Investigating the car case through action research," *Information and Organization* (15:2), pp. 95-124.

Henmon, V. A. C. 1921. "Intelligence and its measurement: A symposium—VIII," *Journal of Educational Psychology* (12:4), pp. 195-198.

Hess, T., Legner, C., Esswein, W., Maaß, W., Matt, C., Österle, H., Schlieter, H., Richter, P., and Zarnekow, R. 2014. "Digital life as a topic of business and information systems engineering?," *Business & Information Systems Engineering* (6:4), pp. 247-253.

Hevner, A. R., March, S. T., Park, J., and Ram, S. 2004. "Design Science in Information Systems Research," *Management Information Systems Quarterly* (28:1), pp. 75-105.

Hildebrandt, B., Hanelt, A., and Firk, S. 2018. "Sharing Yet Caring – Mitigating Moral Hazard in Access-Based Consumption through IS-Enabled Value Co-Capturing with Consumers," *Business & Information Systems Engineering* (60:3), pp. 227-241.

Hinton, G. E., Osindero, S., and Teh, Y.-W. 2006. "A fast learning algorithm for deep belief nets," *Neural Computation* (18:7), pp. 1527-1554.

Hinton, G. E., Sejnowski, T. J., and Poggio, T. A. 1999. *Unsupervised learning: foundations of neural computation*, Cambridge (USA), London (UK): MIT Press.

Ho, T. K. 1995. "Random decision forests," in *Proceedings of 3rd International Conference on Document Analysis and Recognition*, pp. 278-282.

Hochreiter, S., and Schmidhuber, J. 1997. "Long short-term memory," *Neural Computation* (9:8), pp. 1735-1780.

Hong, S., and Tam, K. Y. 2006. "Understanding the adoption of multipurpose information appliances: The case of mobile data services," *Information Systems Research* (17:2), pp. 162-179.

Hormozi, A. M., and Giles, S. 2004. "Data mining: A competitive weapon for banking and retail industries," *Information Systems Management* (21:2), pp. 62-71.

Hu, P. J. H., Hu, H. F., Wei, C. P., and Hsu, P. F. 2016. "Examining Firms' Green Information Technology Practices: A Hierarchical View of Key Drivers and Their Effects," *Journal of Management Information Systems* (33:4), pp. 1149-1179.

Huang, G.-B., Wang, D. H., and Lan, Y. 2011. "Extreme Learning Machines: A Survey," *International Journal of Machine Learning and Cybernetics* (2:2), pp. 107-122.

Huiwen, W., Yuan, W., and Lele, H. 2014. "Incremental algorithm of multiple linear regression model," *Journal of Beijing University of Aeronautics and Astronautics* (11), pp. 1487-1491.

Iivari, J. 2015. Distinguishing and contrasting two strategies for design science research. *European Journal of Information Systems* (24:1), pp. 107-115.

Intelligence 1989. In *The Oxford English Dictionary, Second Edition* (https://www.oed.com/view/Entry/97396?rskey=PgrQzd&result=1&isAdvanced=false#eid, accessed September 04, 2019), Oxford (UK): Oxford University Press.

Intelligence 2003. In *Merriam-Webster's Collegiate Dictionary, 11th Edition* (https://www.merriam-webster.com/dictionary/intelligence, accessed September 04, 2019), Springfield (USA): Merriam-Webster.

Intelligence 2006. In *Columbia Encyclopedia, Sixth Edition* (https://www.infoplease.com/encyclopedia/medicine/psychology/discipline/intelligence, accessed September 05, 2019), New York (US): Columbia University Press.

Intelligence 2011. In *The American Heritage® Dictionary of the English Language, Fifth Edition* (https://ahdictionary.com/word/search.html?q=intelligence, accessed September 04, 2019), Boston (USA): Houghton Mifflin.

Intelligence 2013. In *Cambridge Advanced Learner's Dictionary, Fourth Edition* (https://dictionary.cambridge.org/de/worterbuch/englisch/intelligence, accessed September 04, 2019), Cambridge (UK): Cambridge University Press.

Intelligence 2014. In *Longman Dictionary of Contemporary English, Sixth Edition* (https://www.ldoceonline.com/dictionary/intelligence, accessed September 04, 2019), London (UK): Pearson Education.

Intelligence 2019a. In *Wordsmyth* (https://www.wordsmyth.net/?level=3&ent=intelligence, accessed September 04, 2019).

Intelligence 2019b. In *Wiktionary* (https://en.wiktionary.org/wiki/intelligence, accessed September 05, 2019).

Jamson, S. L., Hibberd, D. L., and Jamson, A. H. 2015. "Drivers' ability to learn eco-driving skills; effects on fuel efficient and safe driving behaviour," *Transportation Research Part C: Emerging Technologies* (58), pp. 657-668.

Janzen, H., Obrzut, J., and Marusiak, C. 2004. "Test review: Roid, G. H. (2003). Stanford–binet intelligence scales, (SB:V)," *Canadian Journal of School Psychology* (19:1-2), pp. 235-244.

Jozefowicz, R., Zaremba, W., and Sutskever, I. 2015. "An empirical exploration of recurrent network architectures," in *Proceedings of the 32nd International Conference on Machine Learning*, pp. 2342-2350.

Kane, G. C., and Labianca, G. 2011. "Is Avoidance in Health-Care Groups: A Multilevel Investigation," *Information Systems Research* (22:3), pp. 504-522.

Kaplan, D. 2008. *Structural equation modeling: Foundations and extensions, Second Edition*, Thousand Oaks (USA): Sage Publications.

Kaufman, A. S. 2016. *Intelligent Testing with the WISC-V*, New York (USA): Wiley.

Ketter, W., Peters, M., Collins, J., and Gupta, A. 2016. "Competitive benchmarking: An IS research approach to address wicked problems with big data and analytics," *Management Information Systems Quarterly* (40:4), pp. 1057-1080.

Khalid, S., Khalil, T., and Nasreen, S. 2014. "A survey of feature selection and feature extraction techniques in machine learning," in *Proceedings of the IEEE Science and Information Conference*, pp. 372-378.

Khosla, A., Cao, Y., Lin, C. C. Y., Chiu, H. K., Hu, J., and Lee, H. 2010. "An integrated machine learning approach to stroke prediction," *Proceedings of the 16th ACM SIGKDD international conference on Knowledge discovery and data mining*, pp. 183-192.

Kim, J., Lim, S., Lee, B., and Lee, J. W. 2015. "Detecting Depression of Cancer Patients with Daily Mental Health Logs from Mobile Applications," in *Proceedings of the Thirty Sixth International Conference on Information Systems*, pp. 1-20.

Kiron, D., Shockley, R., Kruschwitz, N., Finch, G., and Haydock, M. 2012. "Analytics: The widening divide," MIT Sloan Management Review (53:2), pp. 1-21.

Kitchin, R. 2014. "Big data, new epistemologies and paradigm shifts," *Big Data & Society* (1:1), pp. 1-12.

Kohl, C., Mostafa, D., Böhm, M., and Krcmar, H. 2017. "Disruption of individual mobility ahead? A longitudinal study of risk and benefit perceptions of self-driving cars on Twitter," in *Proceedings of the 13th International Conference on Wirtschaftsinformatik*, pp. 1220-1234.

Kohli, R., and Tan, S. S.-L. 2016. "Electronic Health Records: How Can Is Researchers Contribute to Transforming Healthcare?," *Management Information Systems Quarterly* (40:3), pp. 553-573.

Koren, Y., Bell, R., and Volinsky, C. 2009. "Matrix factorization techniques for recommender systems," *Computer* (42:8), pp. 30-37.

Kornhauser, A., Chang, A., Clark, C., Gao, J., Korac, D., Lebowitz, B., and Swoboda, A. 2013. "Uncongested mobility for all: New Jersey's area-wide aTaxi system" (orfe.princeton.edu/~alaink/NJ_aTaxiOrf467F12/ORF467F12aTaxiFinalReport_Draft.pdf, accessed May 15, 2019).

Koukal, A., Gleue, C., and Breitner, M. 2014. "Enhancing Literature Review Methods- Evaluation of a Literature Search Approach based on Latent Semantic Indexing," in *Proceedings of the Thirty Fifth International Conference on Information Systems*, pp. 1-20.

Kovacs, A. F., Megahed, W., Scholz, M., and Sader, R. 2007. "Survival Improvement of a Unicentric Overall Population in 20 Years: 1038 Patients with Oral and Oropharyngeal

Squamous Cell Cancer 1983-2004," *Mund-, Kiefer- und Gesichtschirurgie: MKG* (11:5), pp. 267-283.

Krizhevsky, A., Sutskever, I., and Hinton, G. E. 2012. "Imagenet classification with deep convolutional neural networks," in *Proceedings of the 25th International Conference on Neural Information Processing Systems*, pp. 1097-1105.

Kruse, C. S., Goswamy, R., Raval, Y., and Marawi, S. 2016. "Challenges and Opportunities of Big Data in Health Care: A Systematic Review," *JMIR Medical Informatics* (4:4), pp. 1-11.

Kulkarni, U. R., Robles-Flores, J. A., and Popovič, A. 2017. "Business intelligence capability: the effect of top management and the mediating roles of user participation and analytical decision making orientation," *Journal of the Association for Information Systems* (18:7), pp. 516-541.

Kuderer, M., Gulati, S., and Burgard, W. 2015. "Learning driving styles for autonomous vehicles from demonstration," in *Proceedings of the IEEE International Conference on Robotics and Automation*, pp. 2641-2646.

Lang, K., Shang, R., and Vragov, R. 2013. "Consumer co-creation of digital culture products: Business threats or new opportunity?," *Journal of the Association for Information Systems* (16:9), pp. 766-798.

LaValle, S., Lesser, E., Shockley, R., Hopkins, M. S., and Kruschwitz, N. 2011. "Big data, analytics and the path from insights to value," *MIT Sloan Management Review* (52:2), pp. 21-32.

Le, Q., and Mikolov, T. 2014. "Distributed representations of sentences and documents," in *Proceedings of the International Conference on Machine Learning*, pp. 1188-1196.

LeCun, Y. A., Bottou, L., Orr, G. B., and Müller, K. R. 2012. "Efficient BackProp," in *Neural Networks: Tricks of the Trade*, G. Montavon, G. B. Orr, K.-R. Müller (eds.), Berlin, Heidelberg (Germany): Springer, pp. 9-48.

LeCun, Y., and Bengio, Y. 1995. "Convolutional networks for images, speech, and time-series," in *The handbook of brain theory and neural networks*, M. A. Arbib (ed.), Cambridge (USA), London (UK): MIT Press, pp. 276-278.

Lee, J. G., Kim, K. J., Lee, S., and Shin, D. H. 2015. "Can autonomous vehicles be safe and trustworthy? Effects of appearance and autonomy of unmanned driving systems," *International Journal of Human-Computer Interaction* (31:10), pp. 682-691.

Lefèvre, S., Carvalho, A., Gao, Y., Tseng, H. E., and Borrelli, F. 2015. "Driver models for personalised driving assistance," *Vehicle System Dynamics* (53:12), pp. 1705-1720.

Legendre, A. M. 1806. *Nouvelles méthodes pour la determination des orbites des comètes*, Paris (France): Firmin Didot.

Levinson, J., Askeland, J., Becker, J., Dolson, J., Held, D., Kammel, S., Kolter, J. Z., Langer, D., Pink, O., Pratt, V., Sokolsky, M., Stanek, G., Stavens, D., Teichman, A., Werling, M., and Thrun, S. 2011. "Towards fully autonomous driving: Systems and algorithms," in *Proceedings of the IEEE Intelligent Vehicles Symposium*, pp. 163-168.

Li, H., Cao, J. N., and Love, P. E. D. 1999. "Using machine learning and GA to solve time-cost trade-off problems," *Journal of Construction Engineering and Management* (125:5), pp. 347-353.

Li, Q., Chen, L., Li, M., Shaw, S. L., and Nüchter, A. 2014. "A sensor-fusion drivable-region and lane-detection system for autonomous vehicle navigation in challenging road scenarios," *IEEE Transactions on Vehicular Technology* (63:2), pp. 540-555.

Li, S. S., and Karahanna, E. 2015. "Online recommendation systems in a B2C E-commerce context: a review and future directions," *Journal of the Association for Information Systems* (16:2), pp. 72-107.

Li, Q., Zheng, N., and Cheng, H. 2004. Springrobot: "A prototype autonomous vehicle and its algorithms for lane detection," *IEEE Transactions on Intelligent Transportation Systems* (5:4), pp. 300-308.

Liang, T. P., Lai, H. J., and Ku, Y. C. 2006. "Personalized content recommendation and user satisfaction: Theoretical synthesis and empirical findings," *Journal of Management Information Systems* (23:3), pp. 45-70.

Lin, Y. K., Chen, H., and Brown, R. A. 2013. "MedTime: A temporal information extraction system for clinical narratives," *Journal of Biomedical Informatics* (46), pp. S20-S28.

Lin, Y. K., Chen, H., Brown, R. A., Li, S. H., and Yang, H. J. 2014. "Time-to-event predictive modeling for chronic conditions using electronic health records," *IEEE Intelligent Systems* (29:3), pp. 14-20.

Lin, Y.-K., Chen, H., Brown, R. A., Li, S.-H., and Yang, H.-J. 2017. "Healthcare Predictive Analytics for Risk Profiling in Chronic Care: A Bayesian Multitask Learning Approach " *Management Information Systems Quarterly* (41:2), pp. 473-496.

Linnainmaa, S. 1976. "Taylor expansion of the accumulated rounding error," *BIT Numerical Mathematics* (16:2), pp. 146-160.

Lloyd, S. P. 1982. "Least squares quantization in PCM," *IEEE Transactions on Information Theory* (28:2), pp. 129-136.

Loebbecke, C., and Picot, A. 2015. "Reflections on societal and business model transformation arising from digitization and big data analytics: A research agenda," *The Journal of Strategic Information Systems* (24:3), pp. 149-157.

Lucas Jr, H. C., Agarwal, R., Clemons, E. K., El Sawy, O. A., and Weber, B. W. 2013. "Impactful Research on Transformational Information Technology: An Opportunity to Inform New Audiences," *Management Information Systems Quarterly* (37:2), pp. 371-382.

Lycett, M. 2013. "'Datafication': Making sense of (big) data in a complex world," *European Journal of Information Systems* (22:4), pp. 381-386.

Ma, X., Tao, Z., Wang, Y., Yu, H., and Wang, Y. 2015. "Long short-term memory neural network for traffic speed prediction using remote microwave sensor data," *Transportation Research Part C: Emerging Technologies* (54), pp. 187-197.

Majchrzak, A., Markus, M. L., and Wareham, J. 2016. "Designing for Digital Transformation: Lessons for Information Systems Research from the Study of ICT and Societal Challenges," *Management Information Systems Quarterly* (40:2), pp. 267-277.

Margulieux, L. E., Guzdial, M., and Catrambone, R. 2012. "Subgoal-labeled instructional material improves performance and transfer in learning to develop mobile applications," In Proceedings of the Ninth Annual International Conference on International Computing Education Research, pp. 71-78.

Markus, M. L. 2015. "New games, new rules, new scoreboards: the potential consequences of big data," *Journal of Information Technology* (30:1), pp. 58-59.

Martens, D., Provost, F., Clark, J., and de Fortuny, E. J. 2016. "Mining Massive Fine-Grained Behavior Data to Improve Predictive Analytics," *Management of Information Systems Quarterly* (40:4), pp. 869-888.

Masaki, I. (1992). *Vision-Based Vehicle Guidance*, New York (USA): Springer.

Mayo, R. M., Summey, J. F., Williams, J. E., Spence, R. A., Kim, S., and Jagsi, R. 2017. "Qualitative Study of Oncologists' Views on the Cancerlinq Rapid Learning System," *Journal of Oncology Practice* (13:3), pp. e176-e184.

McAfee, A., and Brynjolfsson, E. 2012. "Big data: the management revolution," *Harvard Business Review* (90:10), pp. 60-68.

McDermott, D. 1976. "Artificial intelligence meets natural stupidity," *SIGART Newsletter* (57), pp. 4-9.

Medhi Thies, I., Menon, N., Magapu, S., and Subramony, M. 2017. "How do you want your chatbot? An exploratory wizard-of-oz study with young, urban Indians," *16th IFIP TC 13 International Conference*, pp. 441-459.

Mertens, P., and Barbian, D. 2015. "Researching 'grand challenges'," *Business & Information Systems Engineering* (57:6), pp. 391-403.

Mery, B., Rancoule, C., Guy, J. B., Espenel, S., Wozny, A. S., Battiston-Montagne, P., Ardail, D., Beuve, M., Alphonse, G., Rodriguez-Lafrasse, C., and Magne, N. 2017. "Preclinical Models in Hnscc: A Comprehensive Review," *Oral Oncology* (65), pp. 51-56.

Metcalf, L., Askay, D. A., and Rosenberg, L. B. 2019. "Keeping Humans in the Loop: Pooling Knowledge through Artificial Swarm Intelligence to Improve Business Decision Making," *California Management Review* (61:4), pp. 84-109.

Meyer, G., Adomavicius, G., Johnson, P. E., Elidrisi, M., Rush, W. A., Sperl-Hillen, J. M., and O'Connor, P. J. 2014. "A machine learning approach to improving dynamic decision making," *Information Systems Research* (25:2), pp. 239-263.

Mikolov, T., Chen, K., Corrado, G., and Dean, J. 2013. "Efficient estimation of word representations in vector space," (https://arxiv.org/abs/1301.3781, accessed July 29, 2019).

Mikolov, T., Sutskever, I., Chen, K., Corrado, G. S., and Dean, J. 2013. "Distributed representations of words and phrases and their compositionality," in *Proceedings of 26th International Conference on Neural Information Processing Systems*, pp. 3111-3119.

Montoya-Weiss, M. M., Voss, G. B., and Grewal, D. 2003. "Determinants of online channel use and overall satisfaction with a relational, multichannel service provider," *Journal of the Academy of Marketing Science* (31:4), pp. 448-458.

Morales, J., Martínez, J. L., Martínez, M. A., and Mandow, A. 2009. "Pure-pursuit reactive path tracking for nonholonomic mobile robots with a 2D laser scanner," *EURASIP Journal on Advances in Signal Processing* (2009:935237), pp. 1-10.

Morimoto, J., and Doya, K. 2001. "Acquisition of stand-up behavior by a real robot using hierarchical reinforcement learning," *Robotics and Autonomous Systems* (36:1), pp. 37-51.

Moy, J. D., Moskovitz, J. M., and Ferris, R. L. 2017. "Biological Mechanisms of Immune Escape and Implications for Immunotherapy in Head and Neck Squamous Cell Carcinoma," *European Journal of Cancer* (76), pp. 152-166.

Muehlfeld, F., Doric, I., Ertlmeier, R., and Brandmeier, T. 2013. "Statistical behavior modeling for driver-adaptive precrash systems," *IEEE Transactions on Intelligent Transportation Systems* (14:4), pp. 1764-1772.

Müller, O., Junglas, I., Brocke, J. V., and Debortoli, S. 2016. "Utilizing big data analytics for information systems research: challenges, promises and guidelines," *European Journal of Information Systems* (25:4), pp. 289-302.

Muus, K. J., Knudson, A., Klug, M. G., Gokun, J., Sarrazin, M., and Kaboli, P. 2010. "Effect of post-discharge follow-up care on re-admissions among US veterans with congestive heart failure: a rural-urban comparison," *International Journal of Rural Remote Health* (10:1447), pp. 1-11.

National Highway Traffic Safety Administration 2017. "Automated driving systems 2.0. A vision for safety," (nhtsa.gov/sites/nhtsa.dot.gov/files/documents/13069a-ads2.0_090617_v9a_tag.pdf, accessed July 18, 2019).

Neisser, U., Boodoo, G., Bouchard Jr., T. J., Boykin, A. W., Brody, N., Ceci, S. J., Halpern, D. F., Loehlin, J. C., Perloff, R., Sternberg, R. J., and Urbina, S. 1996. "Intelligence: Knowns and unknowns," *American Psychologist* (51:2), pp. 77-101.

Nekhlyudov, L., Lacchetti, C., Davis, N. B., Garvey, T. Q., Goldstein, D. P., Nunnink, J. C., Ninfea, J. I., Salner, A. L., Salz, T., and Siu, L. L. 2017. "Head and Neck Cancer Survivorship Care Guideline: American Society of Clinical Oncology Clinical Practice Guideline Endorsement of the American Cancer Society Guideline," *Journal of Clinical Oncology* (35:14), pp. 1606-1621.

Newell, S., and Marabelli, M. 2015. "Strategic opportunities (and challenges) of algorithmic decision-making: A call for action on the long-term societal effects of 'datification'," *The Journal of Strategic Information Systems* (24:1), pp. 3-14.

Newell, A., Shaw, J.C., Simon, H.A. 1959. "Report on a general problem-solving program," in *Proceedings of the 1st International Conference on Information Processing*, pp. 256-264.

Nimavat, K., and Champaneria, T. 2017. "Chatbots: An overview. Types, architectures, tools and future possibilities," *International Journal for Scientific Research & Development* (5:7), pp. 1019-1026.

Parasuraman, R., Sheridan, T. B., and Wickens, C. D. 2000. "A model for types and levels of human interaction with automation," *IEEE Transactions on systems, man, and cybernetics-Part A: Systems and Humans* (30:3), pp. 286-297.

Parker, G. G., Van Alstyne, M. W., and Choudary, S. P. 2016. *Platform Revolution: How Networked Markets Are Transforming the Economy and How to Make Them Work for You*, New York (USA), London (UK): WW Norton & Company.

Payne, A., and Frow, P. 2017. "Relationship marketing: looking backwards towards the future," *Journal of Services Marketing* (31:1), pp. 11-15.

Pazzani, M. J., and Billsus, D. 2007. "Content-based recommendation systems," in *The adaptive web*, P. Brusilovsky, A. Kobsa and W. Nejdl (eds.), Berlin, Heidelberg (Germany): Springer, pp. 325-341.

Pelleg, D., and Moore, A. W. 2000. "X-means: Extending K-means with Efficient Estimation of the Number of Clusters," in *Proceedings of the 17th International Conference on Machine Learning*, pp. 727-734.

Pfeifer, R., and Bongard, J. 2006. *How the body shapes the way we think: a new view of intelligence*, Cambridge (USA): MIT Press.

Piel, J. H., Hamann, J. F., Koukal, A., and Breitner, M. H. 2017. "Promoting the System Integration of Renewable Energies: Toward a Decision Support System for Incentivizing Spatially Diversified Deployment," *Journal of Management Information Systems* (34:4), pp. 994-1022.

Pratt, L. Y. 1993. "Discriminability-based transfer between neural networks," in *Proceedings of the 6th Internationa Conference on Neural Information Processing Systems*, pp. 204-211.

Pratt, L. Y., Hanson, S., Giles, C., and Cowan, J. 1992. "Discriminability-based transfer between neural networks," in *Proceedings of the 5th International Conference on Neural Information Processing Systems*, pp. 204-204.

Priem, R. L., Butler, J. E., and Li, S. 2013. "Toward reimagining strategy research: retrospection and prospection on the 2011 AMR decade award article," *Academy of Management Review* (38:4), pp. 471-489.

Puccinelli, N. M., Goodstein, R. C., Grewal, D., Price, R., Raghubir, P., and Stewart, D. 2009. "Customer experience management in retailing: understanding the buying process," *Journal of Retailing* (85:1), pp. 15-30.

Putnam, H., 1967. "Psychophysical Predicates", in *Art, Mind, and Religion*, W. Capitan and D. Merrill (eds), Pittsburgh (USA): University of Pittsburgh Press, pp. 37-48.

Quionero-Candela, J., Sugiyama, M., Schwaighofer, A., and Lawrence, N. D. 2009. *Dataset Shift in Machine Learning*, Cambridge (USA), London (UK): MIT Press.

Rahman, M. M., and Davis, D. N. 2013. "Addressing the class imbalance problem in medical datasets," *International Journal of Machine Learning and Computing* (3:2), pp. 224-228.

Rai, A. 2016. "Editor's comments: Synergies between big data and theory," *Management Information Systems Quarterly* (40:2), pp. iii-ix.

Reynolds, C. W. 1987. "Flocks, herds and schools: A distributed behavioral model," *Computer Graphics* (21:4), pp. 25-34.

Ricci, F., Rokach, L., and Shapira, B. 2011. "Introduction to recommender systems handbook," in *Recommender systems handbook*, F. Ricci, L. Rokach, B. Shapira and P. B. Kantor (eds.), Boston (USA): Springer, pp. 1-35.

Rochet, J. C., and Tirole, J. 2003. "Platform competition in two-sided markets," *Journal of the European economic association* (1:4), 990-1029.

Romanow, D., Cho, S., and Straub, D. 2012. "Editor's Comments: Riding the Wave: Past Trends and Future Directions for Health It Research," *Management Information Systems Quarterly* (36:3), pp. iii-x.

Rosenberg, L., and Pescetelli, N. 2017. "Amplifying prediction accuracy using Swarm A.I.," in *Proceedings of the 2017 Intelligent Systems Conference (IntelliSys)*, pp. 61-65.

Rosenblatt, F. 1958. "The Perceptron: A Probabilistic Model For Information Storage And Organization In The Brain," *Psychological Review* (65:6), pp. 386-408.

Rosenfeld, A., Bareket, Z., Goldman, C. V., LeBlanc, D. J., and Tsimhoni, O. 2015. "Learning drivers' behavior to improve adaptive cruise control," *Journal of Intelligent Transportation Systems* (19:1), pp. 18-31.

Roweis, S. T., and Saul, L. K. 2000. "Nonlinear dimensionality reduction by locally linear embedding," *Science* (290:5500), pp. 2323-2326.

Russell, S., and Norvig, P. 2010. *Artificial intelligence – a modern approach, 3rd ed.*, New Jersey (USA): Pearson Education, Inc..

SAE International 2016. "Taxonomy and Definitions for Terms Related to Driving Automation Systems for On-Road Motor Vehicles ," (sae.org/standards/content/j3016_201609, accessed July 18, 2019).

Sak, H., Senior, A., and Beaufays, F. 2014. "Long short-term memory recurrent neural network architectures for large scale acoustic modeling," in *Proceedings of the Fifteenth Annual Conference of the International Speech Communication Association*, pp. 338-342.

Salakhutdinov, R., and Hinton, G. E. 2009. "Deep boltzmann machines," in *Proceedings of the Twelfth International Conference on Artificial Intelligence and Statistics*, pp. 448-455).

Sano, A., Amy, Z. Y., McHill, A. W., Phillips, A. J., Taylor, S., Jaques, N., Klerman, E. B., and Picard, R. W. 2015. "Prediction of happy-sad mood from daily behaviors and previous sleep history," in *Proceedings of the 37th International Conference of the IEEE Engineering in Medicine and Biology Society (EMBC)* pp. 6796-6799.

Schapire, R. E. 1990. "The strength of weak learnability," *Machine learning* (5:2), pp. 197-227.

Schepers, R. H., Raghoebar, G. M., Vissink, A., Lahoda, L. U., Van der Meer, W. J., Roodenburg, J. L., Reintsema, H., and Witjes, M. J. 2013. "Fully 3-Dimensional Digitally Planned Reconstruction of a Mandible with a Free Vascularized Fibula and Immediate Placement of an Implant-Supported Prosthetic Construction," *Head & Neck* (35:4), pp. E109-114.

Schilsky, R. L., Michels, D. L., Kearbey, A. H., Yu, P. P., and Hudis, C. A. 2014. "Building a Rapid Learning Health Care System for Oncology: The Regulatory Framework of Cancerlinq," *Journal of Clinical Oncology* (32:22), pp. 2373-2379.

Schneider, C., Weinmann, M., and vom Brocke, J. 2018. "Digital Nudging – Guiding Choices by Using Interface Design," *Communications of the ACM* (61:7), pp. 67-73.

Schultz, A., and Grefenstette, J. 1992. "Using a genetic algorithm to learn behaviors for autonomous vehicles," in *Proceedings of the Guidance, Navigation and Control Conference,* pp. 739-749.

Schwarz, G. E. 1978. "Estimating the dimension of a model," *Annals of Statistics* (6:2), pp. 461-464.

Searle, J. R. 1980. "Minds, brains, and programs," *Behavioral and Brain Sciences* (3:3), pp. 417-424.

Sein, M., Henfridsson, O., Purao, S., Rossi, M., and Lindgren, R. 2011. "Action design research," *Management Information Systems Quarterly* (35:1), pp. 37-56.

Sharma, R., Mithas, S., and Kankanhalli, A. 2014. "Transforming decision-making processes: a research agenda for understanding the impact of business analytics on organisations," European Journal of Information Systems (23:4), pp. 433-441.

Shin, H.-C., Roth, H. R., Gao, M., Lu, L., Xu, Z., Nogues, I., Yao, J., Mollura, D., and Summers, R. M. (2016). Deep convolutional neural networks for computer-aided detection: CNN architectures, dataset characteristics and transfer learning. IEEE transactions on medical imaging, 35(5), 1285-1298.

Shmueli, G. 2010. "To explain or to predict?," Statistical science (25:3), pp. 289-310.

Shmueli, G., and Koppius, O. R. 2011. "Predictive analytics in information systems research," Management Information Systems Quarterly (35:3), pp. 553-572.

Simon, H. 1996. *The Sciences of the Artificial, Third Edition.* Cmbridge (USA), London (UK): MIT Press.

Smith, A., and Krueger, A. B. 2003. *The Wealth of Nations.* New York (USA): Bantam Classics.

Smith, B., and Linden, G. 2017. "Two decades of recommender systems at Amazon.com," *IEEE Internet Computing* (21:3), pp. 12-18.

Sorzano, C. O. S., Vargas, J., and Montano, A. P. 2014. "A survey of dimensionality reduction techniques," (https://arxiv.org/abs/1403.2877, accessed July 29, 2019).

Stilgoe, J. 2017. "Machine learning, social learning and the governance of self-driving cars," *Social Studies of Science* (48:1), pp. 25-56.

Stoekle, H. C., Mamzer-Bruneel, M. F., Frouart, C. H., Le Tourneau, C., Laurent-Puig, P., Vogt, G., and Herve, C. 2017. "Molecular Tumor Boards: Ethical Issues in the New Era of Data Medicine," *Science and Engineering Ethics* (24:1), pp. 307-322.

Su, X., and Khoshgoftaar, T. M. 2009. "A survey of collaborative filtering techniques," *Advances in Artificial Intelligence* (4), pp. 14-32.

Tammemägi, M. C., Katki, H. A., Hocking, W. G., Church, T. R., Caporaso, N., Kvale, P. A., Chaturvedi, A. K., Silvestri, G. A., Riley, T. L., Commins, J., and Berg, C. D. 2013. "Selection criteria for lung-cancer screening," *New England Journal of Medicine* (368:8), pp. 728-736.

Tan, A.-H., and Lai, F.-L. 2000. "Text categorization, supervised learning, and domain knowledge integration," in *Proceedings of the KDD-2000 International Workshop on Text Mining*, pp. 113-114.

Tang, J., Hu, X., and Liu, H. 2013. "Social recommendation: a review," *Social Network Analysis and Mining* (3:4), pp. 1113-1133.

Tavanapour, N. and Bittner, E. A. C. 2018. "Automated facilitation for idea platforms: Design and evaluation of a chatbots prototype," in *Proceedings of the Thirty Ninth International Conference on Information Systems*, pp. 1-9.

Tenenbaum, J. B., De Silva, V., and Langford, J. C. 2000. "A global geometric framework for nonlinear dimensionality reduction," *Science* (290:5500), pp. 2319-2323.

Teubner, T., and Flath, C. M. 2015. "The economics of multi-hop ride sharing," *Business & Information Systems Engineering* (57:5), pp. 311-324.

Thaler, R. H., and Sunstein, C. R. 2008. *Nudge: Improving decisions about health, wealth, and happiness*, New Haven (USA): Yale University Press.

Thongpapanl, N., and Ashraf, A. R. 2011. "Enhancing online performance through website content and personalization," *Journal of Computer Information Systems* (52:1), pp. 3-13.

Thurstone, L. L. 1924. *The nature of intelligence*, London (UK): Kegan Paul, Trench Trubner & Co..

Tibshirani, R. 1996. "Regression Shrinkage and Selection via the Lasso," *Journal of the Royal Statistical Society. Series B (Methodological)* (58:1), pp. 267-288

Tikhonov, A. N. 1963. "О решении некорректно поставленных задач и методе регуляризации," Doklady Akademii Nauk SSSR. 151: 501–504. Translated in "Solution of incorrectly formulated problems and the regularization method," *Soviet Mathematics* (4), pp. 1035-1038

Tilson, D., Lyytinen, K., and Sørensen, C. 2010. "Research commentary – digital infrastructures: The missing IS research agenda," *Information Systems Research* (21:4), pp. 748-759.

Tofangchi, S., Hanelt, A., Kolbe, L. 2017. Towards Distributed Cognitive Expert Systems, in *Proceedings of the Twelfth International Conference on Design Science Research in Information Systems and Technology*, pp. 145-159.

Tofangchi, S., Hanelt, A., and Böhrnsen, F. 2017. "Distributed cognitive expert systems in cancer data analytics: A decision support system for oral and maxillofacial surgery," in *Proceedings of the Thirty-Eighth International Conference on Information Systems*, pp. 1-21.

Traumer, F., Oeste-Reiß, S., and Leimeister, J. M. 2017. "Towards a future reallocation of work between humans and machines – taxonomy of tasks and interaction types in the context of machine learning," in *Proceedings of the Thirty-Eighth International Conference on Information Systems*, pp. 1-11.

Tumbas, S., Berente, N., and vom Brocke, J. 2017. "Born digital: growth trajectories of entrepreneurial organizations spanning institutional fields," in *Proceedings of the Thirty-Eighth International Conference on Information Systems*, pp. 1-20.

Turing, A. M. 1950. "Computing machinery and intelligence," *Mind* (59:236), pp. 433-460.

Valdes, G., Solberg, T. D., Heskel, M., Ungar, L., and Simone, C. B., 2nd. 2016. "Using Machine Learning to Predict Radiation Pneumonitis in Patients with Stage I Non-Small Cell Lung Cancer Treated with Stereotactic Body Radiation Therapy," *Physics in Medicine & Biolology* (61:16), pp. 6105-6120.

Van den Poel, D., and Lariviere, B. 2004. "Customer attrition analysis for financial services using proportional hazard models," *European Journal of Operational Research* (157:1), pp. 196-217.

van der Maaten, L., and Hinton, G. 2008. "Visualizing data using t-SNE," *Journal of machine learning research (9)*, pp. 2579-2605.

Varma, M., and Ray, D. 2007. "Learning the discriminative power-invariance trade-off," In *Proceedings of the 11th IEEE International Conference on Computer Vision*, pp. 1-8.

Vaughan, A., and Bohac, S. V. 2015. "Real-time, adaptive machine learning for non-stationary, near chaotic gasoline engine combustion time series," *Neural Networks* (70), pp. 18-26.

Venkatesh, V., Aloysius, J. A., Hoehle, H., and Burton, S. 2017. "Design and Evaluation of Auto-ID Enabled Shopping Assistance Artifacts in Customers' Mobile Phones: Two Retail

Store Laboratory Experiments," *Management Information Systems Quarterly* (41:1), pp. 83-113.

Venkatesh, V., Morris, M. G., Davis, G. B., and Davis, F. D. 2003. "User acceptance of information technology: Toward a unified view," *Management Information Systems Quarterly* (27:3), pp. 425-478.

Venkatesh, V., Zhang, X., and Sykes, T. A. 2011. "Doctors Do Too Little Technology": A Longitudinal Field Study of an Electronic Healthcare System Implementation," *Information Systems Research* (22:3), pp. 523-546.

Verhoef, P. C., Lemon, K. N., Parasuraman, A., Roggeveen, A., Tsiros, M., and Schlesinger, L. A. 2009. "Customer experience creation: Determinants, dynamics and management strategies," *Journal of Retailing* (85:1), pp. 31-41.

Verschure, P. F., Kröse, B. J., and Pfeifer, R. 1992. "Distributed adaptive control: The self-organization of structured behavior," *Robotics and Autonomous Systems* (9:3), pp. 181-196.

Vodanovich, S., Sundaram, D., and Myers, M. 2010. "Research commentary—digital natives and ubiquitous information systems," *Information Systems Research* (21:4), pp. 711-723.

vom Brocke, J., Simons, A., Riemer, K., Niehaves, B., Plattfaut, R., and Cleven, A. 2015. "Standing on the shoulders of giants: challenges and recommendations of literature search in information systems research," *Communications of the Association for Information Systems* (37:1), pp. 205-224.

Wagner, S., Willing, C., Brandt, T., and Neumann, D. 2015. "Data analytics for location-based services: enabling user-based relocation of Carsharing vehicles," in *Proceedings of the Thirty Sixth International Conference on Information Systems*, pp. 1-16.

Wang, W., and Benbasat, I. 2007. "Recommendation agents for electronic commerce: Effects of explanation facilities on trusting beliefs," *Journal of Management Information Systems* (23:4), pp. 217-246.

Wang, J., Yu, C., Li, S. E., and Wang, L. 2016. "A forward collision warning algorithm with adaptation to driver behaviors," *IEEE Transactions on Intelligent Transportation Systems* (17:4), pp. 1157-1167.

Wang, J., Zhang, L., Zhang, D., and Li, K. 2013. "An adaptive longitudinal driving assistance system based on driver characteristics," *IEEE Transactions on Intelligent Transportation Systems* (14:1), pp. 1-12.

Ward, Michael J., Keith A. Marsolo, and Craig M. Froehle. 2014. "Applications of Business Analytics in Healthcare." *Business Horizons* (57:5), pp. 571-582.

Watkins, C. J. C. H. 1989. *Learning from delayed rewards*, King's College: Cambridge.

Watson, R. T., Boudreau, M. C., and Chen, A. J. 2010. "Information systems and environmentally sustainable development: energy informatics and new directions for the IS community," *Management Information Systems Quarterly* (34:1), pp. 23-38.

Waytz, A., Heafner, J., and Epley, N. 2014. "The mind in the machine: Anthropomorphism increases trust in an autonomous vehicle," *Journal of Experimental Social Psychology* (52), pp. 113-117.

Weber, T. A. 2014. "Intermediation in a sharing economy: insurance, moral hazard, and rent extraction," *Journal of Management Information Systems* (31:3), pp. 35-71.

Weber, T. A. 2017. "Smart products for sharing," *Journal of Management Information Systems* (34:2), pp. 341-368.

Weigel, F. K., Rainer Jr, R. K., Hazen, B. T., Cegielski, C. G., and Ford, F. N. 2013. "Uncovering Research Opportunities in the Medical Informatics Field: A Quantitative Content Analysis," *Communications of the Association for Information Systems* (33:1), pp. 15-32.

Weinmann, M., Schneider, C., and vom Brocke, J. 2016. "Digital nudging," *Business & Information Systems Engineering* (58:6), pp. 433-436.

Wells, J. B., Nowacki, A. S., Chagin, K., Kattan, M. W. 2013. "Strategies for Handling Missing Data in Electronic Health Record Derived Data," *Generating Evidence & Methods to improve patient outcomes* (1:3), Article 7.

Werbos, P. 1974. *Beyond Regression: New Tools for Prediction and Analysis in the Behavioral Sciences.* Ph. D. dissertation, Harvard University.

Wheeler, W. M. 1911. "The Ant-Colony as an Organism," *Journal of Morphology* (22), pp. 307-325.

Wit, J., Crane III, C. D., and Armstrong, D. 2004. "Autonomous ground vehicle path tracking," *Journal of Robotic Systems* (21:8), 439-449.

Woerner, S. L., and Wixom, B. H. 2015. "Big data: extending the business strategy toolbox," *Journal of Information Technology* (30:1), pp. 60-62.

Wolff K.-D., B. F., Beck J., Bikowski K., Böhme P., Budach W., Burkhardt A., Danker, H., E. W., Engers K., Fietkau R., Frerich B., Gauler T., Germann G., Gittler-Hebestreit, N., G. K., Horch R., Ihrler S., Keilholz U., Lell M., Lübbe A., Mantey W.,, Nusser-Müller-Busch R., P. H., Paradies K., Reichert T., Reinert S., Schliephake H.,, and Schmitter M., S. S., Westhofen M., Wirz S., Wittlinger M. 2012. "Diagnostik Und Therapie Des Mundhöhlenkarzinoms (2.0 ed.)," Berlin (Germany): AWMW, Deutsche Krebsgesellschaft e.V., Deutsche Krebshilfe e.V.

Wynn, D., and Williams, C. K. 2012. "Principles for Conducting Critical Realist Case Study Research in Information Systems," *Management Information Systems Quarterly* (36:3), pp. 787-810.

Xu, Z., Li, S., and Deng, W. 2015. "Learning temporal features using LSTM-CNN architecture for face anti-spoofing," in *Proceedings of the 3rd Asian Conference on Pattern Recognition*, pp. 141-145.

Yang, H., Xu, Z., King, I., Lyu, M. R. 2010. "Online learning for group lasso," in *Proceedings of the 27th International Conference on Machine Learning*, pp. 191-1998.

Yarbrough, A. K., and Smith, T. B. 2007. "Technology acceptance among physicians: a new take on TAM," *Medical Care Research and Review* (64:6), pp. 650-672.

Yeow, A., and Goh, K. H. 2015. "Work Harder or Work Smarter? Information Technology and Resource Allocation in Healthcare Processes," *Management Information Systems Quarterly* (39:4), pp. 763-785.

Yi, S. K. M., Steyvers, M., Lee, M. D. and Dry, M. J. 2012. "The Wisdom of the Crowd in Combinatorial Problems," *Cognitive Science* (36:3), *pp. 452-470.*

Yoo, Y. 2010. "Computing in everyday life: A call for research on experiential computing," *Management Information Systems Quarterly* (34:2), pp. 213-231.

Yoo, Y. 2015. "It is not about size: a further thought on big data," Journal of Information Technology (30:1), pp. 63-65.

Yoo, Y., Henfridsson, O., and Lyytinen, K. 2010. "Research commentary – the new organizing logic of digital innovation: an agenda for information systems research," *Information Systems Research* (21:4), pp. 724-735.

Yu, P., Artz, D., and Warner, J. 2014. "Electronic Health Records (EHRs): Supporting Asco's Vision of Cancer Care," *ASCO Educational Book* (34), pp. 225-231.

Zhang, W., Guhathakurta, S., Fang, J., and Zhang, G. 2015. "Exploring the impact of shared autonomous vehicles on urban parking demand: An agent-based simulation approach," *Sustainable Cities and Society* (19), pp. 34-45.

Zhao, Y. 1997. *Vehicle location and navigation systems*, Norwood (USA): Artech House Publishers.

Zhou, S., Jiang, Y., Xi, J., Gong, J., Xiong, G., and Chen, H. 2010. "A novel lane detection based on geometrical model and gabor filter," in *Proceedings of the IEEE Intelligent vehicles symposium,* pp. 59-64.

Zhou, Z.-H. 2012. *Ensemble methods: foundations and algorithms*, Boca Raton (USA): CRC press.

Zhou, Y., Wilkinson, D., Schreiber, R., and Pan, R. 2008. "Large-scale parallel collaborative filtering for the Netflix prize," in *Proceedings of the 4th International Conference on Algorithmic Applications in Management,* pp. 337-348.

Zhuang, Z. Y., Wilkin, C. L., and Ceglowski, A. 2013. "A Framework for an Intelligent Decision Support System: A Case in Pathology Test Ordering," *Decision Support Systems* (55:2), pp. 476-487.

Appendix

The following table shows the author's contribution to the individual articles included in this dissertation.

Appendix A. Overview of the studies included in this dissertation and the contribution of each author.

No	Section	Title	Author	Author's contribution
1	B.I	Towards Distributed Cognitive Expert Systems	Schahin Tofangchi	85
			Andre Hanelt	10
			Lutz M. Kolbe	5
2	B.II	Distributed Cognitive Expert Systems in Cancer Data Analytics: A Decision Support System for Oral and Maxillofacial Surgery	Schahin Tofangchi	65
			Andre Hanelt	25
			Florian Böhrnsen	10
3	B.II	Advancing Recommendations on Two-Sided Platforms: A Machine Learning Approach to Context-Aware Profiling	Schahin Tofangchi	60
			Andre Hanelt	25
			Siyuan Li	15
4	B.II	A Machine Learning Approach to the Efficiency-Comfort Trade-Off in Everyday-Life Automation – The Case of Autonomous Vehicles and Sharing Business Models	Schahin Tofangchi	50
			Andre Hanelt	30
			David Marz	15
			Lutz M. Kolbe	5

Appendix B. Overview of the author's published articles as of December 2019

Peer-reviewed Conferences	Ranking
Tofangchi, S.; Hanelt, A.; Li, Seth. (2019): Advancing Recommendations on Two-Sided Platforms: A Machine Learning Approach to Context-Aware Profiling. In Proceedings of the Fortieth International Conference on Information Systems (ICIS), pp. 1-16.	A
Chatterjee, S.; Saeedfar, P.; Tofangchi, S.; Kolbe, L. M. (2018). Intelligent Road Maintenance: A Machine Learning Approach for Surface Defect Detection. In Proceedings of the Twenty-Sixth European Conference on Information Systems (ECIS), pp. 1-16.	B
Tofangchi, S.; Hanelt, A.; Böhrnsen, F. (2017): Distributed Cognitive Expert Systems in Cancer Data Analytics: A Decision Support System for Oral and Maxillofacial Surgery. In Proceedings of the Thirty Eighth International Conference on Information Systems (ICIS), pp. 1-21.	A
Tofangchi, S.; Hanelt, A.; Kolbe, L. M. (2017): Towards Distributed Cognitive Expert Systems. In Proceedings of the Twelfth International Conference on Design Science Research in Information Systems and Technology (DESRIST), pp. 145-159.	C

Schahin Tofangchi

Göttinger Wirtschaftsinformatik

Herausgeber: Prof. Dr. J. Biethahn • Prof. Dr. L. M. Kolbe • Prof. Dr. M. Schumann

Band 31: Christian Stummeyer
Integration von Simulationsmethoden und hochintegrierter betriebswirtschaftlicher PPS-Standardsoftware im Rahmen eines ganzheitlichen Entwicklungsansatzes
ISBN 3-89712-874-8

Band 32: Stefan Wegert
Gestaltungsansätze zur IV-Integration von elektronischen und konventionellen Vertriebsstrukturen bei Kreditinstituten
ISBN 3-89712-924-8

Band 33: Ernst von Stegmann und Stein
Ansätze zur Risikosteuerung einer Kreditversicherung unter Berücksichtigung von Unternehmensverflechtungen
ISBN 3-89873-003-4

Band 34: Gerald Wissel
Konzeption eines Managementsystems für die Nutzung von internen sowie externen Wissen zur Generierung von Innovationen
ISBN 3-89873-194-4

Band 35: Wolfgang Greve-Kramer
Konzeption internetbasierter Informationssysteme in Konzernen
Inhaltliche, organisatorische und technische Überlegungen zur internetbasierten Informationsverarbeitung in Konzernen
ISBN 3-89873-207-X

Band 36: Tim Veil
Internes Rechnungswesen zur Unterstützung der Führung in Unternehmensnetzwerken
ISBN 3-89873-237-1

Band 37: Mark Althans
Konzeption eines Vertriebscontrolling-Informationssystems für Unternehmen der liberalisierten Elektrizitätswirtschaft
ISBN 3-89873-326-2

Band 38: Jörn Propach
Methoden zur Spielplangestaltung öffentlicher Theater
Konzeption eines Entscheidungsunterstützungssystems auf der Basis Evolutionärer Algorithmen
ISBN 3-89873-496-X

Cuvillier Verlag Göttingen
Nonnenstieg 8 • 37075 Göttingen

Göttinger Wirtschaftsinformatik

Herausgeber: Prof. Dr. J. Biethahn • Prof. Dr. L. M. Kolbe • Prof. Dr. M. Schumann

Band 39: Jochen Heimann
DV-gestützte Jahresabschlußanalyse
Möglichkeiten und Grenzen beim Einsatz computergeschützter Verfahren zur Analyse und Bewertung von Jahresabschlüssen
ISBN 3-89873-499-4

Band 40: Patricia Böning Spohr
Controlling für Medienunternehmen im Online-Markt
Gestaltung ausgewählter Controllinginstrumente
ISBN 3-89873-677-6

Band 41: Jörg Koschate
Methoden und Vorgehensmodelle zur strategischen Planung von Electronic-Business-Anwendungen
ISBN 3-89873-808-6

Band 42: Yang Liu
A theoretical and empirical study on the data mining process for credit scoring
ISBN 3-89873-823-X

Band 43: Antonios Tzouvaras
Referenzmodellierung für Buchverlage
Prozess- und Klassenmodelle für den Leistungsprozess
ISBN 3-89873-844-2

Band 44: Marina Nomikos
Hemmnisse der Nutzung Elektronischer Marktplätze aus der Sicht von kleinen und mittleren Unternehmen eine theoriegeleitete Untersuchung
ISBN 3-89873-847-7

Band 45: Boris Fredrich
Wissensmanagement und Weiterbildungsmanagement
Gestaltungs- und Kombinationsansätze im Rahmen einer lernenden Organisation
ISBN 3-89873-870-1

Band 46: Thomas Arens
Methodische Auswahl von CRM Software
Ein Referenz-Vorgehensmodell zur methodengestützten Beurteilung und Auswahl von Customer Relationship Management Informationssystemen
ISBN 3-86537-054-3

Cuvillier Verlag Göttingen
Nonnenstieg 8 • 37075 Göttingen

Göttinger Wirtschaftsinformatik

Herausgeber: Prof. Dr. J. Biethahn • Prof. Dr. L. M. Kolbe • Prof. Dr. M. Schumann

Band 47: Andreas Lackner
Dynamische Tourenplanung mit ausgewählten Mataheuristiken
Eine Untersuchung am Beispiel des kapazitätsrestriktiven dynamischen Tourenplanungsproblems mit Zeitfenstern
ISBN 3-86537-084-5

Band 48: Tobias Behrensdorf
Service Engineering in Versicherungsunternehmen
unter besonderer Berücksichtigung eines Vorgehensmodells zur Unterstützung durch Informations- und Kommunikationstechnologien
ISBN 3-86537-110-8

Band 49: Michael Range
Aufbau und Betrieb konsumentenorientierter Websites im Internet
Vorgehen und Methoden unter besonderer Berücksichtigung der Anforderungen von kleinen und mittleren Online-Angeboten
ISBN 3-86537-490-5

Band 50: Gerit Grübler
Ganzheitliches Multiprojektmanagement
Mit einer Fallstudie in einem Konzern der Automobilzulieferindustrie
ISBN 3-86537-544-8

Band 51: Birte Pochert
Konzeption einer unscharfen Balanced Scorecard
Möglichkeiten der Fuzzyfizierung einer Balanced Scorecard zur Unterstützung des Strategischen Managements
ISBN 3-86537-671-1

Band 52: Manfred Peter Zilling
Effizienztreiber innovativer Prozesse für den Automotive Aftermarket
Implikationen aus der Anwendung von kollaborativen und integrativen Methoden des Supply Chain Managements
ISBN 3-86537-790-4

Band 53: Mike Hieronimus
Strategisches Controlling von Supply Chains
Entwicklung eines ganzheitlichen Ansatzes unter Einbeziehung der Wertschöpfungspartner
ISBN 3-86537-799-8

Band 54: Dijana Bergmann
Datenschutz und Datensicherheit unter besonderer Berücksichtigung des elektronischen Geschäftsverkehrs zwischen öffentlicher Verwaltung und privaten Unternehmen
ISBN 3-86537-894-3

Cuvillier Verlag Göttingen
Nonnenstieg 8 • 37075 Göttingen

Göttinger Wirtschaftsinformatik

Herausgeber: Prof. Dr. J. Biethahn • Prof. Dr. L. M. Kolbe • Prof. Dr. M. Schumann

Band 55: Jan Eric Borchert
Operatives Innovationsmanagement in Unternehmensnetzwerken
Gestaltung von Instrumenten für Innovationsprojekte
ISBN 3-86537-984-2

Band 56: Andre Daldrup
Konzeption eines integrierten IV-Systems zur ratingbasierten Quantifizierung des regulatorischen und ökonomischen Eigenkapitals im Unternehmenskreditgeschäft unter Berücksichtigung von Basel II
ISBN 978-3-86727-189-9

Band 57: Thomas Diekmann
Ubiquitous Computing-Technologien im betrieblichen Umfeld
Technische Überlegungen, Einsatzmöglichkeiten und Bewertungsansätze
ISBN 978-3-86727-194-3

Band 58: Lutz Seidenfaden
Ein Peer-to-Peer-basierter Ansatz zur digitalen Distribution wissenschaftlicher Informationen
ISBN 978-3-86727-321-3

Band 59: Sebastian Rieger
Einheitliche Authentifizierung in heterogenen IT-Strukturen für ein sicheres e-Science-Umfeld
ISBN 978-3-86727-329-9

Band 60: Ole Björn Brodersen
Eignung schwarmintelligenter Verfahren für die betriebliche Entscheidungsunterstützung
Untersuchungen der Particle Swarm Optimization und Ant Colony Optimization anhand eines stochastischen Lagerhaltungs- und eines universitären Stundenplanungsproblems
ISBN 978-3-86727-777-5

Band 61: Jan Sauer
Konzeption eines wertorientierten Managementsystems unter besonderer Berücksichtigung des versicherungstechnischen Risikos
ISBN 978-3-86727-858-4

Band 62: Adam Melski
Datenmanagement in RFID-gestützten Logistiknetzwerken
RFID-induzierte Veränderungen, Gestaltungsmöglichkeiten und Handlungsempfehlungen
ISBN 978-3-86955-041-1

Cuvillier Verlag Göttingen
Nonnenstieg 8 • 37075 Göttingen

Göttinger Wirtschaftsinformatik

Herausgeber: Prof. Dr. J. Biethahn • Prof. Dr. L. M. Kolbe • Prof. Dr. M. Schumann

Band 63: Thorsten Caus
Anwendungen im mobilen Internet
Herausforderungen und Lösungsansätze für die Entwicklung und Gestaltung mobiler Anwendungen
ISBN 978-3-86955-399-3

Band 64: Nils-Holger-Schmidt
Environmentally Sustainable Information Management
Theories and concepts for Sustainability, Green IS, and Green IT
ISBN 978-3-86955-825-7

Band 65: Lars Thoroe
RFID in Reverse-Logistics-Systemen
ISBN 978-3-86955-902-5

Band 66: Stefan Bitzer
Integration von Web 2.0-Technologien in das betriebliche Wissensmanagement
ISBN 978-3-86955-918-6

Band 67: Matthias Kießling
IT-Innovationsmanagement
Gestaltungs- und Steuerungsmöglichkeiten
ISBN 978-3-95404-104-6

Band 68: Marco Klein
HR Social Software
Unternehmensinterne Weblogs, Wikis und Social Networking
Services für Prozesse des Personalmanagements
ISBN 978-3-95404-247-0

Band 69: Malte Schmidt
Migration vom Barcode zur passiven RFID-Technologie in der automobilen Logistik
Exemplarische Untersuchung am Beispiel eines Automobilherstellers
ISBN 978-3-95404-441-2

Band 70: Janis Kossahl
Konzeptuelle Grundlagen zur Etablierung einer Informationsplattform in der Energiewirtschaft
Ein Beitrag zur Energiewende aus der Perspektive der Wirtschaftsinformatik
ISBN 978-3-95404-524-2

Cuvillier Verlag Göttingen
Nonnenstieg 8 • 37075 Göttingen

Göttinger Wirtschaftsinformatik

Herausgeber: Prof. Dr. J. Biethahn • Prof. Dr. L. M. Kolbe • Prof. Dr. M. Schumann

Band 71: Stefan Friedemann
IT-gestützte Produktionsplanung mit nachwachsenden Rohstoffen
unter Berücksichtigung von Unsicherheiten
ISBN 978-3-95404-606-5

Band 72: Arne Frerichs
Unternehmensfinanzierung mit Peer-to-Peer-gestützter Mittelvergabe
ISBN 978-3-95404-624-9

Band 73: Ullrich C. C. Jagstaidt
Smart Metering Information Management
Gestaltungsansätze für das Informationsmanagement und für
Geschäftsmodelle der Marktakteure in der Energiewirtschaft
ISBN 978-3-95404-696-6

Band 74: Sebastian Busse
Exploring the Role of Information Systems in the Development of Electric Mobility
Understanding the Domain and Designing the Path
ISBN 978-3-95404-727-7

Band 75: Christoph Beckers
Management von Wasserinformationen in der Fleischindustrie
Analyse von Sytemanforderungen zur produktspezifischen Ausweisung
von Water Footprints
ISBN 978-3-95404-809-0

Band 76: Hendrik Hilpert
Informationssysteme für die Nachhaltigkeitsberichterstattung in Unternehmen
Empirische Erkenntnisse und Gestaltungsansätze zur Datengrundlage, Erfassung
und Berichterstattung von Treibhausgasemissionen
ISBN 978-3-95404-908-0

Band 77: Simon Thanh-Nam Trang
Adoption, Value Co-Creation, and Governance of Inter-Organizational Information
Technology in Wood Networks
ISBN 978-3-7369-9031-9

Band 78: Stefan Gröger
IT-Unterstützung zur Verbesserung der Drittmittel-Projekt-Bewirtschaftung an
Hochschulen - Referenzprozessgestaltung, Artefakt-Design und Nutzenpotenziale
ISBN 978-3-7369-9077-7

Cuvillier Verlag Göttingen
Nonnenstieg 8 • 37075 Göttingen

Göttinger Wirtschaftsinformatik

Herausgeber: Prof. Dr. J. Biethahn • Prof. Dr. L. M. Kolbe • Prof. Dr. M. Schumann

Band 79: Johannes Schmidt
Demand-Side Integration Programs for Electric Transport Vehicles
unter Berücksichtigung von Unsicherheiten
ISBN 978-3-7369-9123-1

Band 80: Christian Tornack
IT-gestütztes Nachfolgemanagement in Großunternehmen
ISBN 978-3-7369-9161-3

Band 81: Shanna Appelhanz
Tracking & Tracing-Systeme in Wertschöpfungsnetzwerken für die
industrielle stoffliche Nutzung nachwachsender Rohstoffe
ISBN 978-3-7369-9207-8

Band 82: Henning Krüp
IT Corporate Entrepreneurship – Identifying Factors for IT Innovations
in Non-IT Companies
ISBN 978-3-7369-9253-5

Band 83: Andre Hanelt
Managing the Digital Transformation of Business Models –
An Incumbent Firm Perspective
ISBN 978-3-7369-9254-2

Band 84: Björn Pilarski
Mobile Personalinformationssysteme
Empirische Erkenntnisse und Gestaltungsansätze zum
Einsatz mobiler Anwendungen im Personalmanagement
ISBN 978-3-7369-9291-7

Band 85: Everlin Piccinini
Digital Transformation of Business - Understanding this Phenomenon in
the Context of the Automotive Industry
ISBN 978-3-7369-9323-5

Band 86: Matthias Eisel
Analyzing the Range Barrier to Electric Vehicle Adoption -
The Case of Range Anxiety
ISBN 978-3-7369-9379-2

Cuvillier Verlag Göttingen
Nonnenstieg 8 • 37075 Göttingen

Göttinger Wirtschaftsinformatik

Herausgeber: Prof. Dr. J. Biethahn • Prof. Dr. L. M. Kolbe • Prof. Dr. M. Schumann

Band 87: Gerrit Remané
Digital Business Models in the Mobility Sector: Using Components and Types to Understand Existing and Design New Business Models
ISBN 978-3-7369-9544-4

Band 88: Thierry Jean Ruch
Consumerization of IT –
Studies to Explore the Phenomenon and Implications for IT Management, Information Security, and Organizational Security
ISBN 978-3-7369-9558-1

Band 89: Carolin Ebermann
Die Förderung von nachhaltigem Mobilitätsverhalten durch erhöhte User-Experience und den Einsatz von Informationssystemen
ISBN 978-3-7369-9568-0

Band 90: Sebastian Zander
Interorganizational Information Systems for the Efficient Utilization of Renewable Resources - Insights from Networks in the Wood Industry
ISBN 978-3-7369-9584-0

Band 91: Ilja Nastjuk
The Dark and the Bright Side of Digitalization -
The Case of Sustainable Mobility
ISBN 978-3-7369-9586-4

Band 92: Aaron Mengelkamp
Informationen zur Bonitätsprüfung auf Basis von Daten aus sozialen Medien
ISBN 978-3-7369-9628-1

Band 93: Alfred Benedikt Brendel
Applied Design Science Research in the Context of Smart and Sustainable Mobility
The Case of Vehicle Supply and Demand Management in Shared Vehicle Services
ISBN 978-3-7369-9685-4

Band 94: Markus Mandrella
IT-Based Value Co-Creation in Inter-Organizational Networks
Theory Integration, Extension, and Adaptation to the Wood Industry
ISBN 978-3-7369-9695-3

Cuvillier Verlag Göttingen
Nonnenstieg 8 • 37075 Göttingen

Göttinger Wirtschaftsinformatik

Herausgeber: Prof. Dr. J. Biethahn • Prof. Dr. L. M. Kolbe • Prof. Dr. M. Schumann

Band 95: Benjamin Brauer
Persuasive User-Centric Green IS
Exploring the Role and Paving the Way of Information Systems to Induce Pro-Environmental Behavior Change
ISBN 978-3-7369-9764-6

Band 96: Sebastian Hobert
Empirische Erkenntnisse und Gestaltungsansätze zum Einsatz von Wearable Computern im Industriesektor
ISBN 978-3-7369-9794-3

Band 97: Björn Hildebrandt
Digitalization of Mobility - Understanding the Transformational Impacts of Pervasive Digital Technologies on Business Models in the Mobility Sector
ISBN 978-3-7369-9827-8

Band 98: Jasmin Decker
Micro Learning und Mobile Learning in Unternehmen – Empirische Erkenntnisse und Gestaltungsempfehlungen zum Einsatz mobiler Lernanwendungen
ISBN 978-3-7369-9835-3

Band 99: Jan Moritz Anke
IT-gestützte Lern- und Assessmentmodule für nachhaltiges Wirtschaften
Empirische Erkenntnisse und Gestaltungsansätze zum Einsatz IT-gestützter Lern- und Assessmentmodule
ISBN 978-3-7369-9986-2

Band 100: Daniel Leonhardt
Organizing for Digital Innovation – The Role of the IT Function
ISBN 978-3-7369-7060-1

Cuvillier Verlag Göttingen
Nonnenstieg 8 • 37075 Göttingen